Science vs. Religion

Is It Really That Simple?

by

Trevor Ray Slone

Foreword by **Dr. Winfried Corduan**

Afterword by **Dr. Norman Geisler**

This book is dedicated to my son, Chandler William Slone.

Even though I don't see you much (and that is not by choice)

I want you to know that I will always love you, no matter what.

Table of Contents

Part 2: Intelligent Design, Young Earth Creationism, A Free Thinking Society, and What Needs To Be Done

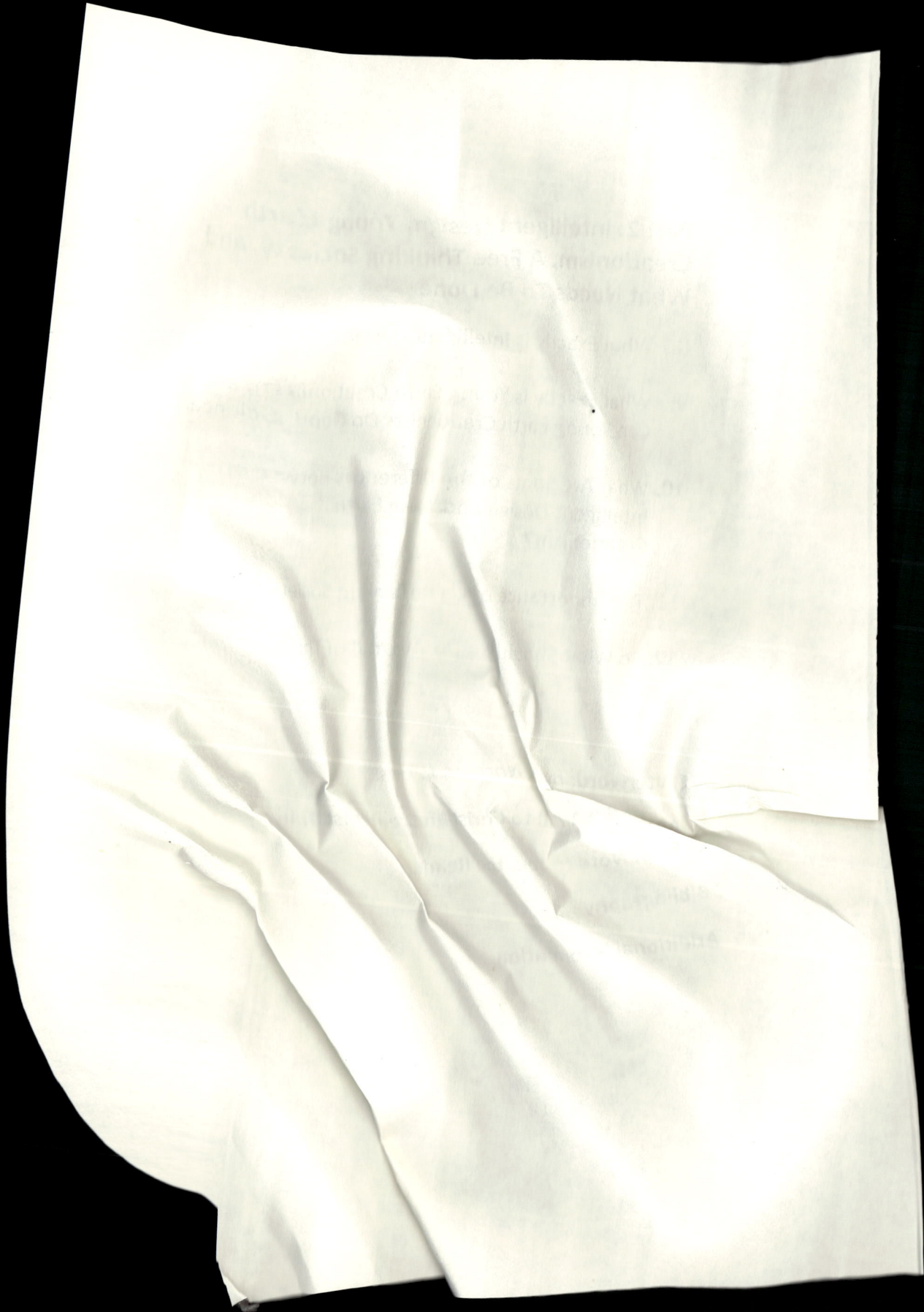

Acknowledgements

Until about 6 years ago I never really thought that I would amount to much, let alone that I would write a book and have two of the greatest Christian minds of the twentieth/twenty-first century write the foreword and the afterword for it. There are, to be sure, people that have made writing this book more feasible for me along the way. For starters, my wife has been great in making sure that I didn't make any major grammatical mistakes in the manuscript, so I would like to thank her for her help. Also, my good friend Tim Stratton, a fellow up and coming Christian apologist who recently finished his M.A. in Christian Apologetics from Biola University, has taken time out of his incredibly busy schedule to occasionally read certain chapters of this book and give me feedback. Tim has been a great encouragement to me along the way, something that I don't often have. I would also like to thank my friends Matt Hale and Aaron Stevens for being a continued source of encouragement to me during the year in which I wrote this book, especially through the hard times when I was manic or depressed. Good friends are hard to find, but when you find them they usually stick around, even if they move away. I would also like to thank Liz Jackson for reading a good portion of this book and giving me feedback. As a theistic evolutionist I am sure that reading this book was not so easy for her, but I am grateful that she took the time out of her busy schedule to do so anyway. I would like to also thank Dr. Norman Geisler for taking the time to write the afterword for this book. I know that he has many other things on his schedule and it really means a lot to me that he did so.

The one who has been the most influential in my life over the last few years has no doubt been Dr. Winfried Corduan. If it wasn't for him I probably would never have decided to go back to school. It is amazing how life can change so quickly with just a little bit of reassurance. Dr. Corduan has been a great encouragement to me during the process of writing this book also. I remember when I first conjured up the idea to write this book and I told Dr. Corduan about my idea he mentioned to me that it was a very ambitious task to undertake, but he never told me that he didn't think I could do it. So, thank you Dr. Corduan for your support and encouragement, and also obviously for writing the foreword for this book.

Lastly, I need to thank, most of all, my Lord and Savior, King and Friend, Jesus Christ for bringing me through everything that I have been through in my life to the point where I am actually stable enough to write a book (I have bipolar 1 disorder and severe ADHD), especially one of this size. I plan on writing many more books in the future, and it would never be possible without my wonderful and amazing Creator who has blessed me with an enduring heart and the ability to persevere. As a side-note, I also, in 2014 published the book "Doing Apologetics Without the Need for Apology: Biblical Principles for Confrontational Relationality," and although I wrote this book, which you are now reading, several years prior to that one, my hope is that this book nevertheless espouses and personifies the principles set forth in that one. Six years ago, in 2009, I was in the hospital for the fourth time in my life on the brink of death because of my debilitating disorders. Now I am a well-educated healthy citizen who is ready to make a difference in the world. I can obviously never thank Christ enough for what He has done for me, but I can acknowledge that without Him I would never have made it past the age of 4, let alone having been born at all and surviving this long with everything that I have been through. We would all do well to give far more credence and glory to our Creator, for without Him there truly would be nothing at all.

Trevor Ray Slone

Foreword

Surely it is an understatement to say that "religion" and "science" have been at loggerheads for the last century or more, particularly over the issue of biological evolution. Or should that last phrase be: "over the interpretation of the first chapters of Genesis"? Or maybe it should read: "over the philosophical assumption of organic evolution"? Come to think of it, there is a lot of ambiguity in this statement. What exactly does "religion" mean in this context, and, for that matter, what exactly is "science"? And who speaks for either endeavor authoritatively?

In short, the statement that "religion" and "science" disagree over such issues as evolution is a platitude whose terms can easily be filled in so as to provide an easy solution. Any would-be William Tell can pierce the apple, any ambitious successor to Alexander can cut the knot, and any modern Christopher Columbus can stand the egg on end, each one to the applause of his peers. Still, as Heidegger has reminded us so many times, in today's world of thought we are prone to confuse cleverness with thinking.

Still, even if we are not looking for simplistic, snappy answers, and if we are willing to clarify our terms sufficiently to engage in a substantial discussion, there are different ways of approaching the issue. Alas! For too many Americans the answer to any controversy has become to moan, "There Ought to be a Law . . . " More accurately, given the nature of our judicial system, this desire translates into "The courts should decide . . . " And so they have. And they have not ruled on the basis of freedom, but on the basis of ideology, just as one would expect any fallen human being to do, whether they are occupying the couches of their living rooms or the benches of their courtrooms, which have become *de facto* throne halls. And, thus, they have told us once and for all (or so they think) that atheistic Darwinian evolution is the only valid scientific paradigm in biology, and that any scheme that even comes close to implying that there is a Creator will damage our school children beyond repair and, thus, may not be mentioned in any class room.

This book places the issue into the context into which it belongs: the clash between two worldviews. It is not a detailed analysis of evolution from a scientific perspective that exposes supposed errors in the lab. It is not a compromise that begins with what we are still "allowed" to say or teach and ends by formulating a give-and-take strategy. It is a no-holds-barred description of the fundamental confrontation between belief and unbelief, or better: between belief in the God of the Bible and belief in the omnipotence of the physical universe. Trevor Slone does not come with his hands stretched out offering a

Introduction

As I sit here writing these opening statements of this book, an article has just been published within the last week in the *Christian Research Journal* titled "The Campaign to Embarrass Christians into Accepting Darwinism." Now, at first glance it certainly seems as though this article would be referring to non-Christian, atheistic evolutionists (the typical type of evolutionist) trying to coerce and bully Christians into believing in evolution. However, this is sadly not the case. Rather, this article was written about a growing group of professing Christians who are trying to bully other Christians into believing in evolution. This is, quite simply, an outrage!

In this article Casey Luskin, research coordinator for the Discovery Institute and an attorney with graduate degrees in science and law, points out that these professing Christians are claiming that "almost two-thirds" of evangelicals are "at war with science" because they reject Darwinian evolution.[1] But is this really true? Is it really necessary to believe in evolution to be in good

---

[1] Karl W. Gerson and Randall J. Stephens, "The Evangelical Rejection of Reason," *New York Times*, October 17, 2011. Quoted by Casey Luskin, "The Campaign to Embarrass Christians into Accepting Darwinism," in *Christian Research Journal* 35, no.3 (2012): 51.

standing with science? Is evolution science? Most people these days certainly seem to think so. We live in a world filled with propaganda and nonsensical mindlessness that demands our allegiance to the most despicable levels of aberration, which includes such notions as that evolution is a proven fact, that anyone who does not believe in evolution is a fool and an imbecile, and that Intelligent Design is religion rather than science. We are also forced to conform to the status quo in our society if we are to get along with those around us, otherwise we are at almost certain risk of losing our jobs, being blacklisted from future job positions, losing funding for research, and so on, especially in the scientific industry. Of course, modern academia has essentially been taken over by secularism in almost every field of study, not just science, but modern "science," it could be said, is where secularism, Naturalism, Materialism, and the humanist agenda really started making headway, primarily starting with the enlightenment philosophers and then gaining exponential acknowledgement following Darwin and his supposed scientific discoveries. Ever since then there has been an increasingly growing hesitation and distain toward believing in the truths of Scripture, believing in the Judeo-Christian God of the Bible (or any god at all for that matter), or relying on anything other than science and reason to provide us with the truth. It is for these reasons and others that I am writing this book to you, in hopes that it may bring to light some of the modern day enigmas regarding why our society has fallen so very far in the last one hundred and fifty years or so, since Darwin wrote his *On the Origin of Species*, from the vital Christian nation that we once were.

The other main reasons for writing this book are: 1) to defeat the modern typical faulty argument that if we teach Intelligent Design in the public school science classrooms that it will lead to teaching Young Earth Creationism in the public school science classrooms, and so therefore we should not teach Intelligent Design in the public school science classrooms; 2) to show that the typical argument that evolution is science and Intelligent Design is religion is fallacious due to the very definitions of the terms "evolution," "science," "Intelligent Design," and "religion"; 3) to show that science, by its very nature, cannot prove anything, but rather science merely deals with various levels of probability, due to the fact that it is founded on inductive logical principles (this is important to understand the problem with the growing belief that we can only learn facts and truth through science); and 4) to stress the crucial need for us all to stand up and defend the truth, our children, ourselves, and our society from the twaddle and peril of the eminence of evolution.

There will of course be other things that we discuss along the way, but those are the primary purposes of this book, for ultimately we want to see that the modern so called "Science vs. Religion" debate is really a debate between two competing worldviews, both of which are fundamentally religious, namely the evolutionary worldview, primarily advocated in conjunction with Naturalism, Atheism, and Materialism, and theistic worldviews, which for our discussion here is chiefly referring to the Christian worldview.

It is my hope and prayer that by the time you are done reading this book you are not only much more informed about the facts surrounding the so called "Science vs. Religion" debate, but that you also feel a yearning and deep desire to take the knowledge that you gain from this book and do something with it in a way that will diminish, if not destroy, the influence of evolution in our society and regain a sense of criticality, sincerity, and decency in our schools, our government, and our society.

It needs to be said here in passing at the outset of this book, although this will be repeated later on, that this book is *NOT* intended to be a scientific refutation of evolution. That is not the purpose of this book. There are many books like that out already, and you can search the Additional Information section at the end of this book for some of those sources. This book is primarily philosophical in nature (but not overly so, I hope), regarding opposing worldviews, as Dr. Corduan made clear in the foreword. Nevertheless, there is some minimal discussion in this book regarding the scientific aspects of the theory of evolution.

Please read carefully as you go through this book, as I discuss a lot of very prominent topics for our current age and they are all in one way or another relevant to the overall aim of this work. May the Lord guide you and open and prepare your mind for what you read in these pages, and may the God of Abraham, Isaac, and Jacob light the same fire in you that He has in me to stand firm against the contemptible, preposterous drivel known as evolution.

must also remember that no amount of time makes the actually impossible possible. We are not dealing with probability here; we are dealing with actual impossibility. But I digress, as we are here discussing the removal of God from America and how evolution played a key role in this feat. Harvard Paleontologist Stephen Jay Gould may have said it best when he stated that "Evolution substituted a naturalistic explanation of cold comfort for our former conviction that a benevolent deity fashioned us directly in his own image."[8]

What this whole idea of life coming from non-life (through random processes) indicates is that there is no need for a Creator of life, such as God, in the history of life on earth. I do not wish to discuss theistic evolution here, as I think that it is one of the dumbest ideas anyone has ever come up with, certainly within the realm of Christianity, for the Bible gives absolutely no allusions to such a process, and it blatantly contradicts the opening chapters of Genesis. This is also not the place for a discussion on panspermia (the idea that life was planted here on earth by some outside source), as that only pushes the question of how life came about one step further back and does nothing in actually answering the question ultimately. What we are dealing with here is a claim that

---

[8] Stephen Jay Gould, cited in Jonathan Wells, *The Politically Incorrect Guide to Darwinism and Intelligent Design* (Washington, D.C.: Regenry, 2006), 62, quoted by Norman Geisler, *Creation & the Courts: Eighty Years of Conflict in the Classroom and the Courtroom* (Wheaton: Crossway Books, 2007), 32.

animals, bacteria, and everything else that is living, ultimately is related to everything else, and everything ultimately comes from one original organism, and that organism started out as a non-living organism.[7] Now the purpose of this book is not to refute evolution on scientific grounds, but I do want to point out that abiogensis (which is essentially the idea of biological life arising from inorganic life, and the belief thereof) is the same thing as spontaneous generation with a whole lot of added time, and spontaneous generation is the idea that things simply come into existence on their own. The problem with this is that the second law of thermodynamics and other scientific principles show that everything in this world is contingent (i.e. dependent; finite), and so anything that exists has to have had something other than itself (because self-creation in nonsensical) bring it into existence which defeats the idea of spontaneity. The term "spontaneous" in this sense means "without help" or "on its own," and the term "generation" necessarily entails action on the part of an actually existing entity, for a non-entity cannot act in any way because it does not possess any attributes that would allow it to do so, since a non-entity is essentially nothing, and nothing cannot possess attributes, and so "spontaneous generation" by definition is a contradiction in terms, and therefore impossible. We

---

[7] There are of course other definitions of evolution, but we are here referring to macro-evolution, and so this definition will suffice for our purposes here.

player in the removal of God from our nation, including in scenarios such as the Dr. King memorial. Back in late 2008 - early 2009 I lived with my older brother and his wife and their three adorable little girls at Fort Belvoir, VA (he is also in the Army, as is my little brother). Fort Belvoir is only about fifteen minutes or so from D.C., so I used to take the bus down to the tram and ride into D.C. to go and visit the Smithsonian museums. If you have never been there you should go as soon as you can, as there are many great things to see in the museums in D.C.[4] Back in 2006 (this may still be there I suppose) in the National Museum of Natural History, when you walked into the Hall of Mammals there was a sign that said "Welcome to the family reunion! Come meet your relatives." You then saw mammals of all sorts.[5] Now this is an incredibly simplified version of evolution. Brock's *Biology of Microorganisms* defines evolution as "Change in a line of decent over time leading to the production of new species or varieties within species."[6] To put it in simpler terms, the general consensus of evolutionary theory among evolutionary scientists is that everything on earth, including all plants,

---

[4] My favorite museum in D.C. was the West National Gallery of Art, as they have many Monet's, Rembrandt's, they have Van Gogh's self-portrait, and many other wonderful pieces of art, although I do not think it is considered part of the Smithsonian.
[5] David Dewitt, *Unraveling The Origins Controversy* (Lynchburg: Creation Curriculum, L.L.C., 2007), 12-14.
[6] Michael T. Madigan and John M. Martinko, *Biology of Microorganisms* (Upper Saddle River: Pearson Education, Inc., 2006), G-5.

public in Washington, D.C., but there is something incredibly important missing from this memorial, for remember that Dr. King was a preacher by profession. According to an article I read online neither this memorial nor the World War II Memorial[3] bare any reference to God whatsoever. Now forgive me for being a bit crass, but how dare the people that built this memorial, and the people involved in deciding what to and what not to include in the memorial, fail to exemplify the very substance of Dr. King's message to the world, which was primarily that God created all of us, and so none of us is any less valuable than any other! This is totally unacceptable and I certainly hope that something is done about this very soon. I remember reading in another article about the Dr. King memorial that Dr. King's relative(s) that are still alive were not even asked for their opinions on anything regarding the memorial or what should be included on it, and they were not happy with this, as they, as myself and so many others, know good and well that Dr. King most certainly would have wanted reference to his God on a memorial built in his honor, if he would have been okay with a memorial being built to honor him at all.

Now before we return to the racism issue, let us talk for a brief moment about how evolution is a key

---

[3] I have seen the WW II memorial in person and I cannot recall any references to God on it either, even in support of the Jews that lost their lives, but my memory may just be failing me. Nevertheless, it is really cool, so make it a point to go see it when you can.

and if there was one thing I knew about people by that point it was that they are all essentially the same. Sure, different cultures have different mannerisms, types of food that they like (I loved the schnitzel in Germany), languages that they speak, and so on, but at the end of the day we all have to eat, sleep, go to the bathroom; we feel the need for friends, family, and to be loved by others, and so on and so forth. I had not seen any indication that some people had feelings and others did not, or that some people were somehow better than other people, especially because of the way they looked. This type of thinking and behaving made absolutely no sense to me then and it makes no sense to me now, nor will it ever. Of course I understand the arrogance of man, and ultimately that is what racism stems from, an unwarranted feeling of superiority. We are going to talk about this in a moment in reference to evolution, but first let us go back to what we discussed in the opening statement of this chapter.

The Removal of God from America

In all of this one thing was made very clear in this biography: Dr. Martin Luther King Jr.'s faith was in God. He was by profession a preacher. He was a mighty man with mighty words, and he stood on the Bible as his rock in times of trouble. This is something that so many people seem to have forgotten today. Bringing us back to the beginning of this chapter, on October 16, 2011 the Dr. Martin Luther King Jr. Memorial was dedicated to the

Then the story went on to talk about Dr. King's days in school and the segregation of that era. I remember thinking about how incredibly foolish it was to make people drink at separate water fountains and use different restrooms just because their skin was a different color. Then the book went on to discuss the boycotts set forth by Dr. King and his followers. I remember thinking that was so cool and brave of them. The book went on to mention a time when someone blew up Dr. King's house because he would not stop his protesting and preaching. Now remember that I was 7 years old when I read this book. I just couldn't fathom someone blowing up someone else's house just because that person was standing up for what was right. I remember thinking of how awful of a thing that was to do. And then I read about the wonderful speech that Dr. King gave in Washington, D.C. I will never forget that the biography said that one man rode many hundreds of miles on his skates to see the speech.

Now, I remember being infuriated against racism as I read this book. I remember thinking of how dumb it was for people to be treated differently just because of the color of their skin. I thought about my friends, like the one from kindergarten and others, and how they were no different than I, aside from their skin color. I had lived in four different states (we lived in Ohio for a few months before moving to Indiana from Washington) and two different countries by the time I read this book when I was 7 years old, and I had met many different kinds of people, remember that I loved to read instantly. I spent much time in my early years after that reading dictionaries and encyclopedias. I mostly just wanted to read stuff that would teach me things about the world, new words, and things of that sort. After kindergarten we moved from Fort Lewis to West Lafayette, IN. My dad was an Army recruiter out there for about three years. Once again one of my best friends was an African-American boy, and we played together during school and after school with our other friends.[2] When I started the second grade at Miller Elementary School in West Lafayette I decided that it was time to move on from reading dictionaries, encyclopedias, and children's books (an odd combination I know) to something different, so I picked out a roughly 220 page biography of Dr. Martin Luther King Jr. from the school library and I began reading it. To this day I have yet to read a book (other than the Bible of course) that I enjoyed more than this one, with the only exception possibly being J.I. Packer's book *Evangelism and the Sovereignty of God*. I remember reading about young Martin Luther King Jr. as he played with his young white friend, and then one day all of a sudden they were no longer allowed to play together. I remember reading about how young Dr. King was very confused as to why they couldn't play together.

---

[2] I have had friends of various skin tones and ethnic backgrounds all throughout my life. Personally I think that the "white people" of America are in general some of the most uncultured people in the world, and that is something that needs to be changed if prejudices are to subside in our nation.

On October 16, 2011 the Martin Luther King Jr. National Memorial was dedicated to the public in the United States capital city of Washington, D.C. I remember as a young boy learning about racism. I knew that there were many different kinds of people in the world, as far as how people looked that is, as I grew up in a military family (my father was in the United States Army). I was born at Fort Stewart, GA, close to Savannah, GA, but when I was about 6 months old we moved to Berlin, Germany. I was very young, but I still remember the Berlin Wall from when we lived over there. It was a very scary sight for a little child. I remember my parents telling me why the wall was there (a simplified version I am sure), and that it was to keep the people in East Berlin out of West Berlin, and vice versa. I remember thinking how terrible things must have been that people had to put up a big wall to keep the citizens from fighting. Then when I was about four and a half years old we moved back to the states to Fort Lewis, WA, close to Tacoma, WA. I started kindergarten the following year, and my best friend was a little African-American boy who was in my class at school. I don't remember his name, but I will never forget him, as he would always call me "Treasure" instead of Trevor. I tried over and over to explain to him that my name was Trevor, but he just didn't get it I guess. Nevertheless, he was a cool kid and I will never forget him as long as I live.

Shortly before we moved back to the states, when we still lived in Berlin, I taught myself how to read. I

2

Why Does the Prominence of Evolution Matter?

"Evolution, when taken to its logical conclusions, leaves no room for rationality, generosity, friendship, humanitarianism, meaning to life, God, or anything else that makes this life worth living."

"According to mainstream biology textbooks, neo-Darwinism is a 'random,' 'blind,' 'uncaring,' 'heartless,' 'undirected,' 'purposeless,' and 'chance' process that acts 'without plan' or 'any goals,' and requires accepting 'materialism' because we are not created for any specific purpose or as part of any universal design,' where 'a god of design and purpose is not necessary."[1]

- Casey Luskin (an attorney with graduate degrees in science and law)

---

[1] Casey Luskin, "Smelling Blood in the Water," in *God and Evolution: Protestants, Catholics, and Jews Explore Darwin's Challenge to Faith*, ed. Jay Richards (Seattle: Discovery Institute Press, 2010), 344, quoted by Casey Luskin, "The Campaign to Embarrass Christians into Accepting Darwinism," in *Christian Research Journal* 35, no. 3 (2012): 52.

the introduction, the purpose of this book is several fold, and it all ultimately fits together in relation to the "Science vs. Religion" debate.

Conclusion

In conclusion, we have looked at how and why logic is fundamental to all reasoning. We have also looked at some specific examples of some forms of informal fallacies, including a look at the informal fallacy known as the slippery slope fallacy, which is paramount to our purposes in this book. So, now that we have got a handle of the basics of logic, let us now move forward on this journey. In the next chapter we are going to take an in depth look at why the prominence of evolution matters so much today. We are going to see that evolution is destroying our nation from the inside out, and that if it is not stopped soon there will be essentially nothing left of us but an anarchical nation of misfits and arrogant domineering culprits and criminals, and those of us who do not fit that mold will be not only the minority, but we will suffer severely for not conforming to such "standards" of animosity.

Young Earth Creationism taught in the public school science classrooms is not necessarily an undesirable consequence. However, we must realize at this point that the terms "desirable" and "undesirable" are primarily, if not completely subjective terms, and therefore my argument that teaching YEC in the school science classroom is desirable will be primarily based off of two *facts* that will be established later in the book. The first of these facts is that Evolutionism, also known as Darwinism, is a belief system (you could even call it a religion) just like creationism, and therefore YEC, in this sense, should be judged and viewed in the same light as Darwinism. The second fact is that YEC, while it is a belief system, has many legitimate scientific contributions to make to the world of modern science. We are going to spend time in various chapters throughout the remainder of this book addressing these two facts, as well as other related topics that are necessary to understand and fully grasp the complexity of the issues surrounding the so called "Science vs. Religion" debate.

Let me also make it very clear that if we can indeed show that the above stated argument commits the slippery slope fallacy, which I intend to do, then we must necessarily, on the grounds of logic and sound reasoning, reject this argument altogether as fallacious and unacceptable. However, before we attempt to take a deeper look into this fallacious argument there are several other things that need to be discussed, for as we saw in perfect many of the Christian virtues within himself, at times went to church, and even gave offerings and tithes to the church from time to time, most probably, based on the way he lived his life, would not have been okay with such a blatant denial of some of the biblical principles that this country was founded on (see Benjamin Franklin's Autobiography). It is no secret that our nation was founded on Christian principles, however skewed they might have been in the minds of some.[16] Of course, many people in the early years of America exclaimed that the Africans were destined to be our slaves because Ham, Noah's son was cursed by God for the immoral act that he committed against his father in his tent, and that God therefore said that he and his descendants would be the servants of his brothers. We know that Ham's descendants ended up in the region of Africa, hence the logic behind the assertion. However, this is not what the Bible says. God actually cursed Canaan, Ham's son,[17] and told him that he would be a servant to his brothers (or possibly Canaan was to be a slave of God[18]). It is generally accepted that this also includes the descendants of Canaan. This

---

[16] I realize that many of our founding fathers were deists, but the principles that our nation was founded on were still largely biblical principles.

[17] There are several theories as to why God did this instead of cursing Ham himself, one being that Canaan was also somehow involved in the wrongdoing of his father, but again, this is another topic for another book.

[18] Walter C. Kaiser Jr., *Mission in the Old Testament: Second Edition* (Grand Rapids: Baker Academic, 2012), 5.

evolution, is ultimately what has caused God to be largely taken out of our country. Of course postmodernism, relativism, pluralism, and many other factors also play into the overall picture of the removal of Christian virtues and the Christian God from the United States of America,[15] but as for the removal of a God prospect in general, and as for the infiltration of anti-supernaturalism in Western society, evolution is undoubtedly the key player and culprit of our time.

It is therefore also not surprising that our President, Barrack Obama, openly mocked Christians and the Bible in a speech that he gave back in 2006 (sections of this speech are readily available on YouTube.com). Granted he was not yet our president, but I think we can rest assured that his anti-Christian sentiments have not changed since that time. Also, just this week (as I write this chapter), our congress is in the process of reaffirming our nations motto, "In God We Trust," and Barrack Obama told them that they should not be wasting their time with such things. This is something that our founding fathers would have found absolutely appalling, and it is most certainly not something that most early Americans would have been okay with either. Even Benjamin Franklin, who never claimed to be a man of God or a Christian, who sought to

---

[15] I am not claiming here that there are not still a lot of devout Christians in America. Rather I am asserting the fact that Christian beliefs and convictions, for the most part, are no longer the dominant beliefs in this country and that they are no longer the primary influence on public policy.

but a meaningless creature free for nothing but to be used by others for their own pleasure. But this would be most disconcerting, for if all human rights are non-existent, then this principle must by necessity be universal, as no man has the power or right to claim self-rights or determine the rights of others, and so if there are no human rights then this would ultimately, based on the way humanity naturally is, namely fallen and inherently devious and evil, lead to universal anarchy, fighting, and as Thomas Hobbes put it, the war of all against all.[12]

Of course, Hitler had many evolutionary beliefs as well, which led him to do many of the things that he did. For instance in his book *Mein Kampf* he says,

> "At the present time there exist upon the earth five races….These are the Ethiopian or negro type, originating in Africa; the Malay or brown race, from the islands of the Pacific; the American Indian; the Mongolian or yellow race, including the natives of China, Japan, and the Eskomos; and finally, *the highest type of all, the Caucasions*, represented by the civilized white inhabitants of Europe and America."[13]

---

[12] Thomas Hobbes, *Leviathan*, pt. 1, chap. 13, quoted by Arthur F. Holmes, *Ethics: Approaching Moral Decisions* (Downers Grove: InterVarsity Press, 2007), 39.

[13] Adolf Hitler, *Mein Kampf* (New York: Reynal & Hitchcock, 1940), 161-162, quoted by Norman Geisler, *Creation & the Courts*, 33.

Everyone is aware of the atrocity that took place during the Holocaust when Hitler killed approximately 6 million Jews, but few people seem to be aware of the fact that Marxism was responsible for over 100,000,000 deaths in the twentieth century. It is to be noted here also that Darwin and Karl Marx were friends.[10] Now I am not insinuating that each one was necessarily corrupt due to their friendship with the other, but it is common knowledge that most of the time people become friends with those who are like themselves, and it is not hard to see the similarities in some of their views on reality, for after all Marxism is founded on Darwinian principles. It should also be noted here that Marxism, which is based on evolutionary principles, rejects human rights as a product of Christianity.[11] This is not surprising though, for after all if evolution, and the Naturalism and Materialism that is so fundamental to it, is part and parcel to the removal of God from a nation, and if Marxism is founded on evolution (which it is), and if human rights are founded on biblical principles (which they are), then it only makes sense that Marxism (and evolution) would deny human rights (and support the idea of a no-God scenario), and to deny human rights is tantamount to claiming that humanity is

---

[9] John Morris, *The Young Earth* (Green Forest: Master Books, 2007), 22.

[10] Geisler, *Creation & the Courts*, 32.

[11] Thomas P. Schirrmacher, "Human Rights and Christian Faith," Patrick Henry College, http://www.phc.edu/gj_schirrmacherv3n2.php (accessed July 24, 2012).

so involved therein can also be found in many popular movies, such as the movie Wall Street (2010), The Green Lantern (2011), the X-Men movies and comics, and others. This is not something that is just a scholastic matter, but rather our nation as a whole is propagating an overwhelming evolutionary dogma that would most likely match many of the communist and socialist nations' propaganda of the twentieth century, and dare I say even the level of propaganda used by Saddam Hussein. This reminds me of a story that geological engineer Dr. John Morris tells in his book, *The Young Earth*. I must quote it at length to provide you with the full effect of the story:

> "I remember one of my graduate students at the University of Oklahoma, who, as a young man growing up in Iran under the Shah's regime, had turned to communism. A leader in the Student Communist Party, he was taken to Moscow for a year's saturation in Communist thought. Do you know what they taught him? Not Marx. Not Lenin. For the whole year, they just filled him with evolution. Evolution is a necessary foundation for Marxism. According to Marxism, evolution is true, and all things come from natural processes (*materialism* is the Marxist word for this) and evolutionary progress through time is inevitable [emphasis original]."[9]

all life on earth originated with a non-life substance by random undirected processes, and so we have a "viable" explanation for the origin of life on earth, at least to some extent, without the need for a Creator of life. Hence, we do not need to posit God as a possible reason for life on earth, and if He did not create us, and since the world is governed by purely naturalistic processes (according to the naturalistic evolutionist), there is no need to even entertain the thought of any sort of God existing. Naturalistic Materialistic Scientism (the main worldview that secular evolutionists espouse) will be discussed in a later chapter, but for now let us just make clear that it is 100% atheistic in nature. We also need to make clear that not all evolutionists are atheists. However, most professional evolutionists are committed to a naturalistic view of evolution, which is an atheistic view, and to be perfectly honest evolution really leaves no room for God, so it is fair to say that evolution is essentially an atheistic view.

I don't know if you have noticed this, but the term evolution is in movie titles, household good brand names, video games, power tool company names, and just about everything else that you can think of in our culture. It is a word that most of us use from day to day in reference to change, without even coming close to pondering the implications of such a nonchalant use of such a loaded term. It is not just a word for the scientists to use in school and in their labs, it is literally everywhere. The worldview

Part 1

The Fundamentals

1

Logic: What Is It and Why Is It Important?

"Were it not for logic we would all be imbeciles."

Although this book is not really about logic, since logic is fundamental to all reasoning in general, and to one of our main purposes in this book in particular, it seems only right to start this book with a chapter on the basics of logic. We will of course address various issues of logic throughout the remainder of the book from time to time, but, for the most part, after this chapter we will be done discussing logic until the final chapter when we recapitulate everything that we have gone over in the book. So, since this chapter is about logic, it will probably seem a bit drier than the rest of the book. Please remain focused and charge through it, and I promise you that you will be much better off for having read it in the future.

If you are like most people that I have come in contact with, especially the college students, when you hear the word "logic" you probably cringe. But what is logic? Well, "Logic is the study of right reasoning or valid inferences and the attending fallacies, formal and informal."[1] Now most of you are probably thinking, "What does that mean?" So, to ease your anxiety a bit, let's just say that logic is the study of how to think properly and how to come to the appropriate conclusions when we think about something, whatever it may be.

Now, you might possibly be thinking back to a time when you had to take a dreaded logic class (or any other type of philosophy class). You know, one of those classes that so many people do so poorly in that the class is graded on a curve. I remember one time my wife took a graduate level biochemistry class, and she said it was so difficult that the curve was actually a five to ten point deviation from the normal grading scale, which meant that an 85 was an A and a 70 was a B (normally a 70 would be one point away from a D). My wife is an excellent student who gets almost perfect grades, but she absolutely hated that class, even though she had already taken almost six years worth of college science classes, because of how hard it was. Maybe your introductory philosophy class was like that for you, or maybe you were so afraid of taking philosophy that you avoided it like the plague. Many people, as I stated above, in my experience, seem to have a deep and passionate disinterest in logic and anything

---

[1] Norman L. Geisler and Ronald M. Brooks, *Come Let Us Reason: An Introduction to Logical Thinking* (Grand Rapids: Baker Books, 1990), 12.

else having to do with phi osophy (if they even know that logic is entailed in philosophy), or so they think.

Or you might be scmeone like me who lives and breathes to use logic whenever and wherever you have the opportunity to do so. I remember when I was in the fourth grade I used to sit in gifted class and spend hours on those logic problems with the statements on the side and the big boxes with the little boxes in them that you had to either put an "X" or an "O" in. I used to do so many of them that I would ask my teacher for extras so I could take them home and do them for fun in my spare time. I even got to the point where I could do the ones with over 20 big boxes in them before I even finished the fourth grade. I love logic! It is like a big game to me where the rules make everything so much clearer and easier to understand. Maybe you are like that. Or maybe you just enjoy making logical connections between different things. I think it is safe to say that we have all at one time or another had an epiphany and have gotten excited when we finally made a connection in our minds between something we knew and scmething else we knew, when we finally figure out how they "fit together." Most of us have probably also gotten excited when we have met someone who knows someone else that we know. These simple mental connections all find their basis in the field of logic.

Now, is logic really that difficult? Is it really something that we should be terrified of? You might be surprised to hear my answer (although hopefully not after reading the previous paragraph), but I would say the answer is an unqualified "*NO.*" Now at this point you may be saying to yourself, "why not?" Well, to better understand why I say that we should not be afraid of logic, consider just one simple practical everyday situation, besides the ones stated in the previous paragraph. Let us say that you are driving down the highway and your gas gauge is almost on empty. You are in the middle of nowhere, so you begin to panic, since you are still 200 miles from your destination, and you do not see a gas station anywhere. Finally, just before you run out of gas, you see a gas station, and the sign reads, "Unleaded - $3.75". Now, do you think to yourself, "I wonder how much the unleaded gasoline is here." after seeing the sign? Do you perhaps keep on driving, hoping to find another gas station to get gas at because you cannot figure out what the sign means when it reads "Unleaded - $3.75"? Of course not! You would automatically assume that this place is a gas station and that the price of the unleaded gasoline at this gas station is $3.75, and assuming you have enough money, you would most likely pull into the gas station and fill your car up with gas. Now, you may be screaming at the page, "What does that story have to do with logic?" It is actually very simple. When you subconsciously decided that the gas price of $3.75 on the sign meant that the gas was $3.75, you were actually using all four laws of logic.[2] Let me explain. When you saw the 3, the 7, and the 5 you assumed that they represented a 3, a 7, and a 5. This is known as the law of identity, which basically states that something is what it is: A is A. In other words, the number 3 is the number 3; the number 7 is the number 7, and so on. Not exactly rocket science is it? Two of the other laws of logic that you used in this instance are the law of non-contradiction and the law of the excluded middle. The law of non-contradiction states that A is not non-A, or more specifically, A cannot be both A and non-A at the same time and in the same sense. So, when you noticed that the 3 in the $3.75 was only a 3 and not also an 8, you were using the law of non-contradiction. The other law of logic, the law of the excluded middle, basically states that something is either one thing or it is something else (either A or non-A). When you noticed that the 5 in the $3.75 was a 5 and not a 7 instead (or some sort of mixture between a 5 and a 7), you were using the law of the excluded middle. The fourth and final law of logic is the law of rational inference, which you used when you deduced from what the sign said that the gas station that owned the sign would actually charge you the price on the sign for unleaded gas, or we could say that you inferred from the fact that the sign was outside of this particular gas station that this particular gas station owned the sign rather than some other gas station further down

---

[2] Ibid, 16.

the road that just happened to place their sign in this gas station's parking lot. This of course seems silly, but it is a classic example of how often we use the laws of logic without even thinking about them or knowing that we are using them. So, in this one simple scenario you have used all four of the laws of logic.

So, let us be realistic with ourselves. Is logic really something that is incredibly difficult? Obviously not, as we have just seen above. Not only is logic not difficult, it is also very important, as we use it practically every time we have a thought. Now that we have seen how the laws of logic are used by us in a seemingly effortless manner much of the time, we are going to move on to see what logic has to do specifically with this book.

First, we will take a brief look at what logical formal and informal fallacies are, and then we will look at a few examples of informal fallacies. Then we will take a closer look at a specific type of informal fallacy called the slippery slope fallacy, followed by a few examples, and then we will discuss how the assertion that "Teaching Intelligent Design (ID) in the public school science classrooms will lead to teaching Young Earth Creationism (YEC) in the public school science classrooms, and so therefore we should not teach Intelligent Design in the public science classrooms," fits neatly and firmly into the category of the slippery slope fallacy and why that is a problem.

Formal and Informal Fallacies

Before we begin looking at formal and informal fallacies, let me just say that, like the laws of logic that we discussed above, formal and informal fallacies are also, in general, not very difficult to comprehend, although formal fallacies are a little more abstract in nature, since they deal with the particular form of an argument, rather than the content of an argument, which is what informal fallacies deal with.[3] Now we do not need to concern ourselves with formal fallacies here, due to the nature of the argument in this book revolving around an informal fallacy and not a formal one, so suffice it to say, as stated above, that formal fallacies have to do with the form of an argument, and not the content. In other words, regardless of what the content of the argument is when dealing with a formal fallacy, if the form of the argument is wrong, then the argument does not work and so it is false.

Now as far as informal fallacies go, there are many different kinds, and they are far more common in everyday life than you probably think. For instance, have you ever gotten into an argument with someone who obviously knew they could not win the argument (perhaps you have even done this yourself), so instead of simply saying that they are wrong, they say something like, "well you're stupid" or "I hate you" (this is classic in the teenage sector) and then they either stand there waiting for you to

---

[3] Ibid, 13.

respond or they leave the area so as to end the argument right then and there, as if they somehow won? This is an extremely simplified form of a specific informal fallacy known as *Argumentum ad Hominem (abusive)*.[4] Basically, when this fallacy is committed, one of the people in the discussion attacks the individual in the discussion instead of actually addressing the argument that they have made. The problem with this, and other informal fallacies, is that the information or assertion presented by the one committing the fallacy is irrelevant to the argument. In other words, to cite the above example, whether your friend thinks you are stupid or not, or further so even if you really are stupid, that does not necessarily mean that your argument is fallacious, whatever your argument may be (unless of course your argument is that you are not stupid, if you really are). To put it another way, the truth or falsity of one's argument is in no way dependent on the character or traits of the one presenting the argument. So, when the *Argumentum ad Hominem (abusive)* fallacy is committed, the person is attacking the character of the other person in the discussion and not their particular argument. This fallacy is all too common in our day and age, so watch out for it. Next time someone commits this fallacy in a discussion with you simply look at them and say, "Ok, but what about my argument?"

---

[4] Ibid, 93.

Another type of fallacy that is incredibly common, especially in political debates and such, is a fallacy known as the genetic fallacy. "The genetic fallacy occurs whenever someone assesses the value of a view or practice on the basis of the origins (genesis) of the view or practice."[5] Have you ever been watching a political debate, and one of the debaters says something to the effect of, "Well you can't believe what he says because he committed check fraud 20 years ago," or maybe you work at a high school and during your lunch hour you heard someone say, "You can't believe her views on raising teachers' salaries because she is a teacher."

Now, in the first example the person opposed to the argument in question is basically saying that since the one making the argument committed check fraud, he is necessarily untrustworthy and therefore his argument must be rejected. But again, the fact that he committed check fraud, and even the fact that he is sometimes untrustworthy (we all are at times), does not necessitate falsity with regard to his argument. Now of course, if it could be shown that he is always untrustworthy, then that would be entirely different, for then one might very well claim that his argument could necessarily be rejected as false, but such an ambitious claim (such as that someone is *always* untrustworthy) is very difficult, if not impossible to prove, and so the genetic fallacy stands and the argument

---

[5] Mark B. Woodhouse, *A Preface to Philosophy* (Belmont: Wadsworth, 2006), 84.

cannot be rejected on the grounds that this man committed check fraud and is sometimes untrustworthy, for the origin of the argument, namely the person making it in the debate, has no direct bearing on the truth or falsity of that argument. Although this example may seem similar to the *Argumentum ad Hominem (abusive)* fallacy, it is actually different since in the *ad Hominem* argument the one committing the fallacy is directly attacking the individual, often times not even addressing the actual argument, while in the genetic fallacy the one committing the fallacy is claiming that the other person's argument is false because of who or where it comes from.

As for the second example of the genetic fallacy listed above, it is often argued in this fashion that the person making the argument is biased and therefore their argument must necessarily be rejected. Now, to be fair, it is possible that the person making the argument is indeed being led by their own bias, and that they have a selfish motive to why they are claiming what they are claiming, but even so, that does not mean that what they are claiming is false. For example, if the teacher is claiming that she and the other teachers at the school she teaches at are underpaid, based on the average pay of other teachers at other schools within the same school district, and her main motivation for claiming this is that she wants to get paid more so she can buy a nicer car, this personal selfish motivator or bias does not in any way necessarily mean that her argument is faulty or fallacious. If the fact is that they do get paid less than the other teachers within the same school district, then all things being equal maybe they should get a pay raise so that they are making the same as the other teachers. The fact that it is a teacher who is making this claim is irrelevant. So we can easily see how this fallacy, known as the genetic fallacy, is basically made up of presumptuous claims that do not necessarily have anything to do with the argument at hand, but rather they are based on the origin of the argument, which in this instance is the person that the argument is coming from and their background or what they do for a living. Now, I must point out here that there are many other ways that the genetic fallacy can be used, and these examples are just two of those ways.

Next, before we move on to discuss the slippery slope fallacy we need to look at one more genetic fallacy example. This example is extremely pertinent with regard to this book and the arguments herein, and it is also a much more personal example. I am not new to this world and how things work. I am not naïve enough to think that someone at some point will not use the fallacious reasoning that I am about to discuss, even though I am going to adequately refute it here and now, but it needs to be addressed nevertheless for the benefit of my overall argument in this book. The fallacy that I am referring to goes something like this: "You can't believe what Trevor Slone says about the slippery slope fallacy that if you teach ID in the public school science classrooms it will lead to teaching YEC in the public school science classrooms, or anything he says about evolution or science, because Trevor Slone is a Christian and a young earth creationist." Now indeed I am a Christian, and I do advocate YEC, on both scientific and biblical grounds, but those facts have absolutely no bearing, as we have seen in the other genetic fallacy examples that we have looked at, on whether or not my arguments, in this book or anywhere else, are valid, sound, truthful and so on, for such arguments depend solely on the facts rather than on my own personal beliefs.

Now, as you will see in the following section, there are two methods to refuting a slippery slope fallacy, and you only need to provide one of these methods of reasonable refutation to prove that the argument is fallacious and that it should therefore be rejected. Therefore, as long as I am able to use at least one of these two methods to show that the argument is fallacious, we will have successfully defeated this slippery slope fallacy regarding ID and YEC and the public science classrooms, and so then we must reject such an argument as false. The most important thing to remember to do when determining whether an argument is truthful or not is to simply let the argument speak for itself, or in other words, just look at the claims within the argument. If they are true and they cohere with one another and with the facts to form a sound and valid argument overall, then accept the argument as true. If not then reject it as false. It is that simple.

The Slippery Slope Fallacy

So, we have looked at two out of many possible informal fallacies, namely the *Argumentum ad Hominem (abusive)*, which is when someone attacks the arguer instead of the argument, and the genetic fallacy, where someone attacks the origin of an argument rather than the argument itself. We are now going to look at the main type of informal fallacy relevant to this book, the slippery slope fallacy.

The slippery slope fallacy may not be quite as common as the fallacies discussed above, but it is nevertheless probably far more common than you think. Let us look at a fairly modern example. I have heard some people recently claim that f we teach sex education in kindergarten, this will just encourage the children to have sex at younger ages and eventually it will lead to an increase in teen or even preteen pregnancies. Now this may very well be true, but is it *necessarily* true? There are two ways to defend against a slippery slope fallacy. The first way is to show that the alleged undesirable consequence does not follow *inevitably* from the proposal. The second is to grant that the consequence does follow but to show that the consequence is not *necessarily* undesirable.[6] Now I think it is safe to say, at least to my knowledge, that few people would be willing to go as far as to argue in the direction of the second way of debunking the slippery slope fallacy in this instance, namely that an increase in teen and even preteen pregnancies is not undesirable, or, put positively, that it is desirable that more teens and preteens become pregnant. That just sounds crazy and wrong to most of us. Of course some would probably disagree with that statement and claim that this is a desirable thing, or that it is the right of the children to decide whether or not they want to be pregnant, but that is another issue for another time and place, and it is outside the scope of the purposes of this book. The other way to discredit the fallacy is to show that the stated consequence does not necessarily follow from the initial hypothetical (If...) statement. This seems like a much more plausible task at this point to me. Now for the record let me just say that I am not an advocate for teaching sex education in kindergarten, for I believe that a child's parents should be responsible and teach their children about sex and the issues involved themselves, at an early enough age that the child can know the facts about such things in time to make adequate decisions regarding such issues, preferably before the child hits puberty, instead of letting them find out some other way, such as from TV shows, or even at school. Nevertheless, It seems to be entirely plausible that teaching sex education in kindergarten could make the children more aware of

---

[6] Ibid, 85.

the pros and cons of having sex at a younger age, and in turn might actually cause more kids to wait longer to have sex for the first time, or at least to be more cautious when doing so, than kids currently are on average, thereby possibly decreasing the number of teen and preteen pregnancies.[7] This is of course assuming that the sex education is taught in a responsible manner. So, the slippery slope that "If we teach sex education in kindergarten, this will encourage the students to have sex at younger ages and eventually it will lead to an increase in teen, or even preteen pregnancies," is not necessarily true, and therefore it is a fallacy. Now before we continue to our next example, it needs to be pointed out that if one can show that the stated undesirable consequence will indeed *inevitably* follow, and that the consequence is *truly* undesirable, then there is no fallacy involved and the claim is simply true, but remember that "inevitably" and "truly" are the key terms here. So, let us look at one more example of the slippery slope fallacy, and then we will move on to discuss one of the primary purposes of this book.

Our next example of the slippery slope fallacy goes as follows: "If you give him an inch, he will take a mile."

---

[7] Having said that, it needs to be noted that the way that sex education is currently taught has in fact greatly increased the number of teen and preteen pregnancies over the last several decades, and so if sex education in the school systems is going to reduce the number of such pregnancies then the curriculum and content of such classes would need to need to be greatly altered first.

Now most of us have heard this one before, and most of us know what this phrase means. It basically means that, for instance, if you give your son a five minute grace period on his curfew, he will eventually start coming home ten, twenty, thirty, forty, fifty minutes, or even an hour late. Let us look at the more specific example of the son and the curfew, as it is a good representation of the slippery slope fallacy. Like the previous example, few of us would argue that it is desirable for our children to start coming home an hour past curfew. My son is only five years old and so he obviously does not have a "curfew," because he is with us all the time, but even I already understand that principle. So we cannot in good conscience refute this argument by using the second method, namely by showing that the consequence is not necessarily undesirable.[8] So, that means we must instead show that the stated consequence, that the son will eventually start coming home an hour past curfew, does not necessarily follow from the initial hypothetical statement. This example is very practical and also fairly simplistic, since most people know that some kids, although maybe not very many, would actually appreciate the five minute grace period and, to show respect in return for the leniency, either make sure they are home within that five minute grace period or even possibly come

---

[8] When I say "necessarily undesirable" I mean within reason. There will always be people with overly lax standards that want to push the envelope. These people and what they desire would be considered out of the ordinary and are not part of our discussion here.

home early from time to time, never taking advantage of the grace period that has been provided to them, and so in this case, as the one above, we have successfully shown that the stated consequence does not necessarily follow, and so this is also a slippery slope fallacy, for remember that we only have to show that the consequence does not *necessarily* follow, not that it will *certainly* not follow.

Do you now understand the basics of informal fallacies, and more specifically the *Argumentum ad Hominem (abusive)* fallacy, the genetic fallacy, and the slippery slope fallacy? I hope so, because it is time to move on to one of the primary issues in this book, the slippery slope fallacy that states: "If we teach Intelligent Design in the public school science classrooms it will lead to teaching Young Earth Creationism in the public school science classrooms." Now this argument is quite obviously the same basic type of argument as our other two examples that we looked at above regarding the slippery slope fallacy. Do you remember what the two methods for disproving a slippery slope fallacy are? That's right, we can either show that the stated consequence does not necessarily follow from the initial hypothetical statement, or we can show that the stated consequence is not *necessarily* undesirable. In the following chapters I will not simply attempt to use one of these methods, but I will actually use both of them, showing that not only does teaching Intelligent Design not necessarily lead to teaching Young Earth Creationism, but I will also show that having curse was ultimately fulfilled when the Israelites destroyed much of the Land of Canaan, and this curse was the reason that God told the Israelites to destroy the Canaanites, for the Canaanites were the descendants of Canaan, the one whom God cursed. So the early Americans, as well as anyone else who uses the false assertion that the book of Genesis justifies enslaving anyone, especially thousands of years after this curse had been settled, is very sadly mistaken. The Bible, and especially the New Testament, does not ever condone racism of any kind, including slavery,[19] and Exodus 21:16 specifically condemns forcing people into slavery. Also, to be sure the Bible does not in fact seek to abolish slavery or openly condemn it, but it does argue throughout that proper treatment of other human beings is vital to living a righteous life that is pleasing to God (Matt. 5:43-48; Mark 12:31; Matt. 7:12; Lev. 19:18). I also think it is safe to say that none of us (who are of sound mind) *want* to be the slave of someone else, we are called to treat others the way we want to be treated (Luke 6:31). And still also, Christianity is for every tribe, tongue, and nation (Rev. 7:9), which means that all the peoples of the world, which we are supposed to go

---

[19] It should be noted here that in Leviticus the Bible does condone slavery, but this type of slavery should not be confused with brutal slavery or slavery that belittles others. This slavery was more like hiring people to work with someone and to live with them. The owner was required to treat their slaves well and to provide for them as if they were part of their family, for God calls us to treat all people with dignity and to love our neighbor as ourselves, and one's slaves would surely count as one's neighbor.

and share the gospel with, as Christians, and be a positive witness to for Christ (Matt. 28:18-20), should be treated with the same mindset, namely that they are all potential brothers and sisters in Christ and so therefore we should not do anything to diminish the chances of them being willing to enter the faith and join us as true believers in Christ. Christians are also all supposed to love their brothers and sisters in Christ (1 John 4:21), and this excludes treating them as less than equal, which slavery and racism inevitably entail. Christianity and the Bible therefore teach that we should all avoid human slavery and racism of all kinds, for we are called to have but one Master whom we should serve, and that is Jesus Christ. Evolution, however, is an entirely different matter altogether when it comes to slavery and racism.

We will now end this section of this chapter with a quote from Charles Hodge, who was principal of Princeton Theological Seminary between 1851 and 1878, about what Darwinism (another name for the evolutionary worldview) is. Hodge said, "What is Darwinism? It is Atheism. This does not mean that Darwin himself and all who adopt his views are atheists; but it means that his theory is atheistic, that the exclusion of design from nature is tantamount to atheism."[20] I could not have said it better myself! Let us

---

[20] Charles Hodge, "What is Darwinism?" in *What Is Darwinism? And Other Writings on Science and Religion,* eds. Mark A. Noll and David N. Livingstone (Grand Rapids: Baker, 1994), 177, quoted in Norman Geisler, *Creation & the Courts,* 32-33.

now turn to examine further how evolution promotes racism.

Evolution and Racism

> "At some future period, not very distant as measured by centuries, the *civilized races of man* will almost certainly exterminate, and replace, the *savage races* throughout the world. At the same time the anthropomorphous apes [that is, the ones which allegedly look like people] ... will no doubt be exterminated. The break between man and his nearest allies will then be wider, for it will intervene between man in a more civilized state, as we may hope, even than the Caucasian, and some ape as low as a baboon, instead of as now between the negro or Australian [Aboriginal] and the gorilla' [emphasis added]."[21]

In addition to the quote from Hitler's book noted earlier, we have here a quote by Charles Darwin himself from his book *The Descent of Man* that also exhibits an incredible amount of racism. Now of course Charles Darwin was not the progenitor of evolutionary theory, but

---

[21] Charles Darwin, *The Descent of Man: 2nd ed.* (: London: John Murray, 1887), 156.

he is definitely the one that we think of when we think of evolution, as he started the "evolution revolution"[22] and he is the one that developed the theory primarily into what it is today, aside from the occasional slight change here and there by others since his time and the additions due to technological advancement and new discoveries. Let it also be clear that Darwin here in this quote is not merely asserting his own beliefs, but rather he is discussing what the *inevitable* results are of such a system of belief as evolution.

First, we will look at the beginning of the above quote, and then the remainder of it in various pieces. Darwin says that it is almost certain that the "civilized races" will exterminate the "savage races" throughout the world. We can see through other writings of Darwin, and also through the earlier quote by Hitler that was influenced by Darwinian evolution, that the civilized races are essentially the white man, but who are the savage races of whom he speaks? Well, if the civilized people are the whites, then the savage people, since Darwin has here presented them as opposites, must be the non-white people.

The next sentence in the quote makes an addition to the first claim and mentions the "anthropomorphous apes" and that they will no doubt be exterminated. What is an anthropomorphous ape? Well, simply put it is a man-

---

[22] Geisler, *Creation & the Courts*, 31.

like ape. Darwin is here referring to a group of people obviously still alive in his time that look like apes (to him), only he calls them apes that look like people. It does not take much of an imagination to figure out what people he is talking about here. He is obviously talking about dark skinned individuals. Now we must keep in mind that this idea that the "savages" and the "man-like ape" will be exterminated is a necessary result of what is known as the "survival of the fittest". Without going into detail for now, as the survival of the fittest is a fairly complicated concept, let us just say that it holds that the more and better evolved will survive, find mates, and thrive, and the less and ill-evolved will die and so will not pass on their genetic information to a succeeding generation. So what Darwin is implying here is that dark skinned people are "less evolved" and therefore not as fit to survive (mind you that less evolved normally includes mental capacity and capabilities also), and so they will be exterminated by the stronger, more evolved races. Well, if dark skinned people are less or worse evolved, then it would seem as though the lighter skinned people are more or better evolved (of course from an atheistic perspective aesthetic terms such as "better" and "worse" are essentially meaningless, since, at least according to Augustine beauty stems directly from the essence of God,[23] but for the purpose of our discussion

---

[23] R. Albert Mohler Jr., *The Disappearance of God: Dangerous Beliefs In the New Spiritual Openness* (Colorado Springs: Multnomah Books, 2009), 50-56.

we must use aesthetic terms anyway), and if the darker skinned people are savages, then it would make perfect sense if we were to treat them as lower class people, if even people at all, for in Darwin's terms dark skinned people are merely apes that look like people, and so they would most certainly not deserve the respect and rights that people deserve, at least on this view. But we have already seen that if evolution is true then humans have no rights regardless of skin tone, and we must also remember that terms like "deserve" and "ought" are meaningless from an atheistic perspective, since these are moral terms and morality in general has its origin in God also, but again for our purposes here we must use such terms. Dr. Ravi Zacharias says it well when he states, "While a naturalist may choose to be a moral person, no compelling rational reason exists why one should not be amoral."[24] Now to be amoral is to be non-moral, or in other words, if one is a naturalist (which most evolutionists are) then, based on his or her worldview, there is no rational reason why he or she should not simply live as if morals do not exist. This would mean that rape is not wrong, nor is murder, theft, adultery, and so on, but this would also mean that loving is not right, nor is sharing, giving, caring for others, helping those in need, and so on. In this light nothing is right or wrong, but rather everything simply is what it is. Let me just say here that Darwin in these first two sentences of

---

[24] Ravi Zacharias, *The Grand Weaver: How God Shapes Us Through the Events of Our Lives* (Grand Rapids: Zondervan, 2007), 76.

the above quote has essentially said that from an evolutionary perspective dark skinned people are inferior to lighter skinned people, and it doesn't take a genius to figure out how that ties into racism.

Next, in the final words of this quote, we see that Darwin is hoping that the break (presumably referring to species branching off in evolutionary terms) between man and his nearest "allies" (genetic relatives) will grow wider due to the extermination of the dark skinned people. It is also made clear in this part of the quote that the "civilized" and the "man-like apes" in the first part of the quote are Caucasians and dark-skinned people, as he makes a parallel comparison between the civilized/savages/man-like apes and the Caucasians/Negros/Australians. Why he hopes for such a gap in genetic relation I do not know, nor do I care to ponder such things. What I am concerned with is what follows that statement, namely the comparison of the baboon as our hopeful closest relative and the "negro" or Australian and the gorilla. We see here that Darwin clearly puts Negros (dark-skinned people) and Australians in the same category as baboons and gorillas in terms of species. If you are a non-white person reading this book right now, take a second and think about these implications of evolution and what they mean for you and your life specifically. What does all this mean for your family? If you have kids, do you want them growing up in a nation that touts such things, even though they don't talk about these unsavory implications? Do you want your kids being taught this stuff, namely evolution, in school? If you are a white person reading this book right now, ask yourself, "Is this an appropriate way to look at people; living, breathing, walking, talking, and feeling people?" I don't know about you, but I get incensed whenever I even think about people being treated or looked at this way. If you are a non-white person who believes in evolution, you are either sadly unaware of the implications of evolution regarding racism, or you don't care about such implications, and I most certainly do not understand why any inquiring mind would subject themselves to either scenario.

In his book *Understanding World Religions* Irving Hexham states that "as a result of growing secularism and the theory of evolution.....the claim that such peoples (Africans) were lower on the evolutionary scale than Europeans" became popular. The claim indicated that the Africans "were not fully human, but were more closely related to monkeys than to men and women. Therefore, slavery and other forms of discrimination and exploitation were fully justified."[25] Hexham also points out that as evolutionist anthropologists made such arguments, they also argued that the Africans who had been in contact with the Europeans were merely imitating them, and that they were in fact "too low on the evolutionary scale to think for themselves."[26] To further this line of argumentation, "*The*

[25] Irving Hexham, *Understanding World Religions* (Grand Rapids: Zondervan, 2011), 79.

Anthropological Review reported that at a meeting of the Anthropological Society in London on 17 November 1863, 'A comparison was drawn between the anatomical differences existing between the Negro and the ape.' Consequently, Africans were said to be nearer to apes than Europeans."[27] That Africans were lower on the evolutionary ladder also justified colonialism.[28] It needs to be said here that comparing anatomical similarities and differences between animals, or between animals and humans has no necessary link as to whether or not they are in fact related or not. After all, we sometimes see on television and in art galleries pieces of fruit and vegetables that very much resemble the faces of different famous individuals, but are we to assume that these fruits and vegetables are somehow related to these people, especially closely related? Absolutely not, as that is clearly absurd, even to the average evolutionist (I would hope at least)! This may sound like something far different from what the evolutionists are doing in comparing the similarities between monkeys and people, but in fact they claim that we are related to the plants as well (although much further on down the line of ancestry), and so this is not really a farfetched question, whether the evolutionist

---

[26] Ibid, 81.
[27] Numerous articles on this topic are to be found in *The Anthropological Review*. See, e.g. vol. 2 (1864):xv-xxlvi; vol 3 (1865): 120 ff, footnoted in Irving Hexham, *Understanding World Religions*, 98.
[28] Ibid, 98.

wants to admit it or not, regardless of how genetically different our DNA may be from those food items, because after all, we are not talking about DNA here, but rather we are talking about similarities and differences in form. Sure one could argue that the fruits and vegetables that are naturally shaped like famous people are an anomaly instead of the norm, as opposed to the monkeys that normally look like certain people, but again the basic principle is the same, namely that form is what is being compared to determine relation. On this particular point, from a strictly morphological standpoint, if we are going to argue that monkeys are related to humans because they look similar, then the fruit and vegetable argument above is equally valid, and I don't think that anyone would actually argue that those famous people are "closely related" to their fruit or vegetable counterparts on that basis, so why should we use such an argument with regards to monkeys and humans? The answer is that we shouldn't! The fact that some monkeys look like some humans means at the very least that, quite simply, some monkeys look like some humans, or it could also mean that those monkeys and humans were all created by the same individual with a similar design in mind when he created them, whoever or whatever this creator may be. I of course am inclined to believe that this creator is the Judeo-Christian God of the Bible, but this is not a necessary inference of this information.

It is no wonder kids are becoming more aggressive. It is no wonder bullying has increased dramatically over the past few decades in our schools around the country. When we teach kids principles like survival of the fittest, we are just asking for them to feel the need and responsibility to "weed out" the weaker kids in their classrooms or on the playground. My wife used to be a GRA (Graduate Research Assistant) for a Principles of Biology class at the institution she was attending for her graduate studies. She told me that one day they had an entire list of games that they could choose from to play to teach the students the concept of survival of the fittest. Actually I think the name of the game that they chose to teach the students was called "Survival of the Fittest." Basically they had several teams and they did several different things, and each time the slowest people on one or both of the teams was eliminated. Now to some extent this is how most games work, but think about it. They are teaching these kids that this is how *LIFE* works, not just a game. They are teaching these kids that these are undeniable principles of how this world works. They are teaching these kids that if you are bigger, faster, stronger, or smarter, you will dominate and take out those smaller, slower, weaker, and less intelligent than yourself, and that is just the way it is. I am 5' 8 1/2", 212 pounds (fairly lean) I can curl around 100 pounds with each arm, and I have an IQ of about 160. According to these principles why should I be nice to almost anyone? Why should I talk to most people like they are my equal? Why should I not go around beating smaller, weaker guys up and taking their girlfriends and wives? Why should I respect even most of my professors in college? Why should I love these other people? Why should I treat them like they matter, or like they have dignity? Why should I not walk around acting like I am better than almost everyone that I come into contact with? Well, from an evolutionary perspective, the answer is just that; for the "why nots" above, "Why not?" Those are precisely the things I would be expected to do according to evolution. And for the "whys", there is absolutely no reason why I should do any of these things. Of course, someone who is stronger and smarter may come along and treat me this same way, and there would of course be nothing wrong with that according to the evolutionary principle of the survival of the fittest. A classic example of this can be seen in that in 1924 a young man was charged with the murder of another young man. His defense attorney "argued that it was the influence of atheist and evolutionist Friedrich Nietzsche on the young man that led him to" murder this other young man. The attorney "also cited Darwin himself (in *The Descent of Man*) approving of savage and barbarous acts in emulation of nature which weed out the weak and inferior breeds."[29] Now, this was merely an argument by the attorney and not necessarily a fact, but as we have already seen this attorney's argument fits squarely with the teachings of

---

[29] Geisler, *Creation & the Courts*, 34.

evolution, and so it cannot simply be dismissed. Contrary to what evolutionary atheist Sam Harris[30] and others assert, there is no basis for morality within a naturalistic evolutionary framework, and there never will be. The main point of life, according to evolution, is to procreate and propagate the species at any cost. This brings me to my next point.[31]

Evolution and Rape

Although rape is something that, unless one is seriously demented, absolutely disgusts us as humans and is a very clear violation of human dignity, it is nevertheless something that, according to the evolutionary worldview, is natural. Remember that objective morals do not exist in a world where naturalistic macro-evolution is true, and so for those who believe that naturalistic macro-evolution is a reality rape is not, by logical implication, wrong, according to their worldview. There is a book that makes this point, namely that rape is a natural part of evolution and humanity, very clear. The book is titled *A Natural History of Rape: Biological Bases of Sexual Coercion*.[32] Of course this book also attempts to argue that rape is somehow

---

[30] See Sam Harris' book *The Moral Landscape: How Science Can Determine Human Values* (New York: Free Press, 2010).
[31] I also realize the absurdity of postulating purpose in a purely random framework such as evolution, but that does not stop the evolutionists from doing so anyway, as they are clearly unconcerned with the truth, which will be seen in a later chapter of this book.
[32] Randy Thornhill and Craig T. Palmer, *A Natural History of Rape: Biological Bases of Sexual Coercion* (Cumberland: MIT Press, 2000).

wrong, and they certainly do not try to justify rape. But nevertheless if rape is just a natural part of life, and if God does not exist, then as we will see below it follows that there is absolutely nothing wrong with it. Now do not mistake what I am trying to say here. I am not saying that all evolutionists are rapists, and I am also not saying that all evolutionists condone rape. What I am saying is that, based on a belief in naturalistic macro-evolution (the most common evolutionary view among scientists), rape is merely another expression of survival of the fittest, for in this view the males who are stronger and more powerful will naturally find women to mate with to procreate and make stronger and more powerful generations in turn. Is this not essentially what animals do? We do not view it as rape though when animals do this because animals are viewed as amoral creatures. But wait! Did we not see earlier in this chapter that from a naturalistic perspective humans are to be looked at as amoral? This is indeed the case, unless of course one is to impose some sort of personal moral standard, but that would be completely arbitrary and there is nothing binding anyone to that standard other than their own arbitrary beliefs at that point, for if we are not created, but rather we are all just cosmic accidents resulting from purely random processes, then what right do we have to attribute any sort of dignity or worth to ourselves or anyone else, or to uphold any sort of morality whatsoever? The fact is that we have no right to do so if we are indeed products of pure randomness, for randomness necessarily is devoid of purpose, and without purpose there is a complete and necessary lack of meaning and value, and meaning without purpose is nonsensical. Also, value is an aesthetic term, and again like we saw earlier aesthetic properties such as beauty and value stem from the essence of God, and if He does not exist, or at least if we are not from Him in some way, such as being created by Him, then value is a meaningless term.

I understand the concept that if you truly believe evolution is real, then if you are going to maintain any level of internal consistency you must follow the implications of such beliefs to whatever end they may so lead you to. That is not the issue here. What is the issue is that our country, our schools, our museums, and our government are preaching the doctrines of evolution as if they are some grand thing to be marveled at. Well, I don't know about you, but for me rape is most certainly not something to be marveled at, at least not in the positive sense. To say that something so hideous and demeaning as rape is simply natural to humans, just as, say, bowel movements or what color our eyes are[33] is about as appalling of a statement as one can make, especially if one is still going to try and uphold the dignity of humanity at the same time. And we must also remember that this statement that rape is natural brings with it the

---

[33] This is essentially what the evolutionists here are claiming, as there cannot be different levels of natural. Something is either natural or it is not.

implication, again from a naturalistic perspective, that it is not wrong, but rather that it is at worst an amoral act. I personally have known many young women who have been victims of this horrendous crime, and all of them are permanently scarred from the experience. Rape is something that is also becoming much more common at universities around the country. People feel that they have a right to take advantage of the weaker, more fragile individuals, and as we saw above, from an evolutionary standpoint there is absolutely nothing wrong with that. That rape is a growing problem on college campuses should also not be surprising based the fact that we have already seen above that they teach such concepts as survival of the fittest as though it is a game at state universities, and as we have also seen above, there is no meaning to the words "right" or "wrong" from an evolutionary perspective.

My mother has been a victim of hundreds upon hundreds of rapes, due to her brother and her father's deplorable habits when she was growing up, as well as another in her adult life when we lived in Germany. I remember when I was 9 years old my mom started having a flash back in the middle of our living room. We did not know what was going on, for none of us, not even my dad, knew about my mom's past. As the days went on the flashbacks got longer and longer. Finally the flashbacks got so bad that the therapist told us that it actually might be possible that she would die while having one, for they were lasting so long that he wasn't sure if she would ever come out them at some point (we are talking flashbacks that lasted hours, sometimes all through the night). She even had one once while she was driving seventy miles an hour down the interstate highway, and she got into a terrible accident and almost got crushed by oncoming traffic.[34] I don't know if you have ever experienced someone you love so dearly having a flashback, especially a 3-6 hour long, (or longer) flashback, especially when you were only 9 or 10 years old, but it is a very scary thing, and it is very unnerving to say the least.[35] I myself developed Bipolar 1 disorder partly due to my mother's past and how she treated me because of it. Let me assure you that rape always hurts someone, and most of the time it hurts many more people than just one. Over the next ten years my mom was in and out of mental hospitals, and I myself have been hospitalized four times since age 15 due to my bipolar 1 disorder.[36] Sometimes we would wake up in the middle of the night and mom would be gone, and we would find her two or three days later in a hospital somewhere across town. Eventually she developed Multiple Personality Disorder, and I assure you that this

---

[34] She did over $8,000 worth of damage to our van in this accident (mind you this was almost 20 years ago too), completely smashing the entire back end.

[35] It is even more unsettling when you are the one trying to talk them out of the flashback for the entire 3-6 hours, as a 9 or 10 year old.

[36] I also have ADHD, and the comorbidity factors for people who have both bipolar 1 disorder and ADHD are very severe, which is partly why my life has been an incredibly difficult one.

too is not something that is easy to deal with, especially for the one who has it. There were times when she would slip into her personality as herself when she was 4 or 5 years old and she would freak out because in her mind she lived in a different state with different people, so she did not recognize our house or any of us, including dad, and so often times she would leave the house in the middle of the night walking all around town by herself, in her pajamas, trying to find her house that she no longer lived in and her family that she no longer lived with. The problem was that she was not 4 or 5, but 40 years old, and she thought she lived in Ohio, but she really lived in Kansas. So whenever we realized that she was gone we would have to get the police to search the streets for her and we would have to run around town looking for her, hoping that she was not abducted or laying in a ditch somewhere, or trying to get into a house that wasn't ours. She also has PTSD, which is all too common these days due to the growing amount of violence in the world. There is much, much more to my mother's story, and I tell what I tell of it only with the utmost respect for my mom. She has been an incredible inspiration to me in showing me that it is possible to persevere through even the most atrocious of events and circumstances.

The point I want to make here is this. Rape is an absolutely unacceptable act that is wrong, illegal, degrading, invasive, and many other things that are all very much on the negative side of reality, but from an evolutionary perspective there is absolutely nothing wrong with it at all. It is just natural! Of course, few if any evolutionists would admit to this, and even fewer would actually go as far as to say that rape is acceptable, for one would have to be a monster to say such a thing, and I am most certainly not accusing evolutionists of saying that, but rather I am simply stating that what they teach implies that rape is an amoral act at worst. Deep down in our hearts we all know that something as horrible as rape is wrong, no matter how many people tell us that evolution is real or the implications so involved therein. We must fight such a notion as that survival of the fittest is ultimately the way that the world works and that we should just learn to live with it and accept it, for the very thriving of the human race along the lines of anything more than simply passing on our genes to the next generation demands that we do so. Now, there is one more issue I want to discuss regarding why the prominence of evolution matters, and that is anarchy. After we look briefly at how evolution promotes anarchy we will conclude this chapter with some closing remarks.

Evolution and Anarchy

This one might sound odd to some people as an implication and outcome of evolution, but give me a few pages to explain and I am sure I will have you convinced.[37]

---

[37] This is of course assuming that you are looking for the truth, and that you are not simply set in your ways of thinking about such things.

Now, we saw a little earlier that if evolution is true then morality goes out the window by implication. What I am really saying here is that if our society purports that evolution is true, and if we teach it in our schools, and if our nation at large gets used to the idea that evolutionary principles are ultimately an accurate representation of the way that things work in this world, then eventually people in our culture are going to realize that there is no good reason to follow rules, laws, or any type of authority, unless of course we just want to, which would be a completely arbitrary decision at best. Take the bullying in American schools that we talked about earlier for example. When I was a kid I got picked on a lot. Between my ADHD, my glasses, being incredibly skinny, then being very fat, and my being smarter than almost everyone around me including my teachers (I say this with full humility, as the Lord alone is to be glorified for my giftedness), I got picked on a lot, mainly because I did not fit in. Of course the fact that I would preach to my friends during recess about Jesus and the Bible probably didn't make me any more popular either during elementary school. Now, mind you that I went to eleven different schools in 6 different states, from the West coast to the East coast to the North and to the South of America, between kindergarten and twelfth grade. Even though I got picked on on a daily basis growing up, as did many other kids in the schools that I went to, the kind of bullying that goes on today was never present, at least to my knowledge, when I was growing up, and most certainly not to the extent that it is present today. Granted the rise of the internet, cell phones, social networks, and technology in general have made people much more aware of the kind of bullying that is prevalent in our society, but these things have also contributed to the number of ways that bullying can occur. I remember a few years ago how appalled and astonished I was when I saw on the news that a group of teenagers had invited a girl from school over to a house, and when she got there they brutally beat her as a group, videotaped the whole thing, and posted the video on the internet so that other people could watch! I simply could not fathom this kind of evil and hatred in such young people. I do not mean that I was unaware that this kind of thing was possible for such young people to do, but rather I have never been able to understand the immense hatred that some people possess toward other people. Even though I have been wronged by a great deal of people, and even though there have been some incredibly evil people even in my own family going only a few generations back,[38] I can honestly say that I do not hate any of them, nor do I hate anyone else, for my Lord God Almighty has taken the ability to hate people

---

[38] My grandpa and uncle on my mom's side were actual Devil worshippers who literally sacrificed dozens of people, often my mom's friends, and then burned them when they were done so as to leave no evidence. They are also the ones who raped my mom on a daily basis as she was growing up from the time she was a baby on. Also, one of my great grandparents was a leader of a chapter of the KKK.

away from me. I love all people, even you, whoever you are as you read this, and I would gladly die for anyone on this planet were it absolutely necessary. But those are not character traits that come from a belief in evolution. Those are character traits that stem from a strong foundation of biblical Christianity and from the God who created us all in His image. Evolution teaches us that if we are to survive then we must exploit and demean those who are weaker than us. Evolution teaches us that the biggest, the strongest, the fastest, and the smartest will be the ones who ultimately survive and thrive. So what are we to tell the children who have diseases or impairments that hinder them from being strong, smart, or fast, or people who are simply genetically less endowed than others? This is ultimately the issue that brought about the eugenics movement of the twentieth century, and it is also most likely the reason for so many teen suicides these days, for if they are not meant to survive and thrive, then why live at all, right? At least that is how the thinking goes as far as the implications of evolution on human thriving. But alas, I digress, for I could go on and on with regard to this discussion, but our topic at hand is anarchy, and so to it we shall now return.

Whether it be bullying in school, gangs on the streets, Arian's spouting there non-sense about white supremacy, the Black Panthers preaching their error of black superiority, or any number of other things, all of these are encouraged by an evolutionary mindset, for if objective moral values are not a viable option, then why do anything other than exactly what we want to do when we want to do it? Why not rape the five year old girl next door simply because it seems fun and desirable? Why not beat the wimpy kid at school until he is unconscious because he wouldn't give you his lunch money, or because he did give you his lunch money? Why not rob bank after bank after bank and kill everyone that stands in your way, just because you don't want to work for a living? Why not? Why Not? WHY NOT? This is ultimately where our nation is headed. There is no need to wonder why when people in Europe these days get mad at the government, instead of protesting peacefully they set buildings and entire city blocks on fire, beat up police officers, and mob the streets for days or even weeks on end. It is because Evolution has become so prevalent in Europe by now that they are experiencing the ramifications of such a worldview.

Also, "in 2006, Gallup published a survey in the Gallup Management Journal showing stats through the second quarter of 2006. At the time they found that among workers eighteen or older in the United States, 15 percent (about 20.6 million people) were actively disengaged. Gallup estimated that it cost employers $328 billion."[39] More recent surveys have shown that more than

---

[39] _____,"Gallup Study: Engaged Employees Inspire Company Innovation," *Gallup Management Journal,* 12 October 2006, http://gmj.gallup.com/content/24880/Gallup-Study-Engaged-Employees-Inspire-Company-Innovation.aspx (accessed 2 July 2010), quoted in John C. Maxwell, *The 5 Levels of Leadership: Proven Steps to*

half of all German employees were disengaged from their work.[40] So we see here that in the countries where evolution has some of the strongest holds on society people are becoming actively disengaged from their work. Of course this could be for other reasons than just an evolutionary worldview, but the fact is that evolution is most likely part of the reason for the crises. If you can't figure out how this information relates to anarchy, think about this: If people are getting paid to do a specific job at a specific level by their bosses and the companies that they work for, yet they are actively disengaged from that work in a way that is costing companies such a large amount of money, do you think they are really that concerned with the stipulations and rules that their bosses have about job productivity and other issues? Absolutely not! And if they are not concerned about what their boss says, it is only a small leap to get to a place where these same people are no longer concerned with what their government says. Now don't get me wrong here, I am not saying that all slackers are anarchists. I am simply saying that if such slacking is already a widespread trend, it is not that much of a leap to see how these same people, if they are continually taught and they continually believe in

---

Maximize Your Potential (New York: Thomas Nelson Inc., 2011), 62-63.
[40] Marco Nink, "Employee Disengagement Plagues Germany," *Gallup Management Journal*, 9 April 2009, http://gmj.gallup.com/content/117376/Employee-Disengagement-Plagues-Germany.aspx (accessed 2 July 2010), quoted by John C. Maxwell, *The 5 Levels of Leadership,* 63.

evolution and its principles, and that God does not exist, will start to care less and less about laws, just like they already don't care about work rules. Dr. Winfried Corduan, the one who wrote the foreword for this book, is from Germany, and he told me that you can find, in Europe, the anarchy symbol plastered all over the place, including all over buildings and other places.

Evolution is also, at least in part, the reason that churches have died out in Europe to a large degree, for after all, if God does not exist, as evolution purports, then why go to church? It is completely inevitable that we, America, in the not so distant future are going to experience the same level of anarchy and godlessness as Europe is experiencing right now if we stay on this preposterous track of telling the world and our countryman that evolution is a proven fact and that we must learn to accept it and its implications. I would strongly argue that the only reason we haven't already experienced what Europe is experiencing in these regards is because many people in America either have not thought through the implications of evolution yet, or they simply do not care enough to live out such implications, but when the day comes, America will undoubtedly have only itself to blame for the destruction of what was once said to be the greatest nation on earth.

Conclusion

We have seen that evolution is at least partially responsible for many negative things in today's American society, including the "removal of God" from our nation and the increase in bullying. We have also seen that evolution is partially responsible for the anarchy that is so prevalent in Europe that will inevitably make its way to America if we don't change what we teach the people of our nation. Still also we have seen that the implications of evolution are, among other things, that rape is nothing more than a Darwinian act of survival of the fittest, and that moral values do not exist, regardless of what the humanists try to tell us. I encourage you to do your own research and, if you do it with an open mind and if you search the right material, you will discover that there is *no* legitimate evidence in support of evolution being real, and there are mountains of evidence that are growing daily against evolution.[41] It would be one thing if evolution really were a proven fact (we will discuss this in a later chapter), but since it is not, and since evidence in favor of evolution is completely lacking, we should be on guard against it at all costs, especially due to the reasons discussed above.

The prominence of evolution is much more serious than most people seem to realize, and that is one of the main reasons that I am writing this book, because America

-----

[41] Check out the section titled "Critiques of Darwinism" in the Additional Information section at the end of this book for further resources on this issue.

needs to know the implications of what we are teaching our children, what we are filling our citizens minds with, and where we are headed as a nation if evolution continues to be the dominating motif of life and industry in our country. The impertinence of evolutionary theory must be addressed, and it must be addressed soon, on a worldwide level, and we must remain persistent until we reach an unmitigated abolishment of such an overarching atrocity, for if we do not, abortion, rape, incest, murder, genocide, and every other unholy thing will ultimately become "just another step in the evolutionary process," and nothing more.

In the first chapter we looked at the basics of logic, and now in this chapter we discussed why the teachings and implications of evolution matter so much. Now we are going to discuss whether the modern mainstream scientific community is really looking for the truth, or whether they have a different agenda of some sort. However, first we must take a brief look at truth and what exactly it is, so as to better understand the nature of the thing, namely truth, which is to what we now turn in the next chapter.

3

What is Truth and Why Does It Matter?

"'What is truth?'"

-          *Pontius Pilate in John 18:38 (HCSB)*

"You will know the truth, and the truth will set you free."

-          *Jesus the Christ in John 8:32 (HCSB)*

Truth is a word that is constantly being thrown around no matter where you go, what you watch on TV, what you read, or who you talk to. It is, in my opinion, one of the most important words in the English language, and, of course, its equivalent in all other languages is equally important. We all want to know the truth about what the weather is going to be like tomorrow wherever we are. We all want to know the truth about what our government is really doing with our tax dollars. And we most certainly all want to know the truth about the war on terror, for we obviously want to be prepared for whatever might happen that might change the very course of our nation, let alone the course of history itself. Everyone wants to know the truth, or so it seems. Do we all really want to know the truth though? And maybe even more importantly than that, do we all want everyone else to know the truth, or are we simply concerned about our own agenda, getting what we want when we want it, and shutting out anyone and anything who might disagree with us, whether the truth is on our side or not?[1] These are some very deep and pertinent questions, and many of us take these questions for granted, especially in our society, where any question we have can be answered a hundred different ways, all of them contradicting one another, simply by getting on the internet and typing in your question in a search engine box. I don't know about you, but I certainly don't want to walk around believing a bunch of rubbish that is not true. Besides, "Virtually all theorists agree that true belief is a necessary condition for knowledge."[2] Now, stop and think about that for a minute. Do you realize what that means? It basically means that for you to be able to legitimately claim that you know anything about anything at all, or put a different way, for you to actually be able to know something, you not only have to believe it, but it also has to be true.[3] Now I remember when I learned that, and it

---

[1] Most of these questions will be addressed, regarding the modern mainstream scientific community, in the next chapter.

[2] Ted Honderich, ed., *Philosophy: The Oxford Guide* (Oxford: Oxford University Press, 2005), 478

[3] I am also of the persuasion that one must be justified in believing something that is true for them to truly know it, but for the purposes of keeping this chapter simple and basic I will avoid a discussion of

immediately changed my entire view on what it meant to know something, let alone what it meant to know a lot of things. The above description of knowledge shows very clearly that if anything you believe is not 100% true, you don't actually know it, because anything that is false is by definition unknowable. Now do not mistake what I am saying here, as I am certainly not saying that it is impossible to know that something is false. Any truthful claim that states a falsehood is by definition a truthful statement, and therefore is knowable. However, what I am saying is that the falsehood itself is unknowable. For instance, you cannot know *that* the moon is made out of cheese, because "The moon is made out of cheese." is a false statement. But, if you were to say, "It is false that the moon is made out of cheese." then that is a true statement and therefore that is something that you can know, namely that it is false that the moon is made out of cheese, or put another way, that the moon is not made out of cheese. Does that make sense? Good.

What we have just discussed, however briefly, is primarily studied and discussed in another field of philosophy known as Epistemology, the study of knowledge and how knowledge is attained. We are also going to talk in this chapter about relativism and the definition of truth, but as far as knowledge is concerned, the above discussion is pretty much as far as we are going

---

justification regarding knowledge, as it is a bit more technical than the issues of belief and truth.

to go. So suffice it to say that, since you cannot know anything unless you believe it, *and* unless it is also true, if you want to know anything at all then you need to be concerned with truth, and more importantly that what you believe is true, otherwise you are just another person who is wrong about something, and nobody wants to be like that, do they?

Now that we understand the nature of knowledge, and also why truth is important with regard to knowledge, let us take a brief look at what exactly truth is. Is it objective? Is it relative to each individual person? Is it specific to a given culture, and therefore possibly different depending on where you are from and what culture you are part of? In the next section, before we move on to some definitions of truth, we will very quickly look at why truth simply cannot be relative, and henceforth why it must be objective.

Why Truth Must Be Objective

First let me just say that there are many wonderful books and articles about this topic already, so I am going to be brief. It is, however, necessary for the sake of my argument throughout this book that I firmly establish to you, the reader, that truth is objective, otherwise you could read this book, not have any problems with any of it, and still decide that you disagree with my argument and go on believing the exact opposite of what is in this book, and I most certainly do not want that, otherwise I probably would not have even bothered writing this book in the first place. To be sure even though truth is objective you could still choose not to believe it, but that would be foolish, and so I strongly urge you to always believe the truth, whatever it may be. My point here is that if truth is objective, and what is in this book is true, then we all, if we are to have and maintain a decent level of intellectual integrity, must necessarily accept what is in this book, and thereby act accordingly.

Now, to show you that I practice what I preach, and that I firmly believe that all truth is objective and therefore is perfectly acceptable and relevant no matter whom or where it comes from, allow me to start things off here by quoting at length a prominent atheist author and avid supporter of evolution, Sam Harris. In his book, *The Moral Landscape*, he says, on page 45:

> "Moral relativism, however, tends to be self-contradictory. Relativists may say that moral truths exist only relative to a specific cultural framework – but *this* claim about the status of moral truth purports to be true across all possible frameworks. In practice, relativism almost always amounts to the claim that we should be tolerant of moral difference because no moral truth can supersede any other. And yet this commitment to tolerance is not put forward

as simply one relative preference among others deemed equally valid. Rather, tolerance is held to be more in line with the (universal) truth about morality than intolerance is."[4]

There it is, plainly and clearly stated. Now although Sam Harris here is primarily discussing moral relativism, his comments are just as relevant to truth claims in general, because the law of non-contradiction (remember chapter 1) that he alludes to in the very first sentence of the above quotation is a universal law of logic, as are all the other laws of logic, and so relativism in any form is self-contradicting, since for two different people to believe differently about something, anything, and both be right, according to the law of non-contradiction is absurd, whether they are discussing morals or anything else. You see, what Sam Harris is basically saying here is that, for instance, when someone claims that something is morally true and right in one culture based on their views and beliefs, and someone else claims that what they believe is true and right in their cu ture, and the two views contradict each other, many people claim that we should simply be tolerant of each cultures beliefs and views and let them each do things their own way, and not tell either one of them that they are wrong, but rather accept both of their view points as right and true. But, as Harris points

---

[4] Sam Harris, *The Moral Landscape: How Science Can Determine Values* (New York: Free Press, 2010), 45.

out, the claim that we should be tolerant of each of the two cultures beliefs is itself not meant to be taken as a relative claim, but rather a universal claim that everyone everywhere should accept and abide by. This is a problem because, if everything is relative, then we cannot have any universal principles, such as tolerance; hence the self-contradicting nature of relativism, for even the claim that "truth is relative" is a universal claim, again showing the farcicality of relativism.

Next, before moving on to discuss more specifically why and how relativism is self-contradictory and therefore should be rejected in favor of objective truth, allow me to quote one more person, at length, on the issue of relativism. Now again the context of the discussion in the quote is moral relativism, but as we have seen above, the principles of relativism, along with the problems thereof, are universal (pun intended) regardless of whatever form it may take, whether moral or otherwise. In his article titled *Is Morality Relative?* Francis Beckwith makes the following statements regarding relativism:

> "The fact that people disagree about something does not mean that there is no truth of the matter. For example, if you and I were to disagree on the question of whether the earth is round, our disagreement would certainly not be proof that the earth has no shape. The fact that a

skinhead (a type of young neo-Nazi) and I may disagree on the question of whether we should treat people equally and with fairness is certainly not sufficient reason to conclude that equality and fairness are not objective moral truths. Even if individuals and cultures hold no values in common, it does not follow from this that nobody is right or wrong about what is moral truth. That is, there could be a mistaken individual or culture, such as Adolf Hitler and Nazi Germany.

If the fact of a mere disagreement were sufficient to conclude that objective norms do not exist, then we would have to believe that there is no objectively correct position on such issues as slavery, genocide, and child molestation; for the slave owner, genocidal maniac, and pedophile have an opinion that differs from the one held by those of us who condemn their actions. In the end, moral disagreement proves nothing.

.....Suppose, however, that the relativist, despite the logical failure of his case, sticks to his guns and maintains that disagreement over objective norms proves the correctness of relativism. But this will not work. For the relativist has set down a principle – disagreement means there is no truth – that unravels his own case. After all, some of us believe that relativism is a mistaken view."[5]

As we said above, although this quote is referring to moral relativism, the principles involved are just as relevant to the discussion of relativism with regard to truth in general. Therefore, from this point on, when we refer to relativism of any form, we will simply refer to it as relativism, whether it be about truth in general or morality, as technically all relativism has to do with truth claims of some sort.

Now here in the above quote Francis Beckwith is discussing the basic concept that I have little doubt you have heard somewhere before, namely that if two people (or three, or four, or however many people it may be) disagree on something, that does not simply mean that no one is right and that there is no objective truth regarding whatever is being discussed, but rather quite the contrary, for indeed they could all be wrong, but they cannot all be right, for "Truth by definition excludes."[6] The very nature

---

[5] Francis J. Beckwith, "Is Morality Relative?" in *Passionate Conviction: Contemporary Discourses on Christian Apologetics*, eds. Paul Copan and William Lane Craig (Nashville: B&H Academic, 2007), 214-215.
[6] Ravi Zacharias, *Jesus Among Other Gods: The Absolute Claims of the Christian Message* (Nashville: Thomas Nelson, 2000), 6.

of truth itself demands, nay, it screams from the mountain tops, that every single claim and view that opposes it must be false and therefore rejected. In other words, when something is true, say, for instance, that on August 3, 2012, as I write this sentence, Barack Obama is president of the United States of America, anyone and anything that disagrees with that truth is necessarily wrong and their disagreeing claim is false, and therefore must be rejected, otherwise we would just be being foolish by accepting and to continuing to believe that which is false, even though we know it is false, for that, like we already stated above, lacks intellectual integrity.

So, if you believe that "religious" people (especially Christians) cannot do real (and good) science, and I believe that they can, we cannot both be right, due to the facts discussed above. All of the above facts about relativism revolve around one of the basic laws of logic, the law of non-contradiction. Two opposing views (both A and non-A) cannot both be true at the same time and in the same sense. For our purposes here, just look at the issue of "the same time and the same sense" as meaning that both opposing claims are referring to the same thing in the same way. The above stated disagreement regarding religious people and science is a prime example of two completely opposing views that cannot both be correct. We will see by the end of this book which side of that argument is right and which one is wrong (I will give you a hint: religious people can and often do do good science), but for now let us stick to the topic at hand, namely truth.

Now that we have discussed relativism and have seen that it must be rejected on the ground of sound reasoning (logic), we can claim that truth must be objective, as it cannot be both subjective (relativism) and objective, but rather it must be one or the other, for there is no other option on the matter, as it certainly, due to the law of the excluded middle, cannot be both. So, we will now move on to elaborate on some definitions of truth. Now remember as we look as these definitions that there can only be one actual correct definition of truth, as it is not a multifaceted word with multiple meanings (at least not for our purposes in this book), and we are going to do our best to figure out what that definition is.

What is the Definition of Truth?

"What is truth?" This question was asked nearly two thousand years ago to Jesus of Nazareth by Pontius Pilate, and although he was most certainly not the first to ask such a question, it has no doubt been the center of an enormous amount of debate throughout history, and it is a question that we must wrestle with here before moving on in this book. Now before we go on let me just say that we are not here concerned with the deep and profound intricacies involved in the concept of truth or certain specific truths. We are simply attempting to get a decent idea of what truth is on a basic level, and we will leave the rest of the issue to books about epistemology.

So, what exactly is truth, and how should we define it? Let us now look at some different ways that a couple of different sources define the word, and then we will briefly discuss which one of these definitions is most viable and why. Webster's New World Dictionary defines the word "truth" in a variety of ways, including: "1. A being true; a) sincerity, honesty, b) conformity with fact, c) reality, actual existence, d) correctness, accuracy; 2. That which is true; 3. An established fact."[7] Now some of these definitions, such as "a being true," and "that which is true" seem to beg the question of what truth is, as they have the word "true" in them, and so we will simply discard these two definitions and move forward. What about "sincerity and honesty?" I think it is safe to say that living in the twenty first century we have all heard someone at some point say something to the effect of, "It doesn't matter what you believe as long as you are sincere." But does sincerity and honesty really constitute truth?[8] This cannot be the case, as what happens when two people sincerely believe two contradictory things? As we have seen above, they cannot

---

[7] Michael Agnes, ed., *Webster's New World Dictionary* (New York: Pocket Books, 2003), 692.
[8] I realize that the dictionary that I cited above was most likely simply giving an example of what it means to "be true" in the sense that it is widely used as a figure of speech, so I am not necessarily accusing this dictionary of claiming that sincerity constitutes truth in the strict sense.

both be right. So sincerity and honesty are also not a sufficient definition of truth. It would seem that definition 1 (d) is also begging the question of a definition for truth by simply rephrasing (giving synonyms for) the word "truth," so we will reject this definition as well. Two of the three remaining definitions are "conformity with fact" and "an established fact." Now these definitions seem adequate, but they are not, as they are primarily circular definitions since a *fact* is generally described as "something that is true." Of course we could just say that a fact is best defined as "something that really is the case," but that would be my personal definition, and so we will not use it here so as to not be accused of creating a definition simply to serve my own purposes. The one definition that is left is "reality, actual existence." The second part of this definition, "actual existence," although most likely a legitimate definition, nevertheless seems to be inadequate for our purposes, as we are not necessarily discussing existence, at least not specifically and directly, so we will reject this definition as well. The other part of this last definition from the above listing is "reality," but we must reject this definition also, as the definition of reality generally has the word "fact" or "truth" in it, and so it to is circular.

So, what now? How can we define truth? Well, the New Testament Greek word for truth[9] is *alaythia* (a-lay-

---

[9] Don't worry. This word is not simply a Bible word. It was and still is a general Greek word with the same basic definition of which I am giving

theea). According to Frederick William Danker in *The Concise Greek-English Lexicon of the New Testament*, this word is best defined as: "That which is really so."[10] That sounds an awful like my definition for the word "fact" given above, namely "something that really is the case," doesn't it? Another way to phrase this definition would be to say that "truth is what is." So, we have found a definition for the word "truth" that is not circular or simply replacing the word "truth" with a synonym, as the above definitions are. It would seem that this is in fact an adequate definition for the word "truth," and since it is adequate, and since all of the other definitions that we looked at above were not, this is the definition that we should accept out of the definitions that we have discussed, and so that is what we shall do.[11]

This definition of "that which is really so" is a pretty good synopsis of what is known as the correspondence theory of truth, which basically says that if the truth claim accurately corresponds to reality, then

---

here, even outside the context of the Bible, church, and Christianity.

[10] Frederick William Danker, *The Concise Greek-English Lexicon of the New Testament* (Chicago: The University of Chicago Press, 2009), 15.

[11] Although there may be other definitions of truth, they would all have something in some way to do with one of the definitions that we have looked at in this chapter, and so there is no need to look at other sources for other definitions of the term, as they could all be summed up under the ones that we have already discussed. I am of course referring to definitions that square with the concept of objective truth, for we have seen that truth must be objective, and so any definition of truth that subverts the idea of objectivity need not even be given the time of day, as it is necessarily an inadequate and fallacious definition.

the truth claim should be accepted as true, and if not then it should be discarded as false. Sounds pretty basic huh? Well, believe it or not there are some people who very adamantly argue against such a theory, although we do not have time to get into that argument here.[12] Suffice it to say that the correspondence theory is a legitimate way to view the concept of truth, and since we have established that truth is not bound by subjectivity in any form, we will move forward in our endeavor with the above definition of truth, viz. "that which is really so," for the remainder of this book. So, we have found a plausible, indeed I would strongly argue the most plausible, definition for truth. Now we will move ahead and look at some specific, practical reasons why it is vitally important to know truth, rather than simply believe what you want to believe.

Why is Knowing and Believing Truth Important?

Suppose that you are a college student (which some of you reading this book may be). The first day of class the teacher passes out a syllabus. Now, if you are like most of the students that I have known thus far in my life, you will most probably take that syllabus and either lose it before you actually read it or throw it away immediately following the class the first time you see a garbage can. If, however, you are a more studious individual you will likely

---

[12] See the section titled "Relativism" in the Additional Information section at the end of this book for further resources on this issue.

read the syllabus shortly after class and possibly even mark down due dates for the class in your calendar, or maybe in your notebook for that particular class.

Now, for our purposes here, let us say that this particular class is a lower level church history class, and on the syllabus it says that you will be having a test over the Council of Nicaea on the third Friday of the semester. You can either choose to believe that there is a test over the Council of Nicaea on the third Friday of the semester in that class, or you can choose to believe that there is not a test over the Council of Nicaea on the third Friday of the semester in that class. Of course, you could choose to believe that this test will in fact take place in this class on the third Friday of the semester and ignore that fact and fail the test for being ill-equipped or missing it altogether for whatever reason, but that is a whole other problem entirely. What do you think is going to happen if you choose to deny that this test will indeed take place on this day in this class? Assuming that the syllabus is correct and all of the test dates are correct and nothing alters the course of the class, on the third Friday of the semester, your teacher, whether you believe it or not, is going to give the class a test on the Council of Nicaea, and if you are not prepared to take it and to do well on it, then you will most likely not do well on that test, and you may even fail it.

While this example of why it is important to know and believe the truth is a valid one, the consequences of such a situation are ultimately minor in retrospect. But what if, say, you had been feeling pretty sick lately and you decided to go to the emergency room. After you got checked in, the doctor, since she could not initially figure out what was wrong with you, ordered a bunch of tests to be done, including an MR , a CAT scan, and blood work. After many hours of going over the results of the various tests, the doctor comes to the conclusion that you have brain cancer. Then the doctor comes into your room and tells you that they are certain that you have brain cancer, and if they don't operate on you immediately you will most likely die in a very short period of time. Now, you can either believe that the doctor has told you the truth and that you really do have brain cancer that needs to be operated on immediately, or you can decide to deny such a belief and leave the hospital and go on about your business. Now, in this particular case let us assume that the doctor really was telling you the truth. What do you think is most likely going to happen to you if you decide to leave the hospital and ignore what the doctor has told you? You got it! You are most likely going to die in a very short period of time. As you can see, the consequences in this scenario are far greater for ignoring truth than they were in the last one (relative to priorities I suppose).

There are of course many, many other reasons that knowing and believing the truth are vitally important, but the principles that we have discussed above are universal in nature and apply to all situations. While every situation may not be a matter of life or death, many of them are, and like we stated earlier, intellectual integrity is at stake whenever choosing to believe or not to believe the truth, which should be very important to all of us, for who wants to associate with someone who lacks integrity, or even more so, what good is a citizen who lacks integrity to the society in which they reside?

As far as knowing the truth goes, the same principles for believing the truth are in order here, for you cannot make the right decisions if you do not know the relevant truth for a given situation. For instance, the majority of the country has a very twisted idea of what Christianity is, mainly because of all of the nonsense that is taught in the public media and by various preachers across the country, not to mention what the state schools and universities teach about it. As another example, most people in academia these days think and teach that polytheism was around long before monotheism was in the history of man, but if you read the Bible you will find that the very first people on earth, Adam and Eve, were in direct and perfect communion with a single God, the God of the Bible.[13] It is important then that we read a lot and study hard, whether we are students in school or not, so

---

[13] Dr. Winfried Corduan's forthcoming book, *In The Beginning God* (Nashville: Broadman-Holman, 2013), should hopefully clear some of this misconception up.

that we know the truth about various issues, otherwise, like we said earlier in this chapter, we are just people who are wrong about something else.

One more thing needs to be mentioned hear regarding the importance of truth. Blaise Pascal, a seventeenth century philosopher, in his infamous "wager," argued that the truth of whether or not the God of the Bible is real and whether or not the Christian teachings are true is so important that we should bet on God and decide to live for Him, because if we end up being right and He is real, and if the Christian teachings are true, then we get to spend eternity in Heaven with Him, and if they are not real, then most likely life ends at death, and so we will have lived a virtuous life and will lose nothing in the end. Now although this is not really sound theology, since one must truly believe the truths of the Bible to be saved, rather than simply taking a gamble on it, it nevertheless is a great example of how truth can have eternal implications, and so it is therefore of infinite importance.

Conclusion

We have seen in this chapter that truth is by necessity objective. We have also seen that relativism is self-contradictory and that it should therefore be rejected as such. We saw that truth can essentially be defined as "that which is really so," and that this definition is an adequate one. Finally, we saw why it is important to know, believe, and accept the truth as truth rather than to ignore or deny it.

In the next chapter we are going to take a look at whether or not the modern mainstream scientific community is actually looking for the truth, or whether they have something different as their goal at this point. So sit back and get reacy for the real truth, because it very well might not be what you were expecting.

4

Is Modern Mainstream Science Really Looking for the Truth, or Do They Have a Different Agenda?

"Mainstream modern science, with its analytical methods and its 'objective' teachings, is the dominant force in modern culture. If science simply discovered and taught the truth about reality, who could object? But mainstream science does not simply 'discover the truth'; instead it relies in part on a set of unscientific, false philosophical presuppositions as the basis for many of its conclusions. Thus, crucial aspects of what modern science teaches us are simply shabby philosophy dressed up in a white lab coat."[1]

- *Senator Rick Santorum, United States Senate*

---

[1] In Rick Santorum's opening comment in William Dembski's book, *The Design Revolution* (Downers Grove: InterVarsity Press, 2004), 2.

"Science and scientists should always seek out the truth no matter where it may lead. Scientific theories should always be open to intense scrutiny, repeated criticisms, and valid revisions, regardless of the source. Scientific thought should never assume the effect before proving the cause – or be a consequence of political correctness, religious fervor, or personal agendas."[2]

-        *Geoffrey Simmons, M.D.*

Now that we have taken a look at what the word "truth" means, we are now going to move on to discuss how this word pertains to modern science. Many, many times throughout my life I have heard people, both lay and professional (in terms of science professions), say that the goal of science is to find the truth. I remember when I was in elementary school and I asked my teachers what the purpose of science was they would happily and enthusiastically respond with the words, "To find the truth about things," or "To figure out how things truly work." Both of these statements, although not exactly the same, are quite similar overall. I have even caught myself saying the same thing to my son, at least until fairly recently when I finally started to see that these assertions are not actually true, for who wants to teach their children lies

---

[2] Geoffrey Simmons, *Billions of Missing Links: A Rational Look At The Mysteries Evolution Can't Explain* (Eugene: Harvest House Publishers, 2007), 17.

and deception, except for the deranged and demented maybe? I would tell him that the purpose of science is ultimately to find the truth, for that is what I was taught growing up and until recently I had no reason that I knew of to question it. But over the last few years, as I have studied somewhat extensively the debate between the evolutionists and the creationists (and the Intelligent Design proponents), and as I have studied worldviews and different philosophical outlooks, I have come to discover that this is indeed no longer the case. But it is not as simple as just making such a statement. This is a slap in the face of what science was originally intended to do. This needs to be addressed thoroughly and immediately, and so that is what we will attempt to do throughout the remainder of this chapter, and also throughout the rest of this book. We are first going to look at some specific quotes from evolutionists that very clearly state that they are not simply, or sometimes even remotely, looking for the truth, followed by a brief look at what this says about modern mainstream science. Then we will look at what the actual goal of modern mainstream science is, followed finally by a brief discussion of what will most likely happen in the very near future if we do not do something about this issue at once.

Some Quotes from Evolutionists

Dr. Scott Todd of Kansas State University made a comment in Nature Magazine in 1999 that is a prime example of the issue we are discussing here. He said, "Even if all the data point to an intelligent designer, such an hypothesis is excluded from science because it is not naturalistic."[3] Dr. Todd here has given us a valuable piece of information that needs to be addressed, for when I first started seeing comments like these a few years ago my mind was completely blown. I had no idea that this kind of nonsense would actually be allowed in our public school systems. I mean think about it, is this not essentially the kind of thing that we ridicule other countries for doing, namely censoring and filtering the "truth" so that it fits a national agenda? But wait, Dr. Todd said nothing about a national agenda, did he? Well, no, but think about this: Without science, how many of the things that you own or need would not exist? TV's, cell phones, the internet, medicine.....we would have no doctors; we would know nothing about space; we would still have to plant our crops like they did in ancient times, essentially tossing the seeds everywhere and hoping that they grow; we would have no clocks or way to know what time it is (referring specifically to the atomic clock); we would not know what weather to expect from day to day; air travel and sea travel, as well as land travel by non-animal means would also not exist. The list goes on and on and on.[4] So what

---

[3] Scott C. Todd, "A view from Kansas on that evolution debate," *Nature* 401, (September 1999):423.

[4] Let me just say that I am not equating science with innovation or inventing things, but rather I am simply stating that science is an integral part of the process of being able to invent, a precursor if you

does that have to do with a national agenda? Everything! Science is essentially the money maker of the modern world, for most advances in life come from one type of science or another, and so every nation, including America, has a very large expressed interest in science. Hence, the national agenda of America, and every other nation, other than possibly some third world countries, revolves around science. Even economics, the stock market, banking, and the like all revolve around science, because they often entail complex algorithms and mathematical formulas that scientists have formulated specifically for those types of applications and systems, and so the world money market itself has an expressed interest in science. Everything everywhere, with few exceptions, revolves, in one way or another, around science. So, what does all of this have to do with Dr. Todd's assertion above? Simply put, Dr. Todd and the rest of the modern mainstream scientific community is censuring facts and essentially controlling the world (in some senses, but obviously not completely. Let's not get too crazy.), including America by asserting that every scientific assertion that we make must be naturalistic. Now, we will look at what exactly Naturalistic Materialistic Scientism is in the next chapter, but for now let us just be clear on the fact that it is essentially the idea that there is no supernatural in the world and that only the observable (presuming we have the means to observe it) exists, tied in

---

will.

with the basic idea that only science can ultimately give us truth, no matter what the topic is. This is necessarily an atheistic worldview as can easily be seen by simply thinking for a second about what it means to say that nothing supernatural, or extra-natural if you will, exists, for this would certainly exclude any non-material entity, such as a god. This is however not a scientific claim, because it cannot be tested. We cannot run experiments to test such a hypothesis, and so Naturalism actually falls outside of the realm of science and instead falls into the category of philosophical worldviews, and really also religion. This will be discussed at greater length later on in the book and is one of the primary points of this book, but for now let us just note that, as Dr. Todd has asserted, and as is also a typical assertion of other modern scientists who espouse evolution, no evidence of any kind of anything anywhere will be admitted to the drawing board or even be discussed if it does not first and foremost fit into a naturalistic framework. There are of course many modern scientists who do not whole heartedly agree with evolution, but let us not forget that some of the most famous museums in the world, including some that are in our nation's capital mind you, are filled with evolutionary propaganda and that, as was made abundantly clear in the documentary made by Ben Stein and Vivendi Entertainment in 2008 titled, *Expelled: No Intelligence Allowed*, even claiming the possibility that evolution might not have all the answers could cause one to lose his/her job in the world of academia, and so for any scientist to express doubts or unbelief regarding evolution is tantamount to denying modern "science" altogether. Of course most people don't think of America as being "run by evolution," and that is not exactly what I am claiming anyway, at least not completely, for to some extent that is exactly what the case in this country is. I am simply trying to get the point across to you that what our culture and country tells us about our past, present, and future, who we are, what we are here for, and other issues of the like are being filtered through an evolutionary lens, and that does not sit well with me and it should not sit well with you because that means that if evolution is not real, as most modern evidence suggests,[5] or even if it is possibly not the whole picture, then we are all being lied to by our nation and our schools, and this includes our children being lied to every day in their schools, on their field trips to museums and zoos, and so on. The other important thing to take note of with regard to the above quote by Dr. Todd is that science and Naturalism go hand in hand for the modern evolutionary mainstream scientist. (Yes, there are some people who believe in theistic evolution, but this is not the mainstream view and is actually largely looked down upon in mainstream scientific culture, as any serious evolutionary scientist will gladly tell you. This is also made clear by viewing the life of former Nobel Prize winner

---

[5] See Additional Information section at the end of this book for further resources on this issue.

Francis Collins. He is the co-discoverer of the structure of DNA and a theistic evolutionist who has recently had his academic and scientific capabilities questioned due to his theistic beliefs. In a 2010 article in *Nature: Immunology*, Dr. Collins was even ridiculed for his book *Belief: Readings on the Reason for Faith*, and the article even questioned whether or not it was a good idea to let him keep his job as the head of the NIH.[6])

The second quote we are going to look at is similar to the one above (which should not be surprising, considering it also represents modern mainstream scientific views), but is more lengthy and also much more complex. We need to see the similarities in the two quotes to experience more fully the seriousness of this censoring and filtering of information. The quote is by an American evolutionary biologist and geneticist named R. Lewontin. He says,

> "We take the side of science in spite
> of the patent absurdity of some of
> its constructs, in spite of its failure
> to fulfill many of its extravagant
> promises of health and life, in spite
> of the tolerance of the scientific
> community for unsubstantiated just-
> so stories, because we have a prior

---

[6] _____, "Of faith and reason," in *Nature: Immunology* 11, no. 5 (May 2010): 357.

commitment, a commitment to materialism. It is not that the methods and institutions of science somehow compel us to accept a material explanation of the phenomenal world, but, on the contrary, that we are forced by our a priori adherence to material causes to create an apparatus of investigation and a set of concepts that produce material explanations, no matter how counterintuitive, no matter how mystifying to the uninitiated. Moreover, that materialism is absolute, for we cannot allow a Divine Foot in the door."[7]

Now, let us take a second to think about the degree to which this man has decided to commit to Materialism[8] and to denying anything that might even remotely promote the idea of a supernatural entity. This sounds an awful lot like the first quote above doesn't it? We should point out here that in the above quote Lewontin is gladly speaking in the plural (we), for he is speaking on behalf of the entire

---

[7] R. Lewontin, "Billions and Billions of Demons," review of *The Demon-Haunted World: Science as a Candle in the Dark*, by Carl Sagan, in the *New York Review of Books* (January 1997): 28-32.
[8] Materialism is the belief that nothing other than what is made up of physical matter exists. We will discuss this view in the next chapter.

modern mainstream scientific community, not just for himself, and he knows that. It should also be noted here that Lewontin is very open here about the fact that much of what the modern mainstream scientific community believes and purports as truth is in fact unsubstantiated, and even counterintuitive. This certainly makes it very clear that their agenda is definitely something other than looking for the truth.

We will now look at two more quotes and then we will move on to take a brief look at what this issue, namely that modern science is not looking for the truth unless it fits their naturalistic materialistic agenda, says about modern mainstream science and the people within that community. These two separate quotes are from the book titled *Unscientific America: How Scientific Illiteracy Threatens Our Future*. This book was written because the authors are disgusted and distraught that so many people in our country still can't seem to get a handle on the "reality" that "evolution is a proven fact," and that without that "knowledge" these people are scientifically illiterate, which is supposedly destroying our society. The first quote is as follows, "science seeks to reveal objective truths about the way the world works."[9] This sounds just like the comments that we saw at the beginning of this chapter that my teachers used to say to me in grade school,

---

[9] Chris Mooney and Sheril Kirshenbaum, *Unscientific America: How Scientific Illiteracy Threatens Our Future* (New York: Basic Books, 2009), 45.

doesn't it? There is however a particular problem in this statement that I would like to address before we move on to the next quote. Science, by definition, cannot discover or prove truths of any kind, because it is done by inductive means. The scientific method functions in such a way that one can only discover answers of probability, not certainty. Let me explain it another way. In science, the scientist essentially makes a hypothesis about something, then tests that hypothesis by conducting experiments, then she repeats the experiments many times until there is either enough evidence in support of or against her hypothesis so that she can either accept or reject that hypothesis on the basis of the evidence from the experiments. However, she cannot ever indefinitely say that her hypothesis is either 100% true or 100% false, which would be needed for a truth to be proven, as there cannot be a less than 100% truth. The only conclusions that she is able to draw from her experiments are probable ones, as in, for instance, there is a 97% chance that this chemical creates this reaction when mixed with this chemical, or there is an 84% chance that this animal will do so and so when put in such a situation. The problem with claiming that science can discover (or reveal) objective truths (all truth is objective, as we saw in the last chapter) is that science is just not set up to do such a thing. It is, as I said above, by nature inductive. What do I mean by inductive? Well, let us look briefly at the opposite of induction, deduction, so as to better understand induction.

Deduction is the kind of reasoning that we generally use from day to day. A basic example of deductive reasoning would be the following.

Premise 1 - I see a sign,

Premise 2 - The sign I see is green,

Conclusion - Therefore, I see a green sign.

This may seem simple, and that's because it is simple. This is called a general to particular argument, because it starts with two general statements and then moves to a more particular conclusion. We all make lots of decisions and form many of our beliefs this way. This type of reasoning is also known as a priori reasoning. "A priori" just means prior to additional knowledge or outside information. For example, in the long quote that we saw earlier Lewontin stated that he has an "a priori commitment to material causes." This means that before he considers any causal evidence at all of any kind it must first meet the criteria of being a material cause, otherwise it simply gets discarded as nonsense. But wait you say, Lewontin is a scientist and you said scientists use inductive reasoning, not deductive a priori reasoning, right? Yes I did. That is precisely my point. Lewontin is using philosophical reasoning to make his scientific decisions and statements. This is unfortunately very common, and also very foolish, because they are two exact opposite types of reasoning and therefore they cannot be reconciled. Now don't get me wrong, for there is nothing wrong with a scientist using philosophical reasoning (deductive reasoning is also called "philosophical reasoning," and inductive reasoning is also called "scientific reasoning"). We all do it every day, but science should be about trying to discover the truth, even if the truth is not 100% attainable by inductive (scientific) means. To do this we need to use means other than purely scientific ones, which of course flies in the face of Scientism, which we will also discuss in the next chapter. Deduction, unlike induction, is a type of reasoning that one can come to *know* truth *with certainty.*

Now, we can make much more complex deductions, but the above syllogism (that is the formal name for an argument with premises and a conclusion) is a good basic depiction of deductive reasoning. This is known as philosophical reasoning, as noted above. Of course this type of reasoning is very well suited for Naturalism and Materialism because they are philosophical worldview systems, but science is not. The problem that we have here is that for far too long now Naturalism and Materialism have been engrained into the thinking of scientists so much that they have come to be viewed as synonymous with science, but in fact, and this is one of the main points of this book, they are not at all synonymous. This is why modern science has come to be known to many as Naturalistic Materialistic Scientism, which is actually a worldview and not science at all, for science can be done within a number of different worldview systems, including a biblical creation worldview, as well as a worldview that espouses intelligent Design but not biblical Creationism, Naturalism, Materialism, and others as well. It is the worldview that differs, and perhaps the method of science being used, but not the science itself, for science is what it is, science.

Inductive reasoning is also known as scientific reasoning, as noted above, and by the nature of this type of reasoning you can only come up with probable and not definitive conclusions. This is primarily because there is what I like to call the "what if factor." This "what if factor" is the idea that even though something certainly seems the way we think it is, there is always the possibility that it is in fact not as it seems, or in other words, "what if the scientist missed something or is wrong." This could essentially be viewed as a mild form of "scientific skepticism," which fits perfectly with the type of reasoning and methods that are used in science, and is healthy to espouse when kept under control, for too much skepticism leads to laziness and a lack of productivity. A prime example of this "what if factor" at work can be seen by looking at the fact that for many centuries scientists and the world thought that the universe was geocentric (the idea that the other planets and the sun revolve around the earth). This was, as far as the scientists could tell, a sure thing. But in the 16th century Nicolaus Copernicus had the idea that the universe is actually heliocentric (the idea that the planets revolve around the sun). Scientists are now pretty sure (they would probably say certain) that planets in our solar system revolve around the sun. It is of course still possible that scientists could be wrong about some or all of this, although this is probably unlikely, but then again I would suppose that is what the ancients thought about the geocentric world that they thought they lived in too. We must remember that from the perspective of science, we cannot ever be 100% certain of anything. This is mainly because science, and inductive reasoning, always starts with the end result and tries to work its way backwards. Scientists do this by seeing the end result and then forming an hypothesis about how the end result came about, and then they try and figure it out by doing and repeating various experiments. But as we should be able to notice, starting with the end result unavoidably means that they have to do some guessing, and that they are to some extent always dealing with historical science, for if one starts with the end result, then that means that the process leading to that result is over, and it is then impossible to know for certain what went on during the process that led to that specific end result. It is also impossible to know for sure, even after all of one's experiments are done, whether or not your end result and the way that it came to be is truly identical to the initial process and end result. And every time a new experiment is done it is impossible to guarantee with absolute accuracy that every single thing happens exactly the same way in each experiment. This is why I call it the "what if factor," because there is always room in science for doubt. Even most complex math formulas, especially when dealing with theoretical math, only give probable conclusions, but we generally think of math as a concrete "science." Of course, math that leads to definitive conclusions would be considered to use philosophical, or deductive reasoning, not scientific, inductive reasoning. The point here is that scientists cannot come up with objective truths by means of science, for it is inductive and so by nature there is always the possibility that the scientist may have missed something or miscalculated something along the way. To be sure, many scientists are very good at what they do and have developed many amazing things, such as medications, computers and so forth, and that is great, but that is inventing and not science, strictly speaking Science, as we will see later on, is a type of studying, rather than inventing, even though often times it is scientists who are the ones doing the inventing. The bottom line, however, is that even if all of the above issues regarding science could somehow be overcome, the fact that science necessarily is done using inductive logic will *always* mean that at best science can only legitimately give us statements of probability, rather than statements of certainty.

The second quote from the book *Unscientific America,* and the final quote that we are going to look at in this chapter is, "A distressingly large number of Americans refuse to accept either the fact or theory of evolution, the scientifically undisputed explanation of the origin of our species and the diversity of life on earth."[10] WOW! Did you catch that definition of evolution? "THE SCIENTIFICALLY UNDISPUTED EXPLANATION OF THE ORIGIN OF OUR SPEICIES AND THE DIVERSITY OF LIFE ON EARTH! Before I continue, I have to say something. I hate to break it to Chris Mooney and Sheril Kirshenbaum, the authors of the above quoted book, but first of all evolution cannot be proven to be a fact, as we will see later on, and so we should not ever claim it as such, especially when dealing with origins issues, because it deals with historical science which is non-repeatable and therefore non-verifiable by definition. We need not get into scientific proofs regarding micro-evolution and so on here, although we will briefly touch on this issue below, as there are many other great books that explain why such leaps are problematic.[11] Also, and more to the point, evolution is becoming increasingly more and more disputed these days. I could name dozens of scientists who flat out reject the idea all together due to its overwhelming absurdity, many of whom will be mentioned in later chapters. There is also a document titled *A Scientific Dissent from Darwinism* that over 700

---

[10] Ibid, 3.
[11] See Additional Information section at the end of this book.

scientists, many of whom still strongly disagree with the creationists and the Intelligent Design proponents, from all over the world have signed saying that they see major problems with the theory of evolution and that they are not convinced that it has all, and for some any, of the answers that it claims to have.[12]

What All of This Says About Modern Mainstream Science

What does all of this say about modern mainstream science? Well, it certainly seems at this point as though modern mainstream science is actually not seeking to find the truth unless it fits into a naturalistic materialistic worldview system. In a later chapter we are going to discuss whether evolution is science or a religious/philosophical belief system (also known as a worldview) and why, but for now let's just look at what all of this specifically says about modern mainstream science, as well as our culture and country.

Now, the above information actually says several things about modern mainstream science. Most importantly it says that modern mainstream science (which of course is represented by modern mainstream scientists) has no integrity. If they are not looking for the truth and only the truth then they lack integrity. Even if they cannot prove the truth, they should nevertheless be

---

[12] _____, A Scientific Descent From Darwinism, http://www.dissentfromdarwin.org (accessed August 4, 2012).

seeking to provide us with the most probable candidates for truth in each of the various areas of science. Otherwise why should they even have jobs, and even more so why should we listen to them or care what they have to say? But it is worse than that. Not only are they not looking for the truth and only the truth, but they are openly and forcefully willing to do their best to make us, the non-scientists, believe whatever they want us to believe, no matter how ridiculous it may be, as long as it fits their agenda. This is an unbelievable power trip. I have personally experienced the unmitigated hatred of staunch evolutionists any time I even mention Creationism or any problem whatsoever with the theory of evolution, no matter how basic a point I may be trying to make. I have seen many professional scientists, both Intelligent Design proponents and creationists,[13] be incredibly disrespected due to their non-evolutionary beliefs. This would even be a problem if evolution were a proven fact, for no human has the right to treat any other human that way! But alas, the evolutionist with his pen filled with ink in hand or a bottle of water at the ready makes his unadulterated and long winded claims of absolute truth that are untouchable by humanity, for evolution reigns supreme and that is that, or so they say! Even Francis Collins, the gentleman we looked at earlier who is the head of the NIH (The National

---

[13] I am not claiming here that someone cannot be both an Intelligent Design proponent and a creationist, because they can, but as we will see later on, Intelligent Design is science, and Creationism is more of a religious worldview.

Institute of Health), a position that is designated by the president of the United States himself, has experienced ridicule for his theistic beliefs by the evolutionary community, and he actually believes in evolution. How ridiculous can people be? Quite, I am afraid. The problem is not that too many people don't believe the truth. The problem is that too many people believe in evolution, something that has virtually no support whatsoever in the scientific realm of evidence. I have taken more than a half a dozen college science courses,[14] from both Christian and secular colleges. I have read the evolution sections of various state approved textbooks, from both my classes and various other biology, immunology, biochemistry, psychology, geology, and other types of science classes. I have watched dozens of lectures on the topic of evolution. I have read books such as Richard Dawkins' *The Greatest Show on Earth* which, aside from the strong animosity toward religion in general, has a primary purpose of explaining the some of the strongest supposed modern evidence for evolution (personally I think Dawkins did a decent job of explaining these evidences the best that they can be explained). My wife and I have over a dozen recent college science textbooks between the two of us, including recent biology and cell-biology textbooks that I have looked through. I have seen many documentaries and

---

[14] This is obviously not nearly as many classes as people with PhDs in scientific fields, but it is still enough classes to learn what I need to know about modern evolutionary dogma.

videos regarding evidence (supposedly) for, and against evolution. I have even been through over 100 power point presentations in one of my college science classes regarding the problems with evolution and evolutionary theory and the supposed evidence thereof. I am well aware of what the evolutionists believe and what they claim is their evidence. Most of the evolutionists, while at varying degrees, for the most part are dogmatic to a fairly high, and for some an extremely high, degree about their evolutionary "evidence" and beliefs. I have heard the talks and the giber-jabbering of the nonsensical evolutionary nitwits who refuse to at least admit that they don't have all of the answers. Now before I continue let it be clearly known that I call them nitwits not because they are inherently unintelligent, but rather because they are openly dogmatic about something that should by necessity be held tentatively, which excludes dogmatism by definition, and they are purposefully acting irrationally in and through their dogmatism, hence, they are nitwits. These are mostly very smart people, but why is it that if someone tries to convince me that I am a hotdog and not a human they are said to be crazy and foolish, but when someone tries to convince me of something with such profound implications as evolution without any major, or even really any minor, evidence to support it, all the while claiming that all of the evidence is out there and that if I just looked at it with an open mind I would see that they are right, and I refuse to believe them, all of a sudden I am the one that is crazy and foolish? I have looked at the evidence. I have spent hundreds of hours watching videos and reading thousands of pages about the evidence, and THERE IS NONE. The curriculum for my 3 credit hour class at Liberty University about origins and evolution (this class curriculum included a textbook, over one hundred power point presentations, and five documentaries, all covering the entire spectrum of major evolutionary "evidence") alone was enough to show me that pretty much everything, if not actually everything, that the evolutionists claim as evidence to support their theory has either been grossly manipulated or substantially misrepresented, and that was just one basic college course on top of all of the other reading and watching videos that I have done over the past few years. The evidence against the "evidence" is out there if you are willing to look for it, and it is not hard to find. But I digress, for my tangent has been made and so now we shall move on to what all of this says about our culture.

What All of This Says About Our Culture

What does all of this say about our culture? Simply put, it says that our culture is in trouble. We will talk more about this specifically at the end of this chapter, but for now let us discuss one main reason why we are in trouble. The fact that the prominence of evolution continues to grow in spite of the rapid decline of real evidence in favor of it shows two things primarily. One, it shows that too many people in our culture either don't care that this is happening or that they are unaware that this is happening. If they don't care, then they either do not understand the implications of what is happening or they just have other priorities ahead of caring about such things. To that I would just like to remind them of the chapter in this book, chapter 2, regarding the prominence of evolution and why it matters, and also that

> Adolf Hitler worked out an "evolutionary ethic in *Mein Kampf* (1924). Applying Darwin's principle of natural selection of survival of the fittest to human ethnic groups, Hitler concluded that since evolution has produced the superior (Aryan) stock, we must work to preserve it. Likewise he believed that inferior breeds must be weeded out. On this basis he killed six million Jews and about five million other non-Aryans."[15]

We have already seen in chapter 2 how the idea of racial superiority was expounded and enhanced greatly by means of evolutionary theory. That does not of course mean that thoughts of racial superiority were absent prior to evolutionary theory. To be fair the Jews themselves in ancient times thought of themselves as being so superior

---

[15] Norman Geisler, *Christian Ethics: Contemporary Issues & Options* (Grand Rapids: Baker Academic, 2010), 25.

to the Samaritans that they would literally walk many extra miles to go around Samaritan villages and avoid walking through them in fear that they may come in contact with one and defile themselves. But something else that most people don't seem to know (we mentioned this briefly in chapter 2) is that the idea of different human races comes from the evolutionary idea that different people groups arose in different parts of the world. If the Genesis account of creation is true, however, then we are all from the same race, namely the human race. I do not think I should have to explain the absurdity and the level of improbability that many different pairs (male *and* female) of humans mysteriously arose all over the world by random evolutionary processes. I doubt that there is a mathematician on the planet who could even fathom coming up with a formula that could even come close to considering all of the possible variants necessary to make such a calculation. I mean come on, the overwhelming improbability (namely 0% probability essentially, as we have no evidence that this is even remotely possible, let alone probable) that even one human would arise from lower life forms is astronomically absurd, but to consider that this happened just right so that a male and a female, who fit together perfectly from a reproductive standpoint, multiple times over all throughout the world, from random processes, is just plain stupefying to even consider. But still, as we saw in the previous chapter, it is not hard to see how feelings of white supremacy could and did arise as a result of evolutionary dogma.

As for those who are unaware of the fact that the influence of evolution is on the rise while the evidence is on the decline, please get them a copy of this book so that they will no longer be ignorant of such an important dilemma, and also please direct them to the Additional Information section in the back of this book for further resources on these issues. Our culture must decide that this is an issue worth fighting over, as it is destroying the humane aspects of our society by causing wide spread feelings of superiority and arrogance. Again, evolution is not the *only* thing causing such feelings, but it is certainly one of the *main* things that is doing so.

What All of This Says About Our Country

What does all of this say about our country? Well, it says that our country is no longer the "Land of the Free." We are not allowed at this point to teach anything other than evolution as science (which we will later see is foolish and a misuse of terms) in our schools, especially the public schools, and even some of the Christian schools are denied the right to accreditation if they do not teach evolution and only evolution as the one true science. The Institute for Creation Research's (ICR) graduate school is a perfect example of this. They used to be fully accredited in California, but recently they moved to the Dallas/Fort Worth, TX area, and after a long battle and several law suits they ended up not being able to regain accreditation because the courts said that evolution is science and what they teach is religion. Now mind you that the teachers at ICR are for the most part fully credentialed scientists with degrees from fully accredited state universities, so if they are not competent to teach science then neither are any of the scientists that work at the state universities and schools. The bottom line here is that the courts have determined that evolution is equivalent to science, and even that evolution *is* science, and so anything that does not square with evolution cannot be science, and so it should not be taught in the science classrooms. Well, as we will see further on in this book, that is not only ridiculous, but it is completely false, and it is a grave misrepresentation of terms such as "evolution," "science," and so on.

This instance and many others like it are destroying our country's right to free thought (we will discuss this more fully in chapter 11). Of course ICR is still allowed to teach their curriculum and award degrees, but those degrees are worthless in terms of getting you a job, or a better paying job, in the mainstream academic world. The bill of rights and the constitution make it abundantly clear that we are to be able to teach, think, and say whatever we wish as long as it is not a detriment to society. But where does that leave evolution? We saw in chapter 2 that evolutionary thought and theory is extremely detrimental to society, and on those grounds alone it should be taught with extreme caution, if at all. I do not need to go into detail regarding the fact that many religious views, especially Christian views, on any subject have never harmed anyone[16] (the crusades were the result of an abuse of human power. They do not stem from a proper understanding of the Bible and its teachings). Sure they may offend people, but let's face it, even passing gas offends those around you, and pretty much everyone does that from time to time and it is most certainly not a crime. Just because something is offensive to some people doesn't make it a crime, but if there is no evidence supporting something that is taught and it is still taught to our children day in and day out as a proven fact, should that not be a crime?[17] But that is exactly what we are doing! And besides, anyone who is offended by someone studying science in a different way, using different scientific methods to do their research, and coming to different conclusions as a result of their research, is simply un-American by nature, for is that not the *kind of thing* that America was founded for, namely scientific freedom? It most certainly is! However, our country has become more focused on protecting itself (from outside, or inside, influence) and the mainstream academicians over and

---

[16] I am not claiming that all religious teachings are un-harmful, but rather only some of them, for there are certainly some religious teachings, such some of the teachings of Islam, that are very dangerous to society. Also, as we will see later on, evolution is also a religious view, and we have already seen that it too is very dangerous.
[17] And even more so if it endangers the lives of others, especially those who are less able to defend themselves.

above the rights of the general population. Is that appropriate? It is essentially no different than the fact that someone can win a presidential election in America these days without winning the popular vote. The American people have no say anymore in what our country does or where it goes or what we teach our children in school. It is not hard to find a Gallup Pole these days that shows very clearly that a lot of Americans do not believe or agree with the idea that evolution is true, especially in the atheistic, naturalistic sense that it is generally taught in the schools. Sure we do not out rightly teach our children to be atheists in our school science classes, but all of the implications are there in the textbooks, and the fact that we are unwilling to allow other theories to be taught alongside evolution shows both the desperate lengths to which modern America will go to maintain its power over what we think and believe and the overwhelming reality that we no longer live in a free society as we once did, at least not when it comes to ideas. Was not Mother Teresa working with the down and out in the name of Religion and Christ? Did not the modern hospital movement come about as a result of Christians and religious people wanting to serve the sick and be more like Christ, the ultimate healer and Great Physician? Even Albert Einstein, whom many mistake as an atheist, said very plainly many times that there must be some supernatural power out there for all of this (the universe and its complexity and enormity) to exist. This information is all out there and readily available to the public. You just have to look for it and use credible sources when doing your research. The belief in Christianity, the Bible, or supernaturalism in general is not a threat to our society and country, but evolution most certainly is! Let me be the first to say that if there were a good deal of real, solid evidence for the reality of macro-evolution, then I would be willing to rethink my position on the issue, but there is no such evidence, and so we mustn't, for the benefit of our children, our society, and our country, act as if there is!

So What Exactly is the Goal of Modern Mainstream Science?

So, now that we have established what the goal of modern mainstream science is not namely to discover truth and only truth with regard to how things work, where we came from, and other issues that science normally addresses, let us take a brief look at what seems to be the goal of modern mainstream science. This section will be fairly short, as we have to some extent discussed this already in the previous pages of this chapter.

It seems to me that modern mainstream science, and therefore our culture, our schools, our museums, and our country, instead of seeking truth, is actually seeking to justify its own ends at all cost. This includes, but is not limited to, trying to convince everyone everywhere that evolution is a reality that cannot be debunked because it is a proven fact and that no one in their right mind really questions the "fact" of evolution. We have, however, already seen that there is no legitimate evidence for the theory of macro-evolution,[18] and let it also be briefly said that evidence for micro-evolution is not now nor will it ever be evidence for macro-evolution, although in reality there is actually no evidence for micro-evolution either in the strict sense, because it is impossible to add information to animals or humans by natural means so as to make new species or subspecies. That is another problem with modern mainstream science. I have read many books and articles and I have seen many quotes in which scientists use the ideas of micro-evolution and macro-evolution as synonymous, and they claim that evidence for one is evidence for the other, without explaining the vast difference between the two. Now, as this book is not meant to be a book of scientific evidence, I will not go into much detail here, but rather it needs only be said that even evidence for micro-evolution (change over time within species) is grossly overstated most of the time. As a brief example, dogs are often used as a proof of evolution, both micro and macro, in turn. The scientists claim that since, over the ast few generations alone, we have come to see many, many new breeds of dogs, this proves that evolution is real. But what they mean by evolution, in part, is the addition of new information (genetic information) over time to make new forms of dog

---

[18] Macro-evolution and evolution, in science, are generally, although not always, synonymous terms especially when dealing with origins.

breeds (in this particular case). But unfortunately what the scientists will gladly fail to mention is that, as a matter of fact, there is no new information being added to the new breeds of dogs, but instead every time we get a new breed we actually have a loss of information. A poodle is an excellent example of an incredible loss in information from previous generations of dog breeds. This is actually therefore the exact opposite of evolution (namely the acquisition of new genetic information over time to "create" new species and subspecies). But the scientists, the modern mainstream scientists, want us to believe that there is new information being added to the new breeds of dogs to make the new breeds of dogs so that we will be more likely to believe that macro-evolution, the generation of new species from other species through random mutations. I don't know about you, but where I come from when someone knowingly tells you something that is the exact opposite of the truth, we call that a lie, deceit, and other words of the sort, not science, and most certainly not a search for the truth. This is just one of many classic examples of the complete falsehood of information that is being taught to our children, and to us, across the country. In truth, "micro-evolution" is more adequately defined as adaptation to the environment within a species. The reason that certain traits in animals can come and go is because God has built into each kind of animal what is known as genetic potential. But the fact of the matter is that once genetic information is gone from a particular species or subspecies it can never return. Traits that have disappeared can only return if there are still some animals within the species or kind that still have the genetic potential for such traits in them, and if they pass such traits onto their offspring, and if those traits are then expressed in those offspring.

Another example that shows that the goal of modern mainstream science is not to seek the truth, although a little off topic here, is the so called "global warming" nonsense that is being purported around the world. All you have to do is watch documentaries like *Global Warming?* or *Global Governance?* to discover that even the basic data for the main assertions and the movement as a whole of global warming proponents is actually false information, such as the "hockey stick" data seen in the temperature measurements in recent years, which actually comes from a glitch in the computer program that they used. When they gathered this information it is a *fact* that essentially no matter what numbers and data you put into this computer program you would get a hockey stick graph (a graph where the data resembled a hockey stick, or a check mark if you will), showing a sharp rise in whatever you were measuring. Al Gore knew this but used the information anyway and has since, along with many other people, probably made countless millions of dollars on such assertions, as well as scared people around the world with his, and the scientists that go along with the idea, nonsensical ideas of global warming. I strongly recommend the above mentioned video to anyone who truly believes in global warming, for it is full of leading climatologists and scientists who completely disagree with the global warming assertions, and they have data and evidence to back up their claims. There was also recently an article published on FoxNews.com that mentioned that those scientists who don't believe in global warming are just as, if not more knowledgeable about science as those who do believe in it.[19] Now do not get confused, this book is not about global warming, but the principal is the same in that modern mainstream scientists[20] are working toward a national agenda that does not necessarily include providing truth to the American public about such things, just like the evolutionists are doing. This is not conspiracy theory here! This is real life and the things that I am telling you are really true. If you do not believe me then feel free to check these things out for yourself, but remember not to get your information from those inside the system of deceit,

---

[19] Maxim Lott, "Global warming skeptics as knowledgeable about science as climate change believers, study says," Fox News, http://www.foxnews.com/scitech/2012/05/28/global-warming-skeptics-know-more-about-science-new-study-claims/?cmpid=cmty_{linkBack}_Global_warming_skeptics_as_knowledgeable_about_science_as_climate_change_believers%2C_study_says (accessed August 4, 2012).

[20] I am not claiming that Al Gore is a scientist, but we must remember that he is, because of his global warming "discovery," an honorary member of the most elite scientific honor society in America, Sigma Xi.

as they no doubt will deny my claims and simply feed you more lies to cover their own, well, bottoms, let's just say bottoms.

As we saw earlier we not only have to believe something to know it, but what we believe also has to be true. So, a lot of what is being taught in our science classes that we know for a fact is false, such as the example of the dogs given above, that is the opposite of providing our children with knowledge But isn't the purpose of our schools to impart knowledge to our children so as to make them more informed citizens? Yes, yes it is, but that is not what is actually taking place! Instead science teachers, and those who decide on science curricula, across the country are making our children dumber by, in essence, teaching their vulnerable minds things that they (the teachers and curriculum committees) know very well are actually false and in turn causing them. and many of us as well, to believe things that are 100% the opposite of the truth. The idea that evolution is a proven fact is another one of those blatant lies being propagated by the modern scientific movement, and it is yet another belief that in turn makes our children, and many of us, dumber for believing it, because it is in fact impossible to prove evolution. We will discuss this issue further in a later chapter, but for now the point is simply that there are many things that modern science is propagating these days that are clearly not in the expressed interest of truth and justice, and henceforth are not in the expressed interest of humanity and civility either. This should bother all of us, especially us Americans, as we go to history class and are told that we are and were founded as a free nation, and then we go to biology or geology class and are told one thing, something with virtually no evidence at all to back it, to the unmitigated exclusion of all other ideas to the contrary. Is that freedom? It most certainly is not! So let it be heard around the world that the modern mainstream scientific community in America has a hidden agenda that does not include the free exchange of ideas and the freedom for parents to choose what should be taught to their children in school. There are enough problems with the modern American family already. We do not need to compound these problems with confusing our children by teaching them one thing at school and another thing that may be completely different at home. Let us agree to teach multiple theories of origin science in our schools at minimum, and to exclude all theories with no viable support at most, and let the children decide for themselves which to believe, with the proper non forceful parental guidance along the way, for that is what freedom looks like in the realm of academia.

What Will Come of All of This if Something is not Done About it Very Soon?

So, what will happen if we continue down this path, this path of the modern scientific community determining what our children are taught in school, and what we are taught on TV, in the news, and in our museums across the country; who is and is not qualified to be accredited, even though they have the same credentials as their evolutionist counterparts; and who is and is not qualified to be employed by state schools simply due to religious or methodological preferences? Well, simply put, it seems to me as though we are currently headed toward being a nation that is much more like the former communist Soviet Union than we are headed to bigger and brighter days of freedom and happiness and to choosing our own destinies and beliefs. This is not just a matter of science you see. If evolution is believed to be true by someone, then that someone has essentially no way of claiming any purpose to life other than the propagation of the human species. We talked about this in chapter 2 did we not? Do we really want our children growing up believing that they ultimately must survive at all costs no matter who they hurt? Do we want more and more Hitlers to rise up and snuff out millions upon millions more people that they decide do not deserve to live simply because they are perceived to be inferior in some way. I do not now, nor will I ever understand how it is that the scientists can ridicule me for my religious beliefs when my religious beliefs (I am a follower of Christ) lead me to love everyone no matter how they treat me, to pray for people that mistreat me, to pray for my president, even if I did not vote for him or like his methods, to love my children and raise them to have manners, respect others, and love people the way that Christ says that we should love them.........., but somehow they are the ones that end up with the last word even though their philosophical outlook on life, which includes evolution, leads inherently to selfishness, arrogance, the diminishment of the less intellectually and physically inclined and less advanced individuals, to disregard family and friends for the ultimate benefit of one's own survival, the annihilation of entire people groups simply because of the color of their skin or their inability to lead "normal" lives (such as the mentally retarded or handicapped), and so on and so forth. Now please do not misunderstand me. I am not in any way claiming that modern mainstream scientists support any of these things necessarily, or that any of them inevitably practice such atrocities in their own lives and families. What I am saying is that if they lived consistently with what they teach about human origins and evolution, then these are the types of things that would fill their lives, because these are the things that inexorably stem from an evolutionary worldview! Did you catch that last phrase, "evolutionary worldview." Good, because that is what we are going to talk about in chapter 6, namely whether evolution is science or whether it is a religious/philosophical belief system.

In short, if we do not want the up and coming generations to grow increasingly more hostile to free thought and the free exchange of ideas; if we do not want our children to grow up to be monsters by way of government teaching and propaganda; if we do not want America to once and for all cease to be a free nation, we must at bare minimum address the issue of being able to teach other scientific theories (as equally viable, all evidence being equal) in our schools for the benefit of letting our children know that it is not as simple as just "believe this" and move on. We need future generations of people who can think for themselves, for if that is not the case, then I abhor the thought of where our nation, and humanity in general, will be several generations from now, namely a bunch of dull minded imbeciles who don't have the slightest idea how to problem solve or make intelligent decisions on their own. We must also address the issue of our children, as well as the rest of us, being lied to in school and on the TVs, news and so on, about the "fact of evolution." The scientific community must be required to speak the truth about just how tentative these scientific theories really are, as well as regarding the overwhelming lack of solid evidence in favor of their beloved evolutionary theories. Otherwise, when the truth no longer has a voice, democracy ineludibly falls, and only evil reigns supreme, and that is, in the end, good for no one, not even the scientists.

Conclusion

In conclusion, first we looked at some different quotes by evolutionary scientists that showed quite clearly that they are in fact more interested in maintaining a high level of comfort within their own worldview system than they are with seeking out and providing the lay population with the truth with regard to matters pertaining to science. Then we took a brief look at what all of that says about modern mainstream science, our culture, and our country as Americans. We followed all of that up by taking a quick look at what exactly the goal of the modern mainstream scientific community is, since we discovered that it is most certainly not the acquisition and portrayal of truth, and we saw that, ultimately, they are simply trying to force everyone to believe whatever they want us to believe, with no regard for what we think or even whether or not what they are teaching us is the truth. Finally, after that we discussed what exactly is going to happen if we do not do something about all of this very, very soon.

Now, before we move on to look at whether or not evolution is science or whether it is more adequately defined as religion and/or philosophy, we are going to take a look at the worldview that the majority of evolutionists espouse, Naturalistic Materialistic Scientism. Don't worry, for although it sounds complicated it will all make sense by the end of the next chapter, so grab a quick glass of water or some coffee, kick up your feet, and get ready to continue on this well needed venture toward discovering the truth about the supposed debate between science and religion.

5

What Is Naturalistic Materialistic Scientism?

"You will find the doctrine of these beliefs expressed throughout our society: in the media, in the educational systems (from grade school to the universities), in our legislatures, and at the local Starbucks. We may not be dealing with traditional religions, but these are nonetheless beliefs and philosophies that impact the questions of faith and destiny. Just like orthodox religions, these current cultural ideologies address questions such as, Where did I come from? What happens after I die? What is the meaning of life?"[1]

- *a quote about Atheism, Darwinism, and Naturalism from*

the book World Religions and Cults 101

In this chapter we are going to take a closer look at the worldview that is so emphatically espoused by many modern mainstream scientists, and more specifically by atheistic evolutionists. This is the worldview that naturally flows from an unmitigated belief in evolution[2] and an unhealthy confidence in science and what it has to offer. It is the worldview known as Naturalistic Materialistic

---

[1] Bruce Bickel and Stan Jantz, *World Religions and Cults 101* (Eugene: Harvest House Publishers, 2002), 233-234.

[2] Again I am ignoring the idea of theistic evolution, because there is neither scientific nor Scriptural evidence of any kind to support such a view.

Scientism. Now more than likely unless you are somewhat schooled in modern scientific and philosophical thought, you probably have not heard of this worldview. As for what a worldview is specifically, that will be discussed in greater detail in the following chapter. For now, we will begin this chapter by examining each one of these three terms (Naturalism, Materialism, and Scientism) individually, followed by a brief look at what they mean when they are put together, and then we will end this chapter with a discussion on some particular issues related to the espousal of such a worldview. Before we get started, however, let me just bring to your attention that this worldview is necessarily an atheistic worldview.

What is Naturalism?

What is Naturalism? Simply put, Naturalism is the worldview that holds that nature is all that exists. This might seem like a fairly straightforward and harmless position to take up, but in reality there are several very important implications involved in this belief system.[3] The first and probably most important implication that stems from such a worldview is that nothing extra-natural, or "supernatural", exists. This can easily be seen by thinking about the negation that is implied by the naturalistic worldview, namely that if only the natural exists, then

---

[3] A belief system and a worldview are essentially the same thing, although they are not necessarily completely identical. This will also be discussed in the following chapter.

anything and everything that would be deemed unnatural does not exist. This would include, as we have already stated, anything that falls outside the category of "natural." But what is natural? If something is natural then it is part of nature, at least in the sense that we are here referring to the term. This includes trees, people, planets, solar systems, cells, macrophages, mitochondria, dogs, cats, buildings, brains, metal, and anything else that possesses some sort of physicality, i.e. a body or physical form of some sort that is detectible[4] by at least one of the senses. Now before we continue let me be clear that this particular worldview, Naturalism, does not necessarily deny the existence of things such as ideas, thoughts, and other abstract concepts that have no physical form, even though that is how the above statements make it seem. These things are generally considered to exist in somewhat of a different sense by the naturalist and so they are not necessarily denied. The worldview that denies these things is known as Materialism, which will be discussed next.

Philosophy: The Oxford Guide defines Naturalism as "the view that everything is natural, i.e. that everything there is belongs to the world of nature, and so can be studied by the methods appropriate for studying that world, and the apparent exceptions can be somehow

---

[4] Assuming we have the proper means to detect it. For instance, we cannot see individual cells with the naked eye, but if we use a microscope we can see them just fine.

explained away."[5] Again we see that everything that belongs to nature exists, and here we also see that everything that falls outside the category of nature can "be somehow explained away." Let me just point out right here before we continue that this last part of the definition of Naturalism, namely that all exceptions can somehow be explained away, is pure presumption that is impossible to prove. This is merely an assumption that all naturalists make based on an element of faith. But wait, how can they use faith in their belief if faith is not part of nature? Again, like we said above, Naturalism does not necessarily deny such things as faith, although few naturalists would probably admit that their belief system entails any element of faith, as most of them argue that their beliefs are purely based on scientific fact.

The book *World Religions and Cults 101* that was quoted at the beginning of this chapter says this about Naturalism and how naturalists view the world:

- Everything that exists is the result of natural causes. All living creatures are the result of a chance collision of atoms that, through time and random, undirected processes, have evolved to their present state.
- As Humans, we are at the top of the evolutionary chain.

---

[5]Ted Honderich, ed., *Philosophy: The Oxford Guide* (Oxford: Oxford University Press, 2005), 640.

- With our intelligence, we can use science to harness nature for our best purposes.
- The solution to society's problems can be found within the scope of intelligence and ingenuity.[6]

This book also points out that, as we discussed in the chapter on the prominence of evolution and why it matters so much, this worldview leaves no room for divinely imposed moral standards, which ultimately means that humans, if they are to have moral standards at all, must make their own.[7] This is known as moral relativism and it is a sure sign of our time here in the twenty first century, although it is not really anything new. I do not want to get into this issue here, as there are many great books on the subject,[8] and we have already seen in chapter 3 that relativism is self-defeating and that it should therefore be rejected as an inadequate way to handle truth and morality. The point I want to make here is simply that Naturalism necessarily implies either moral relativism or a lack of morality all together, and either of these choices is bad news for society. It should also be pointed out here that, as we saw in chapter 2, evolution, since it is an atheistic view, also implies either moral

---

[6] Bickel and Jantz, *World Religions and Cults 101*, 242-243.
[7] Ibid, 243.
[8] See Additional Information section at the end of this book for more resources on relativism.

relativism or no morals at all. This is one of the reasons that Naturalism is often equated with Darwinism, the belief in evolution.

So, what is the second main implication of Naturalism? Since Naturalism denies that anything supernatural exists, those who hold to this view are essentially saying that the vast majority of the world is incompetent and ignorant of the basic facts of reality. "Naturalism disregards and denigrates anyone who adheres to a theistic belief."[9] A theistic belief is simply a belief in a god or gods of some sort. It does not take a genius to look around the world and see that the idea of the existence of something supernatural pervades almost every single culture in the world. Up until a few centuries ago the dominant belief in both mainstream and scientific circles was that God, or a supernatural entity of some sort, did in fact exist. This concept was espoused to some extent by almost all of the "fathers of science," including Kepler, Galileo, Copernicus, Francis Bacon, and even Einstein.[10] So why is it that all of a sudden it is idiotic to believe in the supernatural? I for one am personally offended by such a notion, for as I stated in an earlier chapter my IQ is far higher than most of the people in the world, and yet it makes far more sense in my mind to

---

[9] Ibid, 243.
[10] To be sure all of these men were not Christians, but even Einstein made it perfectly clear that the vast expanses of the universe could not possibly have come to exist on their own.

believe in the supernatural than to deny it based on the evidence that is available to us. Please do not misunderstand me. I am not speaking out of arrogance, and I am certainly not insinuating that people with extremely high IQs are always right about what they believe. What I am getting at is that if myself and others of my intelligence level, such as Einstein,[11] believe in the supernatural then it is not something that should be so easily discarded as rubbish, for the very meaning of intelligence is "the ability to understand" according to Webster's Dictionary,[12] and so one would think that someone of a very high intelligence level would be much more likely to understand things in general, especially things that they have studied a great deal about, and I have indeed studied such issues extensively, as have many other extremely intelligent people, such as Dr. Winfried Corduan who wrote the foreword for this book, and Dr. Norman Geisler, who wrote the afterword for this book.[13] After all, where would we be today if we had ignored and discarded the beliefs and assertions of most of the geniuses of past generations based on a ridiculous a priori

---

[11] It is also suspected that Einstein had Bipolar disorder and ADHD, like me.

[12] Michael Agnes, ed., *Webster's New World Dictionary* (New York: Pocket Books, 2003), 338.

[13] Again please realize that I am not claiming that there are no smart people in the world who disagree with me, for truly there are many. My contention here is rather that those of us who hold theistic beliefs should not be disregarded as unintelligent simply because we hold such beliefs, for that is a foolish branding indeed.

(before the facts) commitment to Naturalism? Where would science be? Quite frankly modern science would not exist, for modern science was started by people who wanted to better understand the creator God by studying His creation. We must not simply explain away things that have more evidence leading to a supernatural explanation or cause than a natural one just because we think that there cannot be anything supernatural out there, for to do so reeks of a complete lack of intellectual integrity.

Nevertheless, this is essentially what Naturalism is, namely the belief that only the natural exists. To sum up what Naturalism is let us return again to the pages of *World Religions and Cults 101* where it says:

> "Naturalism is the worldview that excludes God. It contends that reality is limited to the material and nature. Scientific investigation is the basis on which everything should be evaluated. Matters such as morality and ethics are relative because there is no absolute standard imposed upon humanity. Theists are dismissed from public discourse because they are not dealing with reality."[14]

Now although some of the above quote more accurately describes Scientism, for the most part it is an accurate

---

[14] Ibid, 249.

depiction of Naturalism, and as we will see below, often times Naturalism and Scientism go hand in hand, hence the propensity of the authors of the above quoted book to equate them with each other in this definitional statement. Remember, however, that Naturalism does not necessarily deny the existence of things such as faith, ideas, concepts, and so on. It is Materialism that denies such things, and that is what we are now going to take a look at.

What Is Materialism?

What is Materialism? Materialism, according to *Philosophy: The Oxford Guide*, is "the view that everything is made of matter."[15] Now, there is an ongoing debate as to what exactly matter is, but for our purposes let's just say that matter is an actual physical substance that makes up everything that exists (according to the Materialists). We can see here that the negation implied in this assertion is that everything that is not made up of matter (anything non-physical) does not exist, which would include God, angels, and so on and so forth. These are the same things that Naturalism denies exists.

Although nothing in this definition lends to us the idea of the use of faith, Materialism, like Naturalism, must be espoused by faith, since it is not possible to prove that it is a true belief, for to prove such a belief as Naturalism

---

[15] Honderich, ed., *Philosophy: The Oxford Guide,* 564.

or Materialism presupposes an exhaustive human knowledge, which is impossible to attain. Now, we said above that Materialism denies the existence of anything that is not made up of matter, and we also said in the previous section about Naturalism that Materialism goes a step further in also denying the existence of ideas, concepts, faith, and anything else that is not made up of some sort of physical substance. H.D. Lewis says that Materialism "means that we just cannot recognize any reality which cannot be exhaustively described in material or bodily terms."[16] Also, "Materialism is the end result of reductionism, the widespread methodology operative in contemporary science."[17] Reductionism is essentially the idea that everything that exists can be reduced to particles and the smallest forms of matter. This leaves no room for the immaterial, such as the soul, since the immaterial is not made up of matter, and therefore the Materialist denies that the immaterial exists. This is why Materialism is a monist view, which holds that, among other things, humans are made up of only one substance, namely the physical. This has major implications for the afterlife and supernaturalism, for if humans have no immaterial part then death is the end, and if no non-material substance exists then, like we said above, God does not exist, and if

---

[16] H.D. Lewis, *The Elusive Self* (Philadelphia: Westminster, 1982), 2, quoted by James R. Beck and Bruce Demarest, *The Human Person in Theology and Psychology* (Grand Rapids: Kregel, 2005), 174.
[17] Beck and Demarest, *The Human Person in Theology and Psychology*, 173.

God does not exist then, again, morality is out the window and everyone can do whatever they want whenever they want. But one serious problem with this view is that Hebrews 9:27 in the Bible tells us that after death comes judgment, indicating that we *will all* survive after our physical bodies die, which means that the monist and materialist view must be false, for if we are to survive after death this necessitates that an immaterial aspect of our nature exists!

However, still many therapists tend to claim that they are monistic materialists, meaning basically that they are materialists who believe that the human person is made up of only the body and not also an immaterial soul (as discussed above) but they tend to treat their clients in a way that is conducive of a belief in dualism, the belief that the human person is made up of two substances, a material body and an immaterial soul.[18] Why is this? Most likely it is because it makes more sense to view the human person in dualistic terms, especially since there are still many aspects of the human person that cannot simply be explained by brain chemistry and neurological happenings. So we see here that even on a practical level Materialism is not something that should be viewed in a positive light.

Materialism is also self-defeating, since one must hold to it by faith while at the same time denying that something nonmaterial such as faith exists. Another way

---

[18] Ibid, 178.

to see the incoherence of Materialism is to realize that the very concept of Materialism is itself not made up of matter, for it is merely a concept, and so the very idea of Materialism itself is incoherent and self-defeating right from the start. But the people who hold to a materialistic view of reality crudely ignore the fact that Materialism is an inadequate view of the world, along with the fact that it is illogical and therefore a sham, and continue on believing whatever it is that they want to believe, because to deny Materialism would mean to accept a non-materialistic view of reality, which would open up the possibility of an actually existing non-physical God, to say nothing of admitting that they were wrong regarding their materialistic perspective. Those who hold to Materialism also by deduction indicate that the majority of the world is wrong about reality, due to the pervasive worldwide belief in the supernatural. Of course just because the majority of the world believes something does not make it so, but something believed by so many people, namely the existence of the supernatural, should not be so readily discarded as hog wash. It should also be noted here that to claim that others are wrong is not in itself wrong, but to do so without evidence, or even more so when there is abundant *proof* that the one making such a claim is the one who is in fact wrong, is most definitely immoral and inappropriate. As we saw in an earlier chapter, truth is naturally exclusive, and anyone who disagrees with it is wrong, and we all need to be careful to maintain as high of a level of intellectual integrity as possible. If there is *legitimate* evidence or proof that we are wrong, then we should seek to change our position to the correct one, no matter what consequences may follow.

So, we have seen that Materialism is the belief that only that which is made up of matter exists. We have also seen how and why this v ew of the world is incoherent, and it should therefore be rejected as not being a viable option for those who wish to maintain intellectual integrity. Now we are going to look at a view that few people discuss based on my experience, but that is extremely pervasive in the modern mainstream scientific community in our culture. It is the view known as Scientism.

What Is Scientism?

Going back to *Philosophy: The Oxford Guide* we see that Scientism can entail several different things. The ones that we are concerned with here are the ideas that "only a scientific methodology is intellectually acceptable", "the sciences are more important than the arts for an understanding of the world in which we live, or, even, *all we need to understand* (italics mine)", and "philosophical problems are scientific problems and should only be dealt with as such."[19] Now, *Philosophy: The Oxford Guide* also says that no one actually espouses Scientism, but rather

---

[19] Honderich, ed., *Philosophy: The Oxford Guide*, 858.

some people simply accuse other people of Scientism.[20] However, if someone espouses any one or more of the beliefs mentioned above regarding Scientism, according to *Philosophy: The Oxford Guide* this makes them "open to the charge of Scientism."[21] These three beliefs, either one, two, or all three of them, are essentially held by the majority of the modern mainstream scientific community, and so it is right to charge them with Scientism according to *Philosophy: The Oxford Guide*. Now, even though *Philosophy: The Oxford Guide* does distinguish between espousing Scientism and being charged with Scientism, since it is quite obvious that the majority of the modern mainstream scientific community can rightfully be charged with Scientism, for the remainder of this book we are simply going to speak as though these people do in fact espouse Scientism, contrary to what *Philosophy: The Oxford Guide* says, for the distinction really sounds pretty frivolous anyway.

So, let us now look at each one of these three beliefs related to Scientism. The first thing we need to note is that all three of these beliefs are at best presumptuous. The first two are merely opinions, and the third may also be considered such, although there is somewhat more room for objectivity regarding the third belief. The former part of the second belief does not really concern us, but the latter part of it most certainly does. It

---

[20] Ibid, 858.
[21] Ibid, 858.

states that science is "all we need to understand." Now although I would doubt that very many scientists would truly hold to this belief if pressed on the issue, I would imagine that some do, otherwise *Philosophy: The Oxford Guide* would probably not have even mentioned it. This idea that science is all we need to understand is about as dogmatic of a statement as one can possibly make, but again like we just saw it is merely an opinion and not something that can be proven to be true. This statement, when seen in light of the Naturalism and Materialism that it is normally attached to, openly denies any benefit or purposefulness of studying typical religions, music, art, literature, and so on, and it also assumes that the jobs and interests of millions and millions of people around the world are pointless and foolish, a waste of time if you will, since they have nothing directly to do with science. Now don't get me wrong, I am all for good solid science! My wife is a scientist, and I have great personal interest in areas of science such as the human body, anatomy, kinesiology, physiology, geology, anthropology, psychology, biology, and others, and I have at some length studied these areas of science. I am not trying to show that science is bad. But to say that science is "all we need to understand" is a far cry from any statement about the world that should be considered acceptable, especially on its own merit, based on the number of meaningful and noteworthy things that there are in the world to be understood outside the realm of science, such as music, poetry, art, and so on, for like I said, it is merely an opinion that cannot be proven.

The first belief listed above concerning Scientism, namely that only scientific methodology is intellectually acceptable, is also, like we said above, merely an opinion that cannot be proven. Of course this opinion does not seem to be as big of a deal as the previous one that we looked, but it is nonetheless another extremely dogmatic assertion, and it makes everyone who does not adopt a scientific methodology look as if they are ignorant or foolish in whatever it is that they are doing. This, like the first belief regarding Scientism, should be incredibly disheartening to us as humans, for who are the scientists to tell the sculptor, the musician, and the poet how it is that they must go about their work? If we are to be honest it does not even seem as if many types of professions and undertakings can be done using scientific methodology, and so this particular assertion really implies that all things that are fundamentally non-scientific are worthless. I don't know about you, but that certainly doesn't bode well with me, nor is it something, like we already said, that can be proven, but rather it seems quite counterintuitive.

Now as for the third belief regarding Scientism mentioned above, that all philosophical problems are scientific problems and that they should be dealt with as such, we can see here the influence of Naturalism and Materialism on Scientism, for if all of reality is material and natural, then everything that exists should be able to be figured out on a scientific basis. We will see in the next chapter that philosophy ultimately entails anything and everything that can be thought about. But here we can see a problem with this final belief, since obviously we humans can think of things that are neither part of nature nor made up of matter, such as God, angels, and so on, and so although these things, according to the naturalist and the materialist, do not exist, they can nevertheless be thought about and so they are a part of philosophy that does not fit within the realm of science even according to the Naturalist and the Materialist. Hence the belief that philosophical problems are scientific problems[22] is a false assumption even from the perspective of the Naturalist and the Materialist. Of course all scientific reasoning is a form of philosophical reasoning, namely inductive reasoning, but that in no way means that all philosophical problems are scientific problems.

A Prime example of this third characteristic of Scientism, namely the belief that all philosophical problems are also scientific problems, can be found in Stephen Hawking's book *The Grand Design*. Now, we will discuss this book in more detail in the final section of this chapter, but for now I want to focus on the questions that Hawking attempts to answer within his book. These

---

[22] If this means that they are necessarily so, and since there is no qualifier in this statement we may believe that that is what this belief entails.

questions, as posed on pages 10 and 171 of his book, are as follows: Why is there something rather than nothing? Why do we exist? Why this particular set of laws and not some other?[23] These questions are very obviously philosophical questions, not scientific ones. These questions fit into the philosophical category known as metaphysics. There is in fact no way for science to answer these questions, as there is no way to use the scientific method to come to the truth regarding these questions, especially not without presupposing the belief, coming from outside science, that there is a God who created us. We must also remember that these questions are not something that are part of nature; hence, as we will see in the next chapter, they fall outside the realm of science, since science is the systematic study of nature. Hawking however says, "We claim……that it is possible to answer these questions purely within the realm of science, and without invoking any divine beings."[24] Quite simply, Mr. Hawking is wrong here for the reasons noted above, and he has given us absolutely no reason to legitimately accept his assertion, but rather he simply says at the close of his book, "Spontaneous creation is the reason there is something rather than nothing, why the universe exists, why we exist."[25] One wonders why he uses the word "creation" when he is arguing that the universe is

---

[23] Stephen Hawking, *The Grard Design* (New York: Random House, 2010), 10, 171.
[24] Ibid, 172.
[25] Ibid, 180.

uncreated in the first place, and technically "spontaneous creation" is an oxymoron, since if it is truly spontaneous then there can be no creator, and if there is a creator then it cannot truly be spontaneous.

So, we have seen that all three of the beliefs regarding Scientism are merely opinions, and that the first two can be neither proven nor disproven, although they would seem to be highly unpleasant to consider to those of us who are not committed to such a view. We have also seen that the third belief follows from a naturalistic and materialistic view of the world, and it is also a belief that is false due to the reasons given above. Also, and most importantly with regard to Scientism, it is self-defeating, since it is, fundamentally, the belief that only science can provide us with truth, but that assertion is not even itself scientific and so by its very own standards it cannot be a true statement, hence it is self-defeating, and therefore irrational. And so in short Scientism should also be rejected as an inadequate and even harmful, and irrational view of reality. Now we are going to take a brief look at what it means when you put these three views of the world together.

Naturalistic Materialistic Scientism

We saw that Naturalism is the belief that only the natural exists. We also saw that Materialism is the belief that only that which is made up of matter exists, and we saw that this belief is self-defeating. Finally, we saw what

Scientism entails, and that at least one or more of the beliefs entailed in Scientism are generally held by most modern mainstream scientists.[26] We can easily see that most modern mainstream scientists espouse Naturalism by understanding that the prevailing "scientific" *assumption* is that evolution is a proven fact, and by understanding that sociologists and philosophers tend to refer to Darwinism (the belief in macro-evolution) as Naturalism,[27] and so the terms are largely synonymous, although they do not mean exactly the same thing. Darwinism implies Naturalism, but it is not equivalent to Naturalism. We also saw in the last chapter that many modern mainstream scientists have an a priori commitment to Materialism. And so that is why we can rightfully claim that most, or at least many modern mainstream scientists espouse the worldview known as Naturalistic Materialistic Scientism. In short, Naturalistic Materialistic Scientism is the belief that only the material natural world exists and that science and the scientific method provide the only way of gaining knowledge and meaningful information.

Some Implications of and Problems with Naturalistic Materialistic Scientism

---

[26] I make this statement based on the interactions I have had with scientists over the years and based on the books I have read by scientists and the things I have heard them say on TV and in videos over the years.

[27] Bickel and Jantz, *World Religions and Cults*, 242.

Now, as we have a ready seen this worldview is ultimately incoherent on several levels, but for the sake of argument we are going to talk about it for the rest of the chapter as if it is coherent, because otherwise it would be impossible to expound on it in a rational manner, since the implications of something irrational, if at all even possible, would also be irrational.

The first thing we need to mention is that, as we stated at the beginning of this chapter, this worldview is necessarily an atheistic worldview, for if only the natural and the material exists, then there is obviously no room for God or any sort of creator or supernatural being to exist. This poses a problem since science has in fact shown us in recent years that the earth and the universe had a definite point of beginning. Now I don't want to get into too much technical science or philosophy at this point, but a little philosophy won't hurt.

There is an argument (actually it is a type of argument that can take on many different forms) that basically says that since something exists that is contingent, such as humans or the universe, something else must necessarily exist that is not contingent that our contingency relies on. This is known as the Cosmological Argument. For example, the second law of thermodynamics makes it clear that matter cannot possibly be eternal, and therefore the universe must both have had a beginning in time and it must have an end at some point, since all matter is deteriorating. This shows that the universe is contingent, that it is not self-sustaining and eternal, since the universe is made up of this matter that is deteriorating. Now of course this line of thinking is only valid in a closed system, and some people argue that we are not in a closed system, but there is no proof that we are in an open system, nor is there any evidence of it, and so we may legitimately assume that we are in a closed system. So, something else that is eternal and self-existent had to create the universe, since the universe's existence must necessarily rely on something other than itself, since it is contingent. Of course some people these days postulate that an infinite number of finite gods created each other, and one of them created the universe, but as William Lane Craig points out in his book *On Guard*, an infinite number of anything is impossible.[28] So at some point there has to be an eternal being whose existence is within itself if there is to be anything at all, and since the universe and everything in it exists, and since it is contingent, there must have been something eternal that exists outside of this universe that somehow brought this universe and everything in it into being. Dr. Winfried Corduan gives an excellent example of why this eternal being that exists apart from the material world must exist in the book *Reasons for Faith: Making a Case for the Christian Faith*. In his chapter titled *The Cosmological*

---

[28] William Lane Craig, *On Guard: Defending Your Faith with Reason and Precision* (Wheaton: David C. Cook, 2010), 78-83.

Argument Dr. Corduan uses the following example to make this point clear:

> "Think of the following illustration. Imagine a computer spreadsheet in which the cells (labeled by letters and numbers) have no initial values. You would like cell A1 to have the value of '1.' You can type a '1' on the keyboard, hit 'enter,' and be done with it. But instead you decide to get the value from another cell, say B1. So, you give A1 the formula '=B1' and see what happens. Of course, nothing happens because B1 does not have any value. So you can either give B1 directly the value of '1' of you can derive from yet another cell, say C1 and enter '=C1.' But that doesn't help either since C1 doesn't have any value. The fact is that no matter how long you make the chain of cells referencing each other, unless you input a value from outside the chain, none of the cells will have any value.
>
> Nor does it help to link the cells to each other in a circle. Say that you have gone all the way back to ce l Z256, and you decide that you're tired of the game. So, you tell Z256 that its value is that of A1, where you started. What will you get? You will get an

error message. You will still get no numerical value. To repeat, unless you provide a value from outside the circle of cells, none of them will yet have a value."[29]

So, just like how you cannot get a value in a cell of a spreadsheet without somehow inputting a value from outside the chain of cells, whether it be you or someone else who does it, so also nothing in our contingent universe could exist without something from outside the universe having brought it into existence, or to make a stronger connection to the analogy, the universe could not exist without something outside the universe giving it value (existence).

So we see here that the Naturalistic Materialistic Scientism worldview cannot legitimately account for the existence of the universe, since Naturalism holds that the universe is a closed system *and that nothing outside of that system exists.*[30] There must be something outside of the natural system to account for the existence of the universe and everything in it, as Dr. Corduan's above quote shows us. This is an insurmountable problem for Naturalistic Materialistic Scientism and the people who espouse such a view.

---

[29] Winfried Corduan, "The Cosmological Argument," in *Reasons for Faith: Making a Case for the Christian Faith,* eds. Norman L. Geisler and Chad V. Meister (Wheaton: Crossway Books, 2007), 214.
[30] Bickel and Jantz, *World Religions and Cults 101,* 244.

Another implication of this worldview is that which we discussed above, namely that ideas, thoughts, concepts, faith, and so on and so forth do not actually exist. This is clearly absurd, for as we saw earlier, to even be able to consider Materialism one must utilize the concept of Materialism as well as the words that allow one to define, explain and understand such a term, none of which are made up of matter. But for those who claim to hold to a materialistic worldview, like the men quoted in the previous chapter, they must either ignore such problems with their worldview or they must own up to the fact that Materialism is incoherent and disconnect themselves from that worldview on the grounds that it is irrational. Of course they could also admit that it is irrational and still hold to it anyway for whatever reason, but that lacks intellectual integrity, and those who lack integrity are not worthy of our respect or our time, at least in the sense of discussions. [31]

We are now going to look at one more implication of this worldview, and then we are going to look at a specific example of what espousing this worldview does to an individual's intellectual integrity. The final implication that we need to discuss here is that which we briefly touched on earlier in this chapter, namely that it basically calls all those who are not committed to this worldview

---

[31] I am certainly not claiming that we should not help those who are in need because they lack integrity, for if we did that then we ourselves would also lack integrity, although of a different kind.

ignorant and foolish. Richard Dawkins, an obvious adherent to Naturalistic Materialistic Scientism, in his book *The Greatest Show on Earth: The Evidence for Evolution,* calls those of us who deny what he claims to be the "fact" of evolution "history-deniers."[32] That's right people; Dawkins actually compares those of us who deny that evolution is a fact with those people who deny, for instance, the Holocaust. However, unfortunately for Mr. Dawkins, as we will see in our chapter on whether or not macro-evolution can be proven, by his very own definition of what a fact is it is impossible to prove that macro-evolution is real, especially regarding origins, and so his argument that evolution is a fact of history and that those who deny its reality are denying actual history is cut off and demolished right from the start.

As I said earlier, the majority of the world does not espouse a naturalistic or a materialistic view of the world, as can be seen by the wide variety of theistic and animistic religions across the globe. Should we assume that all of these people are simply ignorant and foolish because they believe in things that they cannot see, touch, hear, smell, or taste? Carbon monoxide is tasteless, odorless, soundless, and you cannot see or touch it (at least not in the general sense of the terms), but we would be incredibly foolish to deny its existence, especially if we are stuck in a garage with a gas powered car running with all

---

[32] Richard Dawkins, *The Greatest Show on Earth: The Evidence For Evolution* (New York: Free Press, 2009), 3-18.

of the doors shut and no ventilation. But even if you don't like that example (since carbon monoxide is made of matter), the fact is that no one can prove the non-existence of anything non-material, and so no one should dogmatically claim that only the natural and/or the material exists, for there are in fact many, many very good reasons to believe otherwise, and so the biggest problem with this implication is that it shows much arrogance and presumption on the part of the one espousing this worldview. Again, like we saw above, there is nothing wrong with telling people they are wrong if they really are wrong, but in this case it is the one who espouses Naturalistic Materialistic Scientism that is wrong, for the reasons mentioned above and others.

Stephen Hawking

Most people in America have probably heard of Stephen Hawking, although many might not know who he actually is. Stephen Hawking, according to his recent book *The Grand Design* was the Lucasian Professor of Mathematics at the University of Cambridge for thirty years, and has been the recipient of numerous awards and honors including, most recently, the Presidential Medal of Freedom (this information can be found on the back fold of the cover of the hardcover version of his book). Hawking is also someone whom we will see is thoroughly committed to the worldview of Naturalistic Materialistic Scientism. We can rest assured that Stephen Hawking is a smart man. I want to make that point clear here, as I am in no way attempting to question his intelligence. My contention rather lies with some of the comments that he made in his book, and also with part of the main argument of the book in general.

In his book Stephen Hawking sets out to argue that the fact that there are numerous universes (this idea is known as a multiverse) explains how we can have a finely tuned universe without having to posit a god or creator who created (or designed) the universe that we live in.[33] He essentially uses a theory established by a man named Richard Feynman in the 1940s that says that when a particle goes from point A to point B it takes every possible route *simultaneously*.[34] Now, this theory might work mathematically somehow, but from a practical point of view, and logically speaking, this is, quite simply, impossible, for something in space and time may not take up more than one space at a time, and it certainly cannot take up every space at the same time,[35] as that involves a contradiction. In essence this is like saying that particle E is in both position B, position C, position D, and so on and so

---

[33] Hawking, *The Grand Design*, 165.
[34] Ibid, 74-75.
[35] This is of course unless you are claiming that it is omnipresent, but then it could not move from point A to point B because it would already be at both point A and point B all the time, and particles do not possess the quality of omnipresence, and even secular physicists do not truly believe that all, or any particles are omnipresent, for that is just also absurd.

forth at the same time, in the same space, and in the same sense, but as we have already seen in this book, the law of non-contradiction holds that something cannot be both A and non-A at the same time and in the same sense. Hence, the particle cannot be in more than one position at any given time, no matter how fast it may be moving. Nevertheless, this is what the Feynman theory says, at least in part.

Stephen Hawking then takes this argument and applies it to the beginning (or the history) of the universe. Now before we continue here I would like to point out that Hawking essentially argues for an eternal universe in this book. He argues that he has gotten around the problem of the universe having a beginning by arguing that in the point of singularity before the big bang – There are actually a growing number of scientists who have serious doubts about the big bang and whether or not it really even happened[36] - time acted as a direction of space rather than one of time due to its being so incredibly warped by the mass of the singularity.[37] So he basically says here that the universe had no beginning, but rather only time at the point of inflation (when the bang happened and the universe began to expand) began to act as time and so time then began, but not the universe, as it has always existed.[38] But on the very next page he says

36 David A. Dewitt, *Uncovering The Origins Controversy* (Lynchburg: Creation Curriculum, L.L.C., 2007), 152-153.
37 Hawking, *The Grand Design*, 134.

that "the beginning of the universe was governed by the laws of science and doesn't need to be set in motion by some god."[39] Now without getting into the rest of what he is arguing here, we can see that he both denied that the universe had a beginning and then talked about the beginning of the universe on the very next page. This is yet another blatant contradiction. Of course some would probably argue that it is simply natural to talk about the beginning of the universe in this way, even though he really doesn't believe that the universe had a beginning, since in his mind the "beginning" is probably just the point at which time began to act as such. To that I would just say two things. One, if he is to be true to his beliefs (i.e. if he is to possess intellectual integrity) then he must not use terms and phrases that represent ideas and concepts that he denies the reality of, unless it is simply to deny the reality of them. Two, why might it be that it "seems natural" to talk about the universe as having a beginning? Might it be because all of the evidence actually points in that direction? The answer to that second question certainly seems to be yes!

To "begin" means to start. Mr. Hawking seems to be equivocating terms here, for he claims that the universe has no "beginning" because it is eternal since

---

[38] Remember, however, that we have already established that the second law of thermodynamics makes it clear that the universe cannot possibly be eternal.
[39] Ibid, 135.

time was essentially non-existent in the pre-inflation point of singularity. The problem with this is that he is using the term "beginning" in two different senses to prove only one point, or rather he is using the term in one way to prove something using the term in another way. This is a logical fallacy known as *equivocation*. The first sense that he is using the term, namely when he states that the universe had no "beginning" (i.e. it is eternal), means that there was never a time in which the universe did not exist, or, put another way, the universe has always existed. But to prove this he equivocates the term "beginning" (although not actually using the term but rather implying it) by arguing that time was non-existent in the point of singularity. In this second sense Hawking is referring to a lack of time, whereas in the first sense he is referring to a lack of existence (or the negation of a lack of existence, i.e. eternal existence). This is not a valid argument. One cannot say that no time existed, therefore the universe is eternal.[40] Christians also believe that prior to the universe being created there was no time, but we do not argue that the universe is therefore eternal, as that is not a valid inference. Nor is the inference that Hawking has made here valid, and so his argument that the universe is eternal fails on the grounds of logic.

Now, as I said above, Stephen Hawking takes the Feynman argument and applies it to the history of the

---

[40] His argument is obviously more complex than this, but this is still a perfectly valid synopsis of the argument.

universe. Remember that the Feynman theory itself is actually illogical and therefore incoherent, even if mathematicians think it works in their theoretical world of abstract concepts. Hawking, however, applies this theory in a specific way and proceeds to argue that just like the particle in Feynman's theory takes every possible route to get from point A to point B simultaneously, so at the time of inflation the universe expanded and did what it did in every possible way simultaneously. This is how he comes to the conclusion that other universes must exist, since all of those other ways and histories could not have led to the reality that we experience in our universe. Now obviously the connection that Hawking has made here is that since the universe was so very tiny (tiny enough for the laws of quantum physics to be in operation) at the point of singularity, just like the particle in the Feynman theory that took every possible route to get from point A to point B, so also at the time of inflation all of the particles in the point of singularity took every possible route to end up where they did. The main problem with this as we have already seen is that this is impossible. What Hawking has essentially argued here implies that the same particles (not similar particles, but rather the actual very same particles) that make up our universe also make up all of these other universes that he claims are out there somewhere, since it was the particles in the singularity that supposedly took every possible route *at the same time*, creating all of the different histories of the different universes. And so this is not different singularities inflating in different ways, but rather it is the same singularity exploding in numerous different ways all at the same time. That, my friends, is absurd, for as we have seen no particle, or anything else, can occupy two or more different spaces at the same time, meaning that something cannot be both somewhere and somewhere else at the same time and in the same sense, especially if it is made up of matter, and we have already seen that Hawking is committed to a materialistic worldview. And so we see here that this theory that other universes exist, at least on this basis, is a farce, since the particles in the singularity can in fact only be in one place at a time, and, fortunately for us, they exist in our universe, and so they cannot exist in any other universe, which removes the possibility on Hawking's grounds that other universes exist.

So we see here that when one, such as Stephen Hawking, is committed to Naturalistic Materialistic Scientism, a worldview that cannot possibly explain reality as it truly is and seems to be, they are destined, if they are to address the profound issues in life, to come up with answers that are, quite simply, incoherent, for to remain coherent you must be willing to be true to all the facts, and you must also be willing to remain logical at all times, something that Materialism is incapable of doing, as we saw above. This is why it is vitally important to reject Naturalistic Materialistic Scientism. Otherwise you are bound to be defeated by illogicalities and inconsistencies somewhere, somehow.[41]

Conclusion

In conclusion, we have looked at Naturalism, Materialism, and Scientism. We have also looked at the worldview that entails all three of these belief systems, Naturalistic Materialistic Scientism. We have seen some implications of this worldview, and we have discussed some of the major problems with it. As we saw in the opening quote of this chapter, Naturalism and Darwinism answer many of the same questions that traditional religions attempt to answer. This leads us to our next chapter where we will determine whether evolution is science, or whether it is better defined as a philosophical/religious belief system, or something else. I hope you are ready, because the next chapter might very well throw you some intellectual curveballs that you never saw coming. We will also assess whether or not science can be done within a system of Evolutionism (hint for the next chapter), just like within a system that utilizes Intelligent Design and/or Creationism. Sit back, kick up your feet, and hold on to your book, because the next chapter might very well just rock your world!

---

[41] Do not mistake my argument here. I am not claiming that since Stephen Hawking's view here is incoherent that every argument that every Naturalistic Materialistic Scientism proponent makes will also be. Rather I am arguing that incoherency stems from the very essence of Naturalistic Materialistic Scientism, as has been shown above.

6

Evolution: Is It Science or Is It Essentially a Religious/Philosophical Belief System?

"Darwin's theory of evolution is indeed a 'scheme or system of ideas or statements.'"[1]

- *Richard Dawkins in his book The Greatest Show on Earth*

Now that we have looked at what truth is, whether or not modern mainstream science is looking for such truth, and what exactly Naturalistic Materialistic Scientism is, we are going to take a look at whether evolution (macro-evolution), should be considered science, or whether it should instead be classified as a religious/philosophical belief system. Now before we continue let me first explain why I use the term "religious/philosophical." Many people, especially, and unfortunately, many Christians, believe that religion and philosophy do not mix, and that in fact philosophy is something evil that we should stay away from, and that religion is on the complete opposite end of the spectrum,

---

[1] Richard Dawkins, *The Greatest Show on Earth: The Evidence For Evolution* (New York: Free Press, 2009), 9-10.

and that we should embrace it. Others simply believe that the philosophers are the smart people and the religious people are the crazy fanatics who need to get a life, and that the two could not possibly mix. That is, quite simply, not the case. For one thing, philosophy is not evil, and the Bible does not say that it is evil or that we should stay away from it, but rather to the contrary there are many passages, such as 2 Timothy 2:7 and 1 Peter 3:15 where we are told to think through things and to always have an answer for the hope that is within us. As we will see below, philosophy most fundamentally involves thinking about things, and so the Bible, far from telling us to stay away from philosophy, actually tells us to embrace it. The passage in Colossians 2:8 where Paul tells us not to get carried away by deceptive philosophies is referring to specific worldviews and types of philosophical thought that go against the teachings of Scripture, not just any philosophy or philosophy in general. Second, and more importantly to our discussion, the questions that are generally brought up and answered in the arena of religion are actually and essentially questions that are dealt with in various philosophical disciplines as well. For instance, what we should or should not do, how we should treat people, whether abortion is right or wrong, and so on are all questions that many different religions have answers to, but these types of questions also fall into a philosophical category known as *ethics*. Another example would be questions like, "Does God exist?," "Why are we here?," or put a different way, "What is man's place in what is real?", and so on. These are also questions that many religions have answers to, and yet these questions generally fall into the philosophical category of what is known as *metaphysics*.[2] So we can see that many, if not all questions that are dealt with in religious systems, such as Catholicism, Christianity, Buddhism, Hinduism, and so on are also dealt with in one category of philosophy or another, and so it seems fair to use the term "religious/philosophical" belief system.

Another reason we are here using both the terms "religion" and "philosophy" is because we are going to show in the following pages of this chapter that evolution can in fact rightly be classified as a "religion" and that it falls under the umbrella of philosophy. Now remember that philosophical reasoning is the opposite of scientific reasoning in the strict sense of the terms, as one deals with certainty and the other only with probability. Of course scientists must use philosophical reasoning to think through their experiments and come up with their conclusions, but that is not science. Science is the doing of the experiments and the studying of nature, which we will see in a few moments. So, to not confuse you any further (assuming you are confused at this point), let us clarify some terms. We are first going to briefly clarify what the term "science" means, followed by a brief look at what the

---

[2] William Hasker, *Metaphysics: Constructing a World View* (Downers Grove: InterVarsity Press, 1983), 16.

terms "philosophy" and "religion" mean. After that we will take a quick look at what exactly evolution is, and then we will move on to the main issue of this chapter, namely whether evolution is better defined as science or whether it is better defined as a religious/philosophical system that science can be done within, or neither. Before we move forward let me remind you of the quote that was at the beginning of the last chapter that mentioned how Darwinism is a system of ideas that answers many of the typical religious questions of life. Also, the fact that Darwinism, the belief system that entails evolution, was given its own chapter in a book about religion such as the one that that quote came from should be very telling as to where this chapter is headed.

What is Science?

What is science? How do we define such a complex discipline? To be sure there are many different types of science, including biology, geology, immunology, chemistry, Intelligent Design (did you catch that? Good! Chapter 8 will explain this in more detail), and so on. However, what we are looking for here is a general definition that overlaps all of the various fields of science.

So, after looking through nearly a dozen college science textbooks, including numerous biology and veterinary medical textbooks, I found but one definition of science and one definition of the scientific method, and so we will look at them both, although in the opposite order.

It seems a bit odd that so many science textbooks have so few definitions of science in them. Might this be because the authors assume (or should I say presume) that the readers should already know what science is? Well, unfortunately as this book hopefully shows, even most scientists do not seem to understand what science is really supposed to be and be about, let alone what it actually is for that matter, hence the reason that modern mainstream scientists are generally not looking for the truth in their labs, and hence the reason for the confusion regarding what exactly Intelligent Design is. This is also most likely the reason that the courts, the museums, the schools, and the scientists think and claim that evolution is science. Well, that is why I have written this chapter, so let's get to it!

First we have, in the *Saunders Comprehensive Veterinary Dictionary*, the following definition of the scientific method:

> "The process of extending knowledge by forming a hypothesis based on observations and epidemiological patterns, which is then tested on a subset of the total population, then generalizing the results to the appropriate population through the process of inductive logic. Before implementation of the hypotheses they should be tested by

studies planned on the basis that the
hypothesis will be proved or denied."[3]

We see here that the scientific method involves creating a hypothesis, followed by experimentation done on a sample of the population involved in the study, which in turn leads to either the acceptance or the denial of the given hypothesis. We also see here that science is done using inductive logic, just as we saw earlier in this book, which leads merely to probable conclusions and not definitive ones. Finally, we can see in this definition of the scientific method that the whole process should be done with the view in mind that the hypothesis will either be proved *or* denied. It does not say that the scientist should do his or her experiment with the presumption that the hypothesis is true *no matter what*, and that there is no way that it can be denied, as many scientists these days do when going about their scientific endeavors. Both proof *and* denial are necessary possibilities for the scientific method to be used correctly. To take this one step further though, since the scientific method entails the use of inductive logic, the hypothesis, contrary to the implications of this definition, cannot actually be proven, but rather it can only be shown to be probable or not.

---

[3] D.C. Blood, V.P. Studdert, and C.C. Gay, *Saunders Comprehensive Veterinary Dictionary: Third Edition* (London: Elsevier Limited, 2007), 1604.

All in all this definition is pretty straight forward, and so we can now move on to briefly discuss what exactly science is and how to define it, but before we go on it needs to be said that all science does not deal with a "population" in the strict sense. However, all science must necessarily entail experiments that are repeated a number of times, and these experiments must include an appropriate sampling of whatever the hypothesis is dealing with, that is of course if the scientific method is to be utilized correctly.

We saw in chapter 4 that the modern mainstream scientific community is not seeking the truth, but what is science supposed to be anyway? How can we correctly identify what science is intended to do, and how should we define it? Well, according to the *Annotated Instructor's Edition of Biology: Concepts and Applications (seventh edition)*, science is defined as follows: "Systematic study of nature."[4] Now since this is a definition that comes from a state approved textbook,[5] we can assume that this definition is widely accepted within the mainstream scientific community, with maybe some minor variations depending on one's preference of terms. This definition also seems to fit quite well with the overall idea of science regardless of who is doing the science and what their

---

[4] Peggy Williams, Jessica Kuhn, and Rose Barlow, eds., *Biology: Concepts and Applications: Seventh Edition, Annotated Instructors Edition* (Belmont: Thomson Brooks/Cole, 2008), Glossary.
[5] This is an instructor's version of a textbook for an introductory biology class called "Principles of Biology" at a major university.

religious beliefs may be. Of course one may argue that we need to define nature in this context so as to better understand the definition given above, but then one need only realize that to the mainstream scientific community Naturalism is the dominant worldview, and so nature here most likely would represent anything and everything that exists, since Naturalism teaches that nothing outside of, or other than, the natural exists. So we can then modify our definition here slightly to mean: *The systematic study of anything and everything that exists in nature.*

Now when we say "systematic," do not get confused with the terms we are using here, as this type of system is not intended to mean the same thing as a belief system, such as we will look at later on in this chapter. Rather, "systematic" in this context refers to a specific way of doing science, namely by means of the use of the scientific method. So we see that science, in its most basic definition, is: *the use of the scientific method to study anything and everything that exists in nature.* This is, it would seem, a reasonable reformative (reformative in reference to the shorter definition given above from the textbook) definition of science based on the above discussion, and so it is the definition that we will be using for the remainder of this book when we talk specifically about science.

What is Philosophy?

Now that we have established a definition for what science is, let us move forward to discuss what philosophy is and how to define it. According to, *Philosophy: The Oxford Guide*, "Most definitions of philosophy are fairly controversial, particularly if they aim to be at all interesting or profound. That is partly because what has been called philosophy has changed radically in scope in the course of history."[6] There are also many, many different types of philosophy. There is the philosophy of science, the philosophy of history, the philosophy of ethics, the philosophy of religion, and many other types of philosophy as well. There is also metaphysics, which is a branch of philosophy that essentially involves the study of what is real. Now all of the different major areas of philosophy, such as the philosophy of science, are simply disciplines that deal with how to think about that particular field. For example, the philosophy of religion is not actually *religious thinking*, as in thinking within a religious system such as Christianity, but rather the philosophy of religion has more to do with "thinking *about* religion (emphasis mine)."[7] This can be done by both those who are religious and those who are non-religious. The philosophy of science is the same in essence in that it

[6] Ted Honderick, ed., *Philosophy: The Oxford Guide* (Oxford: Oxford University Press, 2005), 702.

[7] C. Stephen Evans and R. Zachary Manis, *Philosophy of Religion: Thinking About Faith* (Downers Grove: InterVarsity Press, 2009), 22.

deals with thinking *about* science, as opposed to *scientific thinking*. Some might say that this book, or at least this chapter, would fall into the category of the philosophy of science. But what specifically is philosophy in general? As we have seen above it is hard to come up with a good definition that many people will like, but for the purposes of this book we must try to do so, however carefully we may tread in the process.

We must try not to be too profound, as the quote above from *Philosophy: The Oxford Guide* points out to us. So let us be simple in our definition for what exactly philosophy is. When we take into account all the different philosophical disciplines and all of the different areas to which philosophy may be applied, we see that there is essentially nothing that philosophy cannot touch, and so I think it best to simply define philosophy as: "The discipline of pondering things or something, whether in general or in particular, in which anything that can be thought of is a thing." This definition, I hope, is both limited enough to specifically cover the field of philosophy in particular as well as broad enough to cover the total spectrum of philosophy in general, and since it at least seems as if it is, this is the definition that we will move forward with as our definition of philosophy for the remainder of this book. Now let us remember that philosophy is not to be confused with philosophizing, which would essentially be the actual implementation and expression of doing philosophy, whether in writing, audibly, or even within one's own mind. Philosophy is merely the discipline of pondering things or something, whether general or particular, but not the doing of, or actual execution of that discipline, as that is known as philosophizing.

What is Religion?

We all know of various examples of religions, such as Christianity, Catholicism, Hinduism, Islam, and so on and so forth, but what exactly is religion? How should we define the term? We are going to look at some definitions of the term "religion" here in a minute, but first let us recap over what we said in the initial section of this chapter. Religious systems and philosophical systems often, if not always, overlap in one way or another, especially since, as we saw in our above definition of philosophy, philosophy essentially covers every aspect of everything that can be thought of. This also shows that philosophy can overlap in the area of scientific reasoning. But remember that science itself is not the same thing as scientific reasoning. Scientific reasoning is inductive reasoning, which is a form of philosophical reasoning, as is all reasoning in general. But science itself is a systematic approach to studying the natural world. Let me explain it this way. The *discipline* of science includes scientific reasoning, and therefore philosophical reasoning, but the *definition* of science does not. Science is simply, as we have just stated, a systematic approach to studying the natural world, or in other words, science is essentially the systematic approach to the study of the natural world, while scientific reasoning includes the thinking that is done that is entailed in that approach. I realize that this is a tedious distinction, but it is nevertheless a necessary distinction to show here how, while working together, philosophy and science are still two very distinct disciplines.

We saw in the previous chapter why this distinction is vital to the argument at hand in this book. This also shows more clearly the problem that we raised earlier about science being equated with Naturalism and Materialism. For one thing, science deals with the act and discipline of studying the natural world, while the others, namely Naturalism and Materialism, deal with how one goes about studying and viewing the natural world (with regard to scientific *thought*) based on certain beliefs, which is why we call Naturalism and Materialism belief systems, or worldviews. We will deal with that issue later, but for now simply note the distinctions, as they are incredibly important to our present case, for the main purpose of this chapter is to show that evolution is not science, but rather is fundamentally tied to the concept of a religious/philosophical belief system.

Now, there are many definitions of the term "religion," many of which have something to do with God, a god, or some form of deity or supernaturalism, but these are not necessary components of a definition for religion.

However, let us look at a few of these definitions to get a better idea of why the United States Supreme Court and many, if not most Americans are confused about the so called battle dubbed "Science (evolution) vs. Religion (Creationism, Intelligent Design, etc.)."

One definition of religion that few people would argue against is as follows: "The personal commitment to and serving of God or a god with worshipful devotion, conduct in accord with divine commands especially as found in accepted sacred writings or declared by authoritative teachers."[8] This definition, as the footnote shows, comes straight out of Webster's dictionary and so we should be able to trust this definition as a legitimate definition of the term "religion." Of course there are many other definitions of religion in this dictionary as well, such as: "one of the systems of faith and worship."[9] This definition is a lot broader of course and so it includes more than the above definition of religion that we just saw. Another definition of religion is "a personal awareness or conviction of the existence of a supreme being or of supernatural powers or influence controlling one's own, humanity's, or all nature's destiny."[10] This definition of religion, like the first giver above, involves supernaturalism and so it does not include strict

[8] Philip Babcock Gove, *Webster's Third New International Dictionary of the English Language, Unabridged* (Springfield: Merriam-Webster, Incorporated, 2002), 1918.
[9] Ibid.
[10] Ibid.

Naturalism. It would seem as though these first and third definitions of religion are the kind of definition that the courts had in mind when they deemed Creationism and Intelligent Design religion and not science, like evolution supposedly is. But is this a fair and accurate distinction? We are going to look at this question at a much greater depth before this chapter is over, but first let us look at one more definition of the term "religion." I think you might be surprised with this definition and the implications so involved therein with regard to evolution. However, before we look at this final definition of religion let's take a gander at what one expert of world religions has to say about religion.

In the book *Understanding World Religions* Irving Hexham, an expert on world religions, has this to say as his opening statement for the book in chapter one:

> "Most people have a clear idea of what they mean by *religion* and can usually identify religious behavior when they see it. Nevertheless, when we have to define religion, we soon discover that the task is quite difficult, because religion is manifest in many different ways in our world. Thus, while for most people religion involves a belief in God, this is not true for certain forms of Buddhism. Indeed, to the educated Buddhist, God is quite unimportant."[11]

Buddhism is at its core, contrary to what many people realize and think, both an atheistic and a nihilistic religion.[12] This means that a true Buddhist not only believes that God does not exist, but he/she ultimately also believes that nothing at all, including himself/herself, exists. Now of course this leads to self-refutation ultimately regarding the religion of Buddhism, but that is beside the point here. if Buddhism with such beliefs can still be considered a religion, even though it openly denies the existence of God as well as everything else, why cannot Evolutionism (or Darwinism, whichever you prefer to call it) also be considered a religion? Bruce Bickel and Stan Jantz say it best at the beginning of their chapter titled "Atheism, Darwinism, and Naturalism" in their book *World Religions and Cults 101,* the writing of which was overseen by religion expert Craig Hazen:

> "At first, you might have wondered why we
> are including a chapter on atheism in a
> book about world religions. After all, if
> atheists don't believe in a god, then they
> don't have a religion, right? Well, not so fast
> there buckaroo. Just because they don't
> believe in God doesn't mean that they
> aren't religious. They have a religion. It is a

---

[11] Irving Hexham, *Understanding World Religions* (Grand Rapids: Zondervan, 2011), 15.
[12] Bruce Bickel and Stan Jantz *World Religions and Cults 101* (Eugene: Harvest House Publishers, 2002), 178.

religion of 'no god." There are some pretty interesting ramifications from a belief in 'no god,' and those ramifications are the essence of the atheist's religion (although they aren't quick to admit some of them).

And, you might be thinking, what's the deal with Darwin? How does he merit getting his name in a chapter title? Well, Darwin's theories have been adopted as a belief system by many people; it is a belief system with a doctrine of 'no god.' Without a doubt, there is a religion of naturalism (although its adherents would never characterize their beliefs as a religion since that term smacks too much of god, of which there isn't one).

You won't find a building in your town with a sign that reads: 'First Church of Atheism.' And there won't be a temple dedicated to St. Darwin the Divine. But don't let that fool you. These are real religions....."[13]

We see here in this lengthy quote that Darwinism and Naturalism are in fact belief systems and religions, according to these authors. As we will discover below, I

---

[13] Ibid, 232.

agree wholeheartedly with this assertion. Now let us move on to discuss one more definition of religion.

The final definition of religion that we are going to look at also comes from the same dictionary, namely *Webster's Third New International Dictionary of The English Language Unabridged*, as the above definitions did. The definition is as follows: "a cause, principle, system of tenets held with ardor, devotion, conscientiousness, and faith."[14] Now when we take a look at this definition we see that it is even broader than the second definition that we looked at above. This definition would even include Atheism, which many people consider an anti-religion. It is obvious that the evolutionists are enthusiastic and devoted to the idea of evolution in a conscientious manner, but what about the faith part of the definition? Does evolution entail an element of faith? Well, in the next chapter we are going to see that evolution cannot be proven, which inevitably means that one who believes in it has to believe it based on an element of faith, but for now let us just say that the answer is an unequivocal "YES!" You see, evolution, especially when dealing with origins, is historical science, and as we have already noted historical science is non-verifiable because the instances that we are trying to study cannot be repeated. They are in the past. This is a problem for proving something even as probable, to some extent, because science necessitates repeatable

---

[14] Ibid.

experimentation, which means that historical science is a different type of science, for although we can still do various experiments in the present to somewhat "predict the past," we cannot replay or repeat the actual events of the past, and so historical science inevitably leads primarily to simply interpreting the available data in various ways, rather than doing experiments in the same manner as empirical, or "regular" science does. So, evolution will always fit into the category of religion according to this final definition, because it will always entail an element of faith, along with the other aspects of this definition.

What Is A Belief System?

We will now move on to define one more phrase, namely a "belief system." What is a belief system? How should we define it? Well, without getting too technical, a belief system is equivalent to, but not exactly the same as a worldview. Simply put, a worldview is the lens through which each person sees reality, or, put another way, a worldview is the sum total of one's beliefs that shape our preconceptions and suppositions about reality and how we act and react in and to life, to be a bit more technical. For instance, if someone is a theist, meaning that they believe in God, or a god or gods, then they will necessarily view everything in life in a way that takes that belief into account, or at least they will if they are being consistent with their theistic beliefs. As another example, someone who is a creationist, if they are to be true to such beliefs, will view everything in the universe as having intrinsic value because it was *all* created by something, which necessitates that everything has a purpose for being here. So, for the creationist, his worldview includes, but is not limited to his creationist beliefs, and for the theist, his worldview includes, but is not limited to his theistic beliefs. We will apply this concept of a worldview to evolution, Creationism (again), and Intelligent Design below, but for now it will suffice simply to define the term as we have done above. To be fair though, one can have multiple belief systems within a worldview as one can have different belief systems for different subjects,[15] but for our purposes we will use the term "belief system" in the overarching sense as referring to a single belief system that affects how one looks at all of life in general and each subject therein in particular, which includes all of the beliefs that one holds, which, in essence, is what makes up one's worldview. This is not meant to confuse you, but it is rather meant to emphasize the degree to which Evolutionism (Darwinism) affects one's outlook on life, for although it is a belief system rather than a worldview in the sense that we have defined the terms here, it is a belief system that has ramifications for every single aspect of life and every single subject.

---

[15] For instance one can be a theist, a creationist, and an environmentalist all at the same time. Each of these are belief systems relative to various subjects, and they all fit within a Christian worldview.

We have several more things to discuss in this chapter, so let us sum up this definitive section and move on with our discussion of whether or not evolution is science or whether it is a religious/philosophical belief system, or neither. We have looked at definitions for both science and the scientific method. We have also looked briefly at definitions for philosophy and religion and have seen that religious systems and philosophical systems can and do overlap to a large extent, and so they can be viewed to some extent as the same thing, although they are obviously not 100% equivalent. We have also taken a look at what a belief system and a worldview is. So now let us move on to discuss whether or not evolution is actually science, as many people claim, or whether it can in fact be better defined as a religious/philosophical belief system. This will however require us to first take a brief look at what evolution is and how to specifically define it, and so that is what we shall do next.

What is Evolution?

What is evolution, what is evolutionary theory, and how are they generally defined by the scientific community? Let us look at each of these in turn. First, the term "evolution" is often used as synonymous with change in general. We talk about the evolution of the computer, the evolution of architecture, or the evolution of dance.[16]

---

[16] This is a popular dance routine done by a man named Judson Laipply that shows how dance has changed over the years.

This is, unfortunately, something that has indoctrinated Americans into seeing evolution as just another aspect of life, for if we are aware that change is inevitable (which most intelligent and wise people are), and if we constantly hear that evolution is synonymous with change, then common sense would tell us that evolution (macro-evolution) too is inevitable. This has, to put it ever so plainly, been an incredible detriment to our society, for how can something that has never been, nor can ever be proven be viewed as inevitable from a rational perspective? It cannot! This is yet another way that our society and the people "running the show" have propagandized Americans, as well as people from many other nations, into believing the lie that evolution is a proven fact. Yet this idea that evolution is simply change over time is sometimes even seen in the definitions for evolution found in science textbooks. But not all textbooks give so simple of a definition. The *Brock Biology of Microorganisms (eleventh edition)* textbook published in 2006 by Pearson Education, Inc., defines evolution as follows: "Change in a line of descent over time leading to the production of new species or varieties within a species."[17] Now of course the end of this definition leaves evolution opened to be pretty much any change in any species, which is basically the idea that evolution is

---

[17] Michael T. Madigan and John M. Martinko, *Brock Biology of Microorganisms* (Upper Saddle River: Pearson Education, Inc., 2006), G-5.

synonymous with change, but applied specifically to all living things. This is deceitful, however, because as a matter of fact the evolution that most scientists purport as real is actually defined in terms of origins, as we will see later on in this chapter. What is evolution? For now let us define evolution as an idea that encompasses change within all living things. Did you catch that? An idea! Hold on to that thought, and we will come back to it in a bit.

So what is evolutionary theory? Well, let us first take a quick look at what a theory is, and then we will tie it to the idea of evolution. *Webster's New World Dictionary* defines a theory as "a formulation of underlying principles of certain observed phenomena that has been verified to some degree."[18] Now, if we remember back to our discussion of proof and science we will well remember that anything that has been "verified" can be essentially "unverified" also, at least with regard to science, since science deals only with probability and not actual proof. So right off the bat we see that it is impossible for a scientific theory to become a scientifically *proven* fact, because the theory could be overturned at any time, since no matter how probable something is and no matter how much verification we have regarding a theory, there is always the possibility that someday a different theory will become more probable based on the evidence. This is crucial to understanding science and the scientific method. A good

---

[18] Michael Agnes, ed., *Webster's New World Dictionary* (New York: Pocket Books, 2003), 668.

hypothesis must be both verifiable (to a high degree) and falsifiable (to a high degree). If the hypothesis seems to be verified enough times it will generally be accepted as a reliable hypothesis, but it is reliable at best, because you are dealing with probability, which is always less than 100%, at least in the case of science. This leaves constant room for falsifiability. Of course, this has only to do with non-historical sciences. This is the problem with evolutionary theory when applied to origins and all of life and claiming that it is a proven fact. Even if we find something to be probable today that, if we could trace it back through time would seem to validate our hypothesis regarding past events, that would still only make the hypothesis of past events probable to some degree, but never 100% verified, since again science deals with probability, and even still we cannot actually go back in time and check to see if we are in fact correct and that what we find happening today has happened throughout all of time.

Now before I continue let me say something. This does not mean that good historical science cannot be done, but rather it simply means that if we are to do good historical science, then we need to keep these things in mind and not ignore them and act like they are not part of reality. All scientists, as well as all non-scientists, should do whatever they do with the highest level of integrity possible.[19]

So, with the above definition of "theory" in mind, let us simply state that evolutionary theory is the theory that evolution is true and real. Technically, however, the above definition requires verification of some kind, and since there has been no legitimate verification of evolution, since it is impossible, there cannot, according to this definition of "theory," even be a *theory* of evolution. Rather it is simply a *belief* in evolution that is actually at work in the scientific community. Now let us look at how evolution is generally defined by modern mainstream scientists with regard to origins, because this is where the major speculation, along with the extremely problematic political and ethical theories (such as those espoused by Hitler and Marx), come into play regarding evolution, as we have already discussed in this volume.

In general, the overarching mainstream academic definition of evolution includes something to the effect of, "The descent of all living things from a single common ancestor." This idea is expressed in the state approved high school biology textbook, *Biology*, where the glossary defines evolution as "A change in the characteristics of a population from one generation to the next; the gradual development of organisms from other organisms since the beginning of life."[20] Now although this definition does not

---

[19] Why this is so is another argument for another time and another book, and we do not have time to address it here.

[20] George B. Johnson and Peter H. Raven, *Biology* (Austin: Holt, Rinehart, and Winston, 2004), 1073.

specifically match the one given directly above it in this paragraph, it has the same idea in mind, for as we will see below in the quote from the book *Science* the definition of macro-evolution that is contended by non-evolutionists and espoused by evolutionists involves the common descent of all life forms from lower ones. This is a basic definition that is widely held, but seemingly rarely specifically documented, although I have seen it on occasion in published works. This is what is meant when the evolutionists talk about how the religious people are ignorant because they do not believe in evolution. They are not claiming that we are ignorant because we do not believe in change over time. They are not even claiming that we are ignorant because we do not believe in change within a species. They are claiming that we are ignorant because we do not believe that every living thing, past, present, and future has and will descend from a single common ancestor, which these days is said to have existed billions of years ago. This mockery and disrespect for and of the "religious" can be seen incredibly clearly in a quote taken from the book *Science: The Definitive Visual Guide* edited by a man who is dubbed "one of the world's most popular and respected 'explainers' of science."[21] The quote is as follows: "The *idea* that all creatures on Earth evolved from the same primitive ancestors was rejected in the past for religious reasons (italics mine)."[22] Here the author has

---

[21] Adam Hart-Davis, ed., *Science: The Definitive Visual Guide* (New York: Dorling Kindersley Limited, 2009), 5.

used the term "evolved" as synonymous with "descended", but the idea is still the same overall. The main point that the author is trying to make in this statement is that religion is a setback to science and the acceptance of evolution. However, as this chapter shows, that assertion is problematic on multiple levels. Now, before we move forward to discuss whether evolution is science or a religious/philosophical belief system, let us first return to this issue of evolution and evolutionary theory being ideas. Also, for the purpose of not sounding odd, we are going to continue referring to the "theory of evolution" as such, even though we saw earlier that a theory requires some form of verification and that evolution has no such verification.

Evolution in and of itself is a word, and all words must necessarily have an idea that they correspond to, otherwise the word would be meaningless, and so the word cannot be detached from its corresponding idea if it is to remain intelligible. However, it is the idea that matters most, for one can have an idea without a name for that idea, but, as seen above, if one is to remain coherent, then he cannot have a name/word without an idea attached to it, and so it is the idea of evolution that we are here concerned with. Now the theory of evolution is basically a compilation and intermingling of the ideas associated with how evolution supposedly works, and also

---

[22] Ibid, 200.

the idea that evolution is actually true. While this could be a definition of evolutionary theory, it is also the idea that is attached to the phrase "evolutionary theory." While this may seem like a mute distinction, it is not. My point here is to show that it is the idea of a thing that is believed and not the thing itself, and so it is important to remember that the definitions, or ideas, that we attach to words are what we are actually dealing with. If we are going to analyze something such as evolution, we must analyze the idea attached to it. Sometimes etymology is also important, but not for our purposes here. So, what I meant above when I said that evolution and evolutionary theory are ideas was that the ideas attached to those words/phrases are what is important, and not the words/phrases themselves. This is important because it is the ideas attached to words and phrases that have consequences, and, as stated above, it is the ideas that we believe or disbelieve, not the words or phrases themselves. Also, some words and phrases have ideas attached to them that are directly associated with some type of action. Other words and phrases are more abstract and are not directly related to any sort of action, but rather mostly, or perhaps merely, relate an idea through nomenclature. Allow me to give examples now of each type of words and phrases mentioned above and then hopefully you will have a better understanding of where we are going with this line of argument.

Now, an example of the first type of words/phrases mentioned above that are more associated with actions would be something like the word "pitching," or the phrase "playing catch." While these words and phrases have certain ideas associated with them, such as the idea of throwing a ball from a mound to a catcher behind home plate for the word "pitching," or two or more people throwing a ball back and forth repeatedly for the phrase "playing catch," these ideas involve physical human actions that can be controlled by us in a general sense, for it is the one who is pitching who is throwing the ball to the catcher and so on, and so these types of words are more closely associated with actions, and more specifically actions involving an agent or agents. Science is another one of these types of words, since it is invariably associated with the use of the scientific method, a series of actions that are done by humans.

Other types of words and phrases, such as "reason" or "moral obligation" are less directly associated with actions and more connected specifically to abstract ideas. "Reason" of course is directly related to the idea of cognition, or rational thinking, but it is only indirectly linked to the actual action of thinking rationally, at least in the way that we are here using it, as we are using "reason" here in the sense of being defined as an attribute, not an action. "Moral obligation" in the same way is directly linked to the idea that something has been established as right or wrong by a given source and is either forbidden or commanded by that source, but this phrase is only indirectly linked to the actions involved in living up to, or not living up to, such obligations.

So we can see that the first type of words and phrases are directly linked to actions by an agent (often times human agents), and the second type of words and phrases are only indirectly associated with actions by an agent (again often human agents). The idea of "macro-evolution", as we will substitute here for the basic term "evolution," since that is the type of evolution that we are concerned with, would seem to be in the first category of words and phrases, since it deals with change over time, which requires action, as change in the strict sense requires a causal agent of some sort, for change cannot truly happen without influence. However, "macro-evolution", according to modern mainstream science, is led by random chance, natural selection, and so on. Now chance is nothing more than another abstract term that refers to the idea of probability, and so it cannot rightly be viewed as being an agent, and so it also cannot cause change. But what about natural selection? Well, natural selection is a phrase that is associated with the idea of a process that is guided by random chance, which again is illusory at best, since chance cannot produce change. Also, natural selection cannot be viewed as an agent causing change, for an agent must possess certain qualities, such as actual existence, and for an agent to be an acting agent, it must also possess the ability to act, and therefore also it must be living in some sense, but natural selection is a process, not an actually existing agent, and so it does not, indeed it cannot possess attributes such as these. And still also, how can a process be guided by a non-agent, such as probability or chance, in the first place?[23] That is the height of folly with regard to the idea of macro-evolution in conjunction with natural selection. But I digress, for that is not the topic at hand, and so now we will move forward.

So, "macro-evolution" is a term that essentially is associated *directly only* with the abstract ideas involved therein, such as change from simple to complex organisms over long periods of time, and ultimately it is not even remotely associated with the actions of an agent (which is why it leads so clearly and unequivocally toward Atheism). Hence, "macro-evolution" falls into the second category of words and phrases, namely phrases and words that are directly linked only to abstract concepts, and merely

---

[23] These few arguments regarding chance and natural selection singlehandedly destroy the very possibility of non-theistic evolution as it is presented by modern scientists. Christian theistic-evolution is impossible because it flies in the face of the Genesis account of creation relative to any appropriate hermeneutical approach. Non-Christian theistic evolution could be posited, but at that point one would have to provide evidence that the god or supernatural force associated with evolution actually exists, because natural selection and random chance, as we have seen, are not viable options for mechanisms for evolution. At best one would have to posit Pantheism, the idea that nature and everything in the universe is god, for evolution to become viable, but again there are major problems with Pantheism also. For arguments against Pantheism see Winfried Corduan, *No Doubt About It* (Nashville: Broadman-Holman, 1997), 92-95.

indirectly, if at all, linked to actions. And therefore since "science" falls into the first category of words and phrases, namely those that are directly linked to action, "macro-evolution", and "evolution", since one was substituted for the other in our discussion above, cannot be considered science, for they fall into two separate categories of word types.

Now that we have established the above information, we will be able to better understand how evolution is in fact associated with the idea of a religious/philosophical belief system, and that it is not science. This should however already be fairly clear to you at this point, that is if you have paid attention to the definitions throughout this chapter thus far. For the remainder of this chapter we will first take a brief look at how evolution does not in fact fit into the category of science, followed by how evolution actually fits very well into the categories of religion and philosophy, and then we will look at whether or not evolution is a belief system, followed finally by our conclusion for this particular part of our discussion.

Why Evolution is Not Science

If you would take a moment to remember back to the earlier section in this chapter listed under the heading, "What is Science?" you would recall that our finalized definition of "Science" was as follows: *the use of the scientific method to study anything and everything that exists in nature.* We also saw just moments ago that the terms "science" and "evolution" are different kinds of terms, and that therefore they cannot be viewed as synonymous with one another. But now we are going to take a deeper look into why evolution is not science, contrary to the opinion of many people, including the majority of modern mainstream scientists.

Now, we defined evolution several different ways above, but the two definitions that we need to look at here are "an idea that encompasses change within all living things," and "the descent of all living things from a single common ancestor." Now it doesn't really matter which one of these definitions we use, because neither of them square well, or at all, with the definition that we have established for "science." However, since the second definition of "evolution" is more widely used in scientific academic circles these days, and since it is essentially macro-evolution that we are referring to here in this book, and also since this second definition is a fairly standard definition for macro-evolution, that is the one that we will here compare to our definition of "science."

First, we have seen above that the "use of the scientific method" is a necessary component of something being classified as "science." This phrase is what we substituted for the term "systematic" in the definition of "science" that we discussed from a particular mainstream biology teachers textbook, based on our elaboration regarding the variety of definitions and things that we looked at regarding the terms "science" and "scientific method." So the first thing that must ineludibly be a part of a particular idea or term to make qualify as being "science" is the use of the scientific method. Well, it is no doubt that the evolutionists who espouse an evolutionary worldview use the scientific method in their research, but that is not what we are looking at here. Rather we are discussing whether or not "evolution" is the same thing as "science," or put another way, if "evolution" can rightly be viewed as synonymous with "science." Put differently, we are looking at the question: "is evolution science?" So, look closely at this definition of evolution and tell me if there is any possible way to fit this phrase, namely the "use of the scientific method," or the idea associated with the use of the scientific method, into it. Evolution is "the descent of all living things from a single common ancestor." What do you think? You got it! There is absolutely no way to mesh the phrase, "the use of the scientific method," with the definition given here for "evolution." Why? Because they are two clearly different types of ideas, as we said earlier. Evolution (macro-evolution) is an *idea about ancestry and origin*, namely the ancestry and origin of all living things. Science, on the other hand, is an *idea involving a specific way to do something*, namely how to study anything and everything in nature. The difference should be incredibly obvious at this point in our discussion, and so if you still cannot see it then go back and read this chapter one more time from the beginning, and then if you still don't see it, you might want to evaluate your personal biases that you may be bringing to the table for this particular discussion, as they can often times blind us from even the clearest of truths.

Second, another aspect of the definition of "science" that we have established is the term "study." Now again, of course there can be studies done to support or refute evolution, but this is also not what we are talking about here. The same exact thing that we just saw above is also the case for this term regarding integrating it into or with the definition of "evolution." It just won't work, because, as we just saw, evolution (macro-evolution) is an *idea about ancestry and origin*, namely the ancestry and origin of all living things, and science is an *idea involving a specific way to do something*, namely how to study anything and everything in nature. Put another way, there is not even a hint of an idea directly related to the term "study" in the definition of evolution that we are looking at, namely "the descent of all living things from a single common ancestor."

I think, at this point, that we need not look any further into whether or not evolution is science, for the case has now been made to the contrary, and although the case that has been made is certainly not exhaustive, it is nevertheless rock-solid and so we can rest assured that evolution is *not* science. We will now move on to look at why evolution *is* in fact a religion, why it falls under the umbrella of philosophy, and how it relates to the concept of a belief system and whether or not true science can be done within this system.

Why Evolution is Essentially Philosophical

This section will be brief, since the points have already been made, and so all we need to do is to tie them together. Recall back in the section of this chapter under the heading "What is Philosophy?" that we established that philosophy is the discipline of thinking *about* different things, namely anything and everything. Well, does evolution fall under the category of anything? Of course it does, but the discipline of thinking about evolution is not evolution, it is the philosophy of evolution. Also, the philosophy of evolution entails the thoughts and ideas about evolution, but not the actual thinking itself, for as we said earlier that is called philosophizing. So how are evolution and philosophy the same? If you recall our above discussion you will notice that we established that evolution (macro-evolution) is an *idea about ancestry and origin*. Evolution is in fact a thought (idea) about something, namely ancestry and origin, which obviously falls into the category of anything, and so evolution is entailed in philosophy, since it directly involves thoughts *about* something, and not just involves, but is an idea about something, namely origins and ancestry, or, stated differently, evolution is a thought about something, which means that it is entailed by philosophy, or it falls under the umbrella of philosophy. And so while evolution cannot actually be classified as philosophy, since philosophy is a discipline and evolution is an idea about some something, it is, as an idea, entailed in the discipline of philosophy, since philosophy includes the thoughts and ideas, but not the thinking itself, of whatever is being pondered.

Why Evolution is Essentially Religious

In a letter to Asa Gray on June 5, 1861, Charles Darwin called natural selection his "deity."[24] Now it doesn't take a genius to know that the word "deity" is strictly a religious term, regardless of how you are looking at it. Of course Darwin was not necessarily saying that he was worshipping natural selection, but he was obviously keenly aware of the implications that natural selection necessitated regarding evolution since it is supposedly the driving force of evolution. However, we have already seen that the idea of natural selection is itself purely fictional and an impossibility, for if something is purely natural (this includes being purely material) and random, as we saw in a previous chapter it necessarily lacks purpose, and selection implies purpose. Of course it could be random selection, but then uniformity of selective decisions (which is what the evolutionists argue for when they argue that

---

[24] Charles Darwin, in a letter to Asa Gray, June 5, 1861 [in Francis Darwin, ed., *The Life and Letters of Charles Darwin*, 2 vols. (New York: Basic Books, 1959), 2:165], quoted in Norman Geisler, *Creation & the Courts* (Wheaton: Crossway Books, 2007), 31.

natural selection selects for positive and beneficial change, mutations, and adaptations) becomes so incredibly improbable that it is not even remotely worth being considered as a viable possibility, and it most certainly is not probable enough to call it likely. Actually, from a mathematical perspective the likelihood that something such as natural selection, if it did "exist", would make such uniform decisions over the course of billions of years (this is how old most scientists claim that the world is) is so absurdly low that we might as well say that it is impossible. The bottom line here is that natural selection is itself an incoherent concept, for as the evolutionists see it it is nature that is doing the selecting. But nature is not an actually existing entity, unless one posits Pantheism, which, as we saw in an earlier footnote in this chapter is self-refuting, and "selection" requires an actually existing entity, an agent to do the selecting, and so since nature is not an actually existing entity, but rather an abstract term that we use to identify the sum of what is in the universe, it cannot "select" anything.

Ninian Smart argued that "we ought to call something a religion when it conforms to certain general characteristics found in similar phenomena which are also called religions."[25] We saw in the opening quote of the last

---

[25] Ninian Smart, "Towards a Definition of Religion," unpublished paper, Lancaster University, 1970. Cf. Ninian Smart, *The World's Religions* (Englewood: Prentice-Hall, 1989), 10-21, quoted by Irving Hexham, *Understanding World Religions: An Interdisciplinary Approach* (Grand Rapids: Zondervan, 2011), 16-17.

chapter that Darwinism, Naturalism, and Atheism answer many of the same questions that other religions answer. We will also see below that these religions, which are all a part of the modern non-theistic evolutionary worldview, include the necessity of a certain level of faith, as well as holding such beliefs with devotion. All of these things, and others, are aspects that Darwinism, Naturalism, and Atheism all share in common with other religions, and so according to the statement above by Ninian Smart we should classify these worldviews as religions, and since evolution also answers many of these same religious questions, and since it is also held by faith and with devotion by those who believe it, it too should be classified as a religion.

Now, earlier in this chapter we established "religion" as "a cause, principle, system of tenets held with ardor, devotion, conscientiousness, and faith."[26] Now some of you at this point might be saying to yourself, "How can this possibly be synonymous with evolution?" Well, we will look at that in just a second, but first let me just say again that this should be quite obvious by now. For the last several chapters we have established the principles that I am about to use here to show that evolution is essentially a religion, or at least that it can be rightly classified as a religion.

---

[26] Gove, *Webster's Third New International Dictionary*, 1918.

We have established in previous chapters that anything dealing with historical sciences cannot be proven or verified, since it is impossible to repeat past events through experimentation. Sure someone can create and do an experiment simulating a past event, but since it is in the past there is no way to be *100%* certain that you have all of the factors exactly as they were in the past, since we cannot go back in time and check. Therefore, all ideas dealing with historical science, including macro-evolution, must necessarily be held on faith, since there can be no concrete evidence to *prove* the idea. We have also already seen that any hypothesis involving science and the scientific method also cannot be made 100% certain, and so those things too must be held with a level of faith, however great or however little that faith may be. Now the "principle" (referring to the above definition of religion) of evolution would be that all living things descended from a single common ancestor. This principle is held in (with) faith by all those who believe it, since it is impossible to prove, since it deals with science, and more specifically since it deals with historical science. This fits perfectly with the definition of religion given above. But I want to talk also about another aspect of this definition of religion before we continue. This definition says that the particular principle is held with "ardor, devotion, (and) conscientiousness." Does that sound to you like so many of the outraged and hardcore evolutionists around today? It certainly sounds like them to me. Of course these people hold the principle idea of evolution with ardor and devotion! For many of them their careers and livelihoods depend on such devotion. Also, many of them have been brainwashed to the point that they think it is a proven fact, and so they are naturally devoted to something that they see no reason to question. But what about the third word, "conscientiousness." This is something that many evolutionists do on the surface, namely hold the principle idea of evolution in a conscientious manner, but they are also ultimately inconsistent in the way they live their lives, for if there is nothing but random mutations and molecules, why get up in the morning? How can one find purpose in a world of nothing but chance? The answer, quite simply, is that no purpose can rightly be found when such a principle as evolution is held to be true, and so at least in some sense most evolutionists do not consistently hold their evolutionary beliefs in a conscientious manner, but that is another argument for another time, and so I digress. Our argument still holds, and at least in some sense there is a conscientious decision to believe in evolution for the evolutionists, and so, due to the arguments above, evolution can rightly be classified as a religion.

Okay, so we have seen here that evolution, along with being entailed in philosophy, is also religion. This is two thirds of the proposition that evolution is a philosophical/religious belief system, and so we will now move forward to discuss how evolution fits in with the category of a belief system.

Is Evolution a Belief System?

We established earlier in this chapter that a belief system, or a worldview, is the sum total of one's beliefs that shape our preconceptions and suppositions about reality and how we act and react in and to life. Now of course we can see right away that "evolution" as we have defined it cannot possibly be "the sum total" of the beliefs that one holds,[27] but since a belief in macro-evolution is necessarily a fundamental belief, since it deals with ultimate origins, including human origins, we may rightly adjust the term evolution to "Evolutionism" to make it a more fitting title for a belief system, since a belief system can appropriately be named after its most basic principle, and what could be more basic than a belief about one's origin? This "Evolutionism" is necessarily a religious and philosophical belief system, since its most fundamental principle, evolution, is religious and philosophical, and so while evolution itself cannot rightly be classified as a belief system, Evolutionism, which is a necessary belief system to uphold for anyone who truly espouses macro-evolution, is indeed a belief system, and a religious/philosophical belief system at that, since it is founded on its most basic

---

[27] That is unless of course that is literally the only belief that someone holds, which is highly unlikely, of not impossible.

principle of evolution (macro-evolution), which is both religious and philosophical, as we have seen above.

Can Science Be Done Within the Belief System of Evolutionism?

Now that we have established that evolution fits into the concept of a belief system by way of Evolutionism, let us take a quick look at whether or not science can be done within this system. We must remember though, before we continue, that Evolutionism (non-theistic) necessarily implies Atheism and Naturalism also, so we are not just dealing with one belief system here, but three (at least). Remember, as we said earlier, one can have more than one belief system within one's overarching worldview (the overarching worldview being the sum total of one's beliefs).

Finally, and one more time for now, our definition of science in this chapter is *the use of the scientific method to study anything and everything that exists in nature.* We also established earlier that science is an idea involving a specific way to do something, that is, to use the scientific method to study nature. We did not set any other barriers or boundaries on science, since none would seem appropriate.[28] Therefore, if there are no barriers or boundaries as to the use of the scientific method relative

---

[28] I am speaking practically, not ethically, as there most certainly should be ethical boundaries to science and the study of nature.

to worldview consideration, I see no reason why good, true, and accurate science cannot be done within the worldviews of Evolutionism, Naturalism, Atheism, Materialism;[29] or Creationism either for that matter, which is one of the main points of this book.

Conclusion

In conclusion, we have established definitions for the scientific method, science, philosophy, religion, evolution, and belief systems. We have also seen how all of these definitions play into one another. It should be clear to us by now that evolution can rightly be classified as religion, but more importantly we have seen that evolution ***cannot*** rightly be classified as science. Also, we have established that, while evolution itself cannot be considered a belief system, Evolutionism, a necessary belief system of anyone who espouses a belief in evolution (macro-evolution), is founded upon the most basic principle of evolution, since evolution deals with origins and nothing is more basic and fundamental than origins, and so evolution is directly related to the belief system that bears its very name (plus an "ism"). This belief system is also known as Darwinism, which we saw above. Finally, we have seen that good, true, and rational science can be done within the bounds of any belief system (unless the

---

[29] Having said that, I must also point out that attempting to live consistently within a materialistic, naturalistic, or atheistic worldview *could* most certainly hinder the doing of good science, but again that is another argument for another book.

belief system denies the possibility of doing science, or something to that effect), whether it be Evolutionism, Naturalism, Creationism, or whatever else the belief system may be.

In the next chapter we are going to take a closer look at whether or not macro-evolution can be proven, even though we have already touched on it some in previous chapters. This is very important to grasp so as to better understand why it is so un-kosher for the majority of the ruling bodies in our country to be refusing to allow alternative scientific explanations to be taught in our schools alongside evolution (as they currently are doing), which is happening mostly because everyone is constantly told that evolution is a proven fact, for after all, if it is a proven fact then all opposing views must necessarily be wrong and therefore should not be taught to anyone, especially our children, right?

7

Can Macro-Evolution Really Be Proven?

"...I am quite conscious that my speculations run beyond the bounds of true science. .....t is a mere rag of an hypothesis with as many flaw[s] & holes as sound parts."[1]

- *Charles Darwin*

*"**Fact:** ......a particular truth known by actual observation of authentic testimony, as opposed to what is merely inferred."*[2]

- *Richard Dawkins' personal definition of the term "fact" in his book The Greatest Show On Earth*

---

[1] Charles Darwin to Asa Gray, cited by Adrian Desmond and James Moore, *Darwin* (New York: W.W. Norton and Co, 1991), 456, 475, quoted by unknown author, *Answers to Evolution: 16 Reasons to Doubt Darwinism* (Torrance: Rose Publishing, 2004), back page of pamphlet.
[2] Richard Dawkins, *The Greatest Show On Earth: The Evidence For Evolution* (New York: Free Press, 2009), 14.

Before we discuss the above quote by Darwin, let me just say that the definition for the term "fact" given by Richard Dawkins above is not only pure propaganda on behalf of his evolutionary agenda, but it is also an inadequate definition. It is not mandatory that something be known to be true for it to be a fact. Something *can* be a fact apart from any such knowledge. Anyone who studies epistemology should know that. But even more to the point here regarding this quote by Dawkins is the *fact* that he is claiming in his book, *The Greatest Show On Earth*, that evolution is a fact, based on this definition of the term. However, as we will see below macro-evolution, which is what Dawkins has in mind, cannot possibly be proven, and has never been observed, and so by his own definition, even though it is an inadequate one, his argument that evolution should be espoused by all because it is a fact falls apart and should therefore be rejected.

Now, the above quotation by Charles Darwin shows that even Darwin himself was aware that his *theory* of evolution went "beyond the bounds of true science," meaning primarily that his speculations could not possibly be wholly proven from scientific exploration and methods. Unfortunately many of us are shocked when we see statements like this from Charles Darwin because we are unaware that he was ever skeptical of his theory of evolution. This is no doubt at least in part because the scientific community at large does not want anyone questioning them when they claim that macro-evolution is a proven fact, and so they do their best to hide these types of quotes from the public. However, the fact is that many of these types of statements were made by Darwin, especially in his later years in life. In this chapter we are essentially going to look at, as the title of the chapter suggests, whether or not macro-evolution - the belief in common descent for all life on earth and also the belief that species can evolve into new, different species - can be proven, although by this point in the book you, the reader, should be keenly aware that macro-evolution deals with historical science and so it *cannot* actually be proven (sorry to spoil it for you if you haven't caught on to that point by now). We are going to do this by first discussing what exactly historical science is, what empirical science is, and how they are different. Then we will take a look at some specific claims that various specific evolutionists, and evolutionists in general make about specific things related to evolution, such as the age of certain hormones, rocks and so on, and then we are going to end the chapter with a discussion on why these claims, along with the claim that macro-evolution is a proven fact, are either untrue claims or claims that cannot be proven, followed finally by a conclusion to the chapter, as always.[3]

---

[3] Do to the nature of this chapter, as well as several later chapters throughout the rest of this book, it will be necessary to quote many sources at length. This is so that you, the reader, can get a fuller picture of the issues being discussed without simply reading my statements and taking my word for what I am saying. In this chapter

What Is Historical Science?

> "Historical sciences include archeology,
> geology, forensics, and other disciplines
> that work to explain past events. Whereas
> empirical sciences test one hypothesis at a
> time with an experiment, historical sciences
> make use of multiple competing
> hypotheses. These represent a variety of
> different explanations that "compete" with
> each other as the best one. Each hypothesis
> serves as a framework for interpreting data.
> Since questions of a historical nature
> address singular events in the past, it is
> impossible to repeat them. No experiments
> can be done today to test them in the same
> way that empirical sciences are tested."[4]

This quote is taken from a book titled *Unraveling the Origins Controversy*. It was written by the head of the department of biology at Liberty University, Dr. David A. Dewitt. He has a Bachelor of Science degree in biochemistry from Michigan State University and a PhD in Neurosciences from Case Western Reserve University. He

---

we will have many quotes by evolutionists themselves (as well as some creationists) on the issues that we are here discussing. Please realize that if it were not pertinent to my argument here I would not be quoting so many sources at such great length.
[4] David A. Dewitt, *Unraveling the Origins Controversy* (Lynchburg: Creation Curriculum, L.L.C., 2007), 38-39.

actually has been doing important research on Alzheimer's disease for quite some time now. But I digress, as my point is simply to show that Dr. Dewitt is credible in speaking on issues of science.[5] We will see in a later chapter that Dr. Dewitt is a young earth creationist. But wait! You probably thought that all young earth creationists were crazy stupid people who don't know anything about anything, right? Well, quite frankly that is exactly what the secular scientists, as well as, unfortunately, many Christian scientists, claim about young earth creationists, even though it is very, very far from the truth, especially when referring to the young earth creation scientists, or at least most of them. But again that is an argument for a later chapter in this book. I promise you we will come back to that issue, but for now let us get back to discussing historical science.

Now, I would assume that you noticed that biology was not mentioned specifically in the list of historical sciences above. Well, that is because biology has traditionally been considered an empirical science. We will discuss what an empirical science is below, but for now let us just say that it is a science that deals directly with observable and repeatable events. Historical science, on the other hand, as we saw in the above statement made

---

[5] Do not misunderstand me here. I am not claiming that people without scientific degrees are not credible when speaking on matters of science. I am simply claiming that Dr. Dewitt and his above quoted statement, even though he is a young earth creationist, are still credible when talking about scientific matters.

by Dr. Dewitt, deals with past events, events that have already happened that can no longer be observed. Of course these days we have video cameras and regular cameras that we can use to take pictures and video of events and then view them later on in time, but cameras have only been around for about the last three-hundred and fifty years or so, and video cameras have been around for only about one hundred years or so, and macro-evolution is said to take far, far longer than that to take any perceivable steps at all. And so we are left, in biology (the study of life), with aspects that are empirical, and also aspects that are of the historical nature, with regard to which type of science the scientists are actually doing, and since macro-evolution is a biological theory involving both past events and present events, it is, at least in part, dealing with historical science. Ultimately, all theories dealing with the distant past, and most especially origins in general, are pure conjecture at best, albeit with varying levels of evidence to back up such theories.

> "As soon as we leave living animals, the methods of investigation open to us are much more limited. Since we cannot directly observe the faunas of past ages, their hereditary mechanisms, their behavior and to a large extent their ecology and organization into species and smaller units are outside our knowledge. From the structures preserved in fossils and the rocks

in which they are found, we must deduce as much as we can of the animal's biology. Except in rare series of strata in which we can observe the microevolution of the past, we have only occasional fossils preserved at long intervals of time, and must try to link these by hypothetical intermediates...........Nevertheless we must push our interpretation of these larger evolutionary changes as far as it will go if we are to reach any broad view of animal evolution as a whole."[6]

Notice here the statements that claim that certain types of information are outside the knowledge of the scientists. Also note the fact that this author also refers to "hypothetical intermediates" (animal species linking one species to another genetically as a sort of in between step in the evolutionary pathway) and says that we must "push our interpretation of these larger evolutionary changes (meaning macro-evolutionary changes) as far as it will go." The author here says nothing of staying within the bounds of integrity or only pushing the interpretation as far as the actual evidence allows. He only says that they *must* take their interpretation as far as it will go.

---

[6] G.S. Carter, *Animal Evolution: A Study of Recent Views of Its Causes* (London: Sidgwick and Jackson Limited, 1951), 264.

The statement above was made by G.S. Carter, an evolutionist, in 1951 in his book entitled *Animal Evolution: A Study of Recent Views of Its Causes*. Now of course 1951 is no longer recent, at least not in the way most of us think when we use the term "recent," but the principles set forth in this quote are nonetheless still 100% relevant to the theory of macro-evolution, just as much today as they were back in 1951. Note in this quote that historical science, implied by the phrase "as we leave living animals," is said to deal with interpreting data, not actually analyzing empirically verified information or facts. This is not to say that empirical scientists do not also interpret their data, but there is a major difference, as empirical science deals with observable and repeatable events and experiments and the data directly drawn from those events and experiments. Historical science deals instead with what we might call "aftermath data," or data that comes after the event has occurred. For instance, forensics is one of the historical sciences mentioned in the earlier quote from Dr. Dewitt above. Allow me to use an example using crime scene forensics to demonstrate how historical science works.

Let us say that a team of forensic scientists are trying to figure out how a person, let us call him Tim, was killed on the street, which we will name 34th street, in a particular city, which we shall say is East St. Louis, after they got a call from someone, let us call her Jill, that informed them that she found Tim's body lying on the sidewalk. Now first off I am sure that you noticed that I could have simply given you the name of the persons, street, and city in the last sentence without adding all the other statements and words that I added to the sentence that I did. I did this merely to emphasize that each piece of information is vital to the job of the forensic (historical) scientists. The fact that Tim is the one that is dead and Jill is the one that called, and not the other way around is very important to their case, for if they got just those two facts screwed up it would destroy their ability to come to a proper conclusion as to what really happened. Also, the name of the city must be known along with the name of the street, for how many cities have a 34th street? A lot! Now when the scientists arrive on the scene, all they see at first is Tim lying dead on the sidewalk. This scene is essentially what they have to work with. Let us assume that there is no video or pictures involving what happened to Tim, and there are no witnesses of what happened to Tim either. So, the scientists must use clues (pieces of evidence, or data if you will) from the scene to come to their conclusion, and ultimately, even if they find someone guilty of killing Tim and that person confesses to the crime, that will still not be anything more than a theory in the minds of the scientists, since they were not there when Tim was killed. This idea of a conclusion involving historical science only being able to be, at best, a theory, and never a proven fact is precisely the point of this chapter, and we will discuss this concept more later on. For now let us discuss what types of data the scientists might have to use for their investigation and what they might do in analyzing that data.

The scientists would need to view the actual scene where Tim was found. They would have access to his body, the sidewalk that it was laying on, the blood still in his body, and so on, but they would not have the ability to repeat the event of Tim's death, since he is already dead. Now suppose that the scientists/investigators find a hole going all the way through the chest of Tim from front to back. This is a hole that if you put your hand on one side of the hole and looked through the other side of the hole you could see your hand through the hole. Now the investigators' immediate impression upon this first bit of evidence is that Tim was shot in the chest with a gun that shoots fairly large bullets at a high speed.[7]

One of the investigators, let us call him Joe, decides to go ahead and assert that Tim definitely was shot in the chest by a high powered gun. Now, this initial reaction by Joe is equivalent to what the evolutionists did with their theory of evolution when they started calling it a proven fact. Joe has only very limited evidence (and it is not really evidence that supports his theory at all, as we will later see) to support his conclusion, and yet he went ahead and

---

[7] Please excuse the graphic nature of this example, but it is really one of the best examples of how one deals with historical science and how historical science differs from empirical science.

asserted his conclusion as a definite fact. There are two major problems with this assertion of Joe's though. First, as we saw earlier, since Joe was not at the scene of the crime when it took place he can only have but a theory, and his theory cannot truly be proven as a fact (although it might actually be the truth), since he did not observe the event and since the same event, namely the death of Tim in this same way, is non-repeatable. Now the second problem with Joe's assertion is, quite simply, that he is wrong, for in fact Tim did not get shot but instead, while walking down 34th street in the middle of the night he stopped and turned toward the street to yell at a friend that he saw on the other side of the street, and at that very moment a big truck with a V10 engine in it shot a rod out of the engine, through the side of the truck, and the rod hit Tim right in the chest, went through his chest, and buried itself in the brick wall behind Tim.[8] When the man Tim saw across the street (who was actually not Tim's friend, but instead someone who looked like one of Tim's friends) heard the noise of the rod shooting out of the truck engine he ran away as fast as he could and did not come back because the sound scared him. There was no one else within a half of a mile besides the man driving the truck, and the man driving the truck was going one hundred miles an hour when his engine stopped running after the rod shot out, and so he coasted over a thousand

---

[8] Whether or not this is likely, or even possible is irrelevant to my argument here.

feet down the road, and thankfully there was a mechanics shop right in that area and he was able to get his truck into the parking lot of the shop and call a cab to take him home. The man driving the truck, let us call him Bill, did not find out what happened to his truck until three days later, since it was dark that night (the street and parking lot lights were all burnt out) and he was tired and drunk when it all happened, and the mechanic's shop was a few days behind in their work, so it took them a while to have a chance to look at his truck to figure out what was wrong with it, and so he knew of no reason to go back and see if his truck had injured anyone or damaged anything. No one was on the section of 34th street that Tim was on for several more hours until Jill was walking to work to begin preparations to open up her coffee shop when she found Tim lying on the sidewalk with blood all around him, dead.

Now of course this is a fictional story, and an unlikely, yet possible one, but we can see here some similarities in this situation and the one involving the historical science done by the evolutionists who attempt to study origins and other past events, such as the event of the genetic ancestors of both ourselves and modern monkeys evolving into humans.[9] First, just like with Joe,

---

[9] It is important to understand what evolutionists really believe. They do not believe, for instance, that what we now know as monkeys somehow evolved into humans millions of years ago. Rather they believe that a common ancestor of both modern monkeys and humans, namely something that was most likely not yet like either, "split off genetically" at some point in the distant past, and one of the

the evolutionists claim that macro-evolution is a proven fact, that it is definitely true, when in reality they were not present millions and billions of years ago to observe these so called evolutionary changes, and so, like Joe, they cannot rightfully claim that their theory is anything more than just that, a theory. Second, these evolutionists are basing their assertion that macro-evolution is a proven fact on evidence that, not only is minimal, but doesn't actually exist at all. Also, another similarity between the evolutionists and Joe is that Joe has evidence, but he is misinterpreting that evidence because he is neglecting other evidence that points in other directions, and the evolutionists do the same thing with their "evidence." They simply fail to address the issues such as the problems with the idea of natural selection and random chance being a mechanism for evolution that I have raised in previous chapters of this book.

The evolutionists are claiming that macro-evolution is a fact when in fact they have no real evidence to support such a conclusion, for evidence that is misinterpreted to favor a theory is not really evidence in favor of that theory at all. Sure, just like Joe, they think they have real evidence, but just like Joe who was apparently ignorant of the necessity to wait until more research and investigation was done, and until more solid evidence was gathered, the

---

animals resulting from that genetic split ended up evolving, down the line, into monkeys, and another animal involved in that genetic split, albeit ever so slow, eventually evolved into us, humans.

evolutionists go about touting that macro-evolution is a proven fact without any evidence at all to truly support their conclusions. I took a course in undergraduate school called *The History of Life* at Liberty University, and one of the main purposes of the class was to look at the supposed evidences for evolution. We had to sit through over one hundred power point presentations, at least 4 video documentaries, and we had to read our textbook mentioned earlier, *Unraveling the Origins Controversy*, and I can honestly say that after sitting through all of that, plus everything else that I have learned and read both in school (including secular schools) and on my own time, I know for a fact that there is no evidence supporting the idea of macro-evolution that cannot also be explained and interpreted in a way that supports other origins claims, such as Creationism. Even the supposed transitional fossils do not exist, especially not at the bottom of the "evolutionary tree."[10] The further down on the tree you go, the less evidence there is, and there actually comes a point on the tree where there is literally a dotted line (a line indicating no evidence has been found) that runs the entire length of the tree, showing that it is absolutely impossible with the available evidence that we have to support on any level the conclusion that all living things are related biologically. There is also absolutely no

---

[10] See also the book entitled *The Fossil Record: Unearthing Nature's History of Life*, written by Dr. John D. Morris (PhD in Geological Engineering) and Frank J. Sherwin (M.A. in Zoology) published in 2010.

legitimate evidence supporting the idea that species can change into other species, and to be perfectly honest the idea doesn't even make sense to begin with based on what we know (actual knowledge, not mere speculation), since no two species can interbreed anywhere in the world right now and produce offspring representing a completely new species, especially offspring that can reproduce. Sure someone might claim that. given enough chances and time certain species could change enough to mate and develop a new species, but there are many major problems with that. One of those problems is that the chances that both a male and a female of similar enough species would evolve into the same species capable of producing fertile offspring is not just astronomically low, it is impossible based on what we know from empirical science about animal reproduction and micro-evolution. Micro-evolution, which is actually better labeled as adaptation within a species, always happens in a circle, within a species, and has never, ever been shown to happen between species or to the extent that a new species is formed. So those people, l ke Richard Dawkins in his book *The Greatest Show on Earth: The Evidence for Evolution*, that claim that micro-evolution is evidence supporting the idea of macro-evolution are 100% wrong when they say such things, as that is completely and utterly untrue. But don't just take my word that micro-evolution does not prove macro-evolution. According to the *Animal Behavior Desk Reference: A Dictionary of Animal Behavior, Ecology, and Evolution, Second Edition*, macro-evolution can rightly be defined as "a change in species composition within a monophyletic group within space and time."[11] There is however also a note in this same book below this definition that says exactly what many, many non-evolutionists have been trying to say for years and years, and what I just said above, about macroevolution. It says, "If species are discrete reproductive units, microevolutionary processes cannot logically be extrapolated, in a reductionist manner, to explain macroevolutionary patterns."[12] Mind you that this book was not written by creationists, but rather it is a secular reference guide for evolution and other topics, and on the copyright page at the beginning of the book it says, "This book contains information obtained from authentic and highly regarded sources." Notice that this statement says, "If species are discrete reproductive units." The idea that species are discrete reproductive units, in the sense that no two different species can produce a fertile offspring, is in exact accord with what we do in fact know about the animal kingdom. Henceforth, micro-evolution cannot rightfully be used to support the idea of macro-evolution, by the standards of the secular community mind you, since the processes and things that take place within a micro-evolutionary framework are not the same processes and

---

[11] Edward M. Barrows, *Animal Behavior Desk Reference: A Dictionary of Animal Behavior, Ecology, and Evolution, Second Edition* (Boca Raton: CRC Press LLC, 2001), 220.
[12] Ibid.

things that are said to take place within a macro-evolutionary framework.

Dr. John Morris says the following regarding vertical evolution, or evolution from one species to a more advanced species, "There is no evidence whatsoever – past, present, or possible – that *vertical* evolution of one kind of organism into a more complex kind of organism has ever occurred, or ever can occur (emphasis original)."[13] Dr. Geoffrey Simmons, M.D., makes a similar statement in his book *Billions of Missing Links* when he states that "there are no published experiments that clearly show one species naturally evolving into another species."[14] Dr. Simmons goes on to say,

"No scientist has ever observed a natural collection of organic chemicals spontaneously linking up to form a protein, or thousands of different proteins, fats, sugars, and minerals combining to create a functional cell, or millions of different living cells fusing into a jellyfish, or a clam escaping its sHell to become an octopus, or a fish evolving into anything remotely similar to an amph bian, or a frog transitioning into a lizard, or a bear

---

[13] John Morris, *The Young Earth* (Green Forest: Master Books, 2007), 4.
[14] Geoffrey Simmons, *Billions of Missing Links* (Eugene: Harvest House Publishers, 2007), 18.

developing a blowhole on the top of its head and an anus along its belly as it went for a millennium-long swim, or a monkey giving birth to anything humanoid. If Darwinian research cannot get past step 1 (observation), then step 4 (testing of predictions) can never be fulfilled."[15]

Many, if not all of these things mentioned in this quote are essentially things that the evolutionists claim have taken place at some point in the past, and yet, as Dr. Simmons here states, no one has ever seen any of it happen (or at least we do not have any credible records of anyone seeing such things), and you would think that if anything like these things had been witnessed by someone in the distant past that we would know about it one way or another, especially if these types of things are supposed to be normal, regular types of events, albeit taking long periods of time to develop. We must remember that no matter how slow the steps are said to take place, the steps still must actually take place, and the types of things mentioned in the above quote have never been witnessed because, quite simply, they are impossible, and until someone proves me wrong on that, we have every reason to believe that they are in fact impossible, for the evidence supports such a conclusion 100% at this time, and if a scientist or someone else tells you otherwise, ask him or

---

[15] Ibid.

her to show you their evidence. I am not talking about a fossil that they make claims about, for as we will see later on in this chapter any claims made about fossils are pure speculation, especially when dealing with fossils that were not observed before, during, and after the fossilization process. I mean real hard evidence. The simple fact of the matter is that there is none.

But again I digress, as the task at hand is to discuss what exactly historical science is. As we have seen above historical science is a lot ike, and actually includes forensic science. We have also seen that historical science is something that deals with past events, events that cannot be repeated or observed and so any claims dealing with historical science must necessarily remain theories, however much or however little they may be supported by the evidence, and can never actually be considered proven facts, for facts they may be, but we cannot prove them to be such. This is a far cry from empirical science, which we are now going to briefly discuss.

What Is Empirical Science?

Unlike historical science, empirical science deals directly with repeatable and observable events. For example, while a geologist who is trying to figure out how old an igneous rock is is dealing with past events, such as when the rock was formed, a neuroscientist who is trying to determine which section of the brain controls movement in a certain part of the body does not have the same limitations that the geologist has. The geologist has to make some pretty strong presumptions about his rock and his methods of dat ng, as well as having to maintain a high level of faith in his conclusions and his presumptions regarding the age of the rock, for he most likely did not observe the rock as it formed, nor can he repeat the process (we will come back to this example later on in this chapter when we discuss some of the claims of evolutionists). The neuroscientist, on the other hand, while he will inevitably have to make some basic presumptions regarding his research, is not necessarily going to be dealing with past events, for she can simply open up someone's skull on the operating table, send a slight shock to different parts of the brain, and continue to do so until the specific body part she is studying moves.[16] You see, the neuroscientist is dealing with empirical data (data that is derived from the five senses). This is essentially what empirical science is all about, namely researching repeatable, observable events to come to specific conclusions about various issues regarding those events.

How Are Historical Science and Empirical Science Different?

There are several ways in which these two types of science are different. One of these ways is that they each

---

[16] The entire process would be a bit more complicated than this of course.

attempt to answer different types of questions. For instance, empirical sciences attempt to answer questions like, "What is it?", "Why does it happen?", "How does it work?", and "Can we change it?" Historical science, on the other hand, attempts to answer questions such as, "What happened?", "Why did it happen?", "How did it come to be?", "What/Who did it?" and "When did it happen?"[17] Note that the empirical science questions are essentially concerned with the present, while the historical science questions are all in the past tense. This is, of course, because historical science deals with events in history, the past, which is why it is called "historical science." Empirical science, on the other hand, deals with present events, because empirical data, as we saw earlier, comes through the five senses, hearing, touching, smelling, tasting, and seeing, which necessitates that someone be physically present, hence the reason for the present tense questions for empirical science listed above.

As we saw above, historical science and empirical science are also different in that they use and analyze different types of data. The historical scientist must use data that ultimately consists of the consequences of the past event being pondered, such as the Petrified Forest found on the northeast corner of Yellowstone National Park. This forest contains many layers of trees buried in the rock and dirt. This has traditionally been interpreted

---

[17] Dewitt, *Uncovering the Origins Controversy*, 39.

by most scientists as an indication that there were many successive volcanic eruptions throughout history that buried each layer of trees in the wake of each eruption.[18] Now, this is a prime example of historical science at work. The scientists have the aftermath data, namely the petrified trees buried in many layers all over the mountain, but none of those scientists were around to witness the eruptions that they claim caused the layering of the trees, and neither can they repeat such events. Whether or not this is the correct interpretation of the Petrified Forest at Yellowstone is not the issue here, although we will return to it in our chapter on Young Earth Creationism. The point here is that this is a classic example of how historical science works.

Empirical science, on the other hand, would be something akin to certain aspects of physics. For example, if a physicist is trying to determine how fast a baseball goes from the pitcher's hand to the catcher's mitt he needs only to have the distance that the ball traveled and the amount of time that it took the ball to get from the pitcher's hand to the catcher's glove. He can then divide the distance that the ball traveled by the time that it took the ball to travel from point A to point B, and then he has the answer to his question, namely how fast the ball traveled from the pitcher's hand to the catcher's mitt.

---

[18] John Morris and Steven A. Austin, *Footprints in the Ash: The Explosive Story of Mount St. Helens* (Green Forest: Master Books, 2003), 100.

These pieces of data, both the amount of time that the ball travels and the distance that it travels can both be measured and observed by the physicist in the present, and so while the historical scientist is merely dealing with the consequences, or aftermath data of past events, the empirical scientist gets to deal with information that is directly observable. A similar comparison would be that while the empirical scientist was present when the ball was thrown and personally measured the distance and time that the baseball traveled, the historical scientist did not show up on the scene until just after the ball was thrown and so he has to try to determine how fast the ball was moving by information such as the size and depth of the indentation in the catcher's glove that the ball made when it hit the glove (the consequence of the pitcher throwing the ball to the catcher). Now of course that information would be hard to get, but it is a great example of the difference in the types of data used by the empirical scientist and the historical scientist.

Now that we have looked at what historical science and empirical science are and how they differ, namely both in the questions they seek to answer and the data that they use in their investigations and research, we are going to discuss several claims made by evolutionists and see both how they fit into the category of historical science, and also therefore how they cannot be touted as proven fact. Some of these claims may seem a bit outlandish to you, as they should, and some of the things that we discover in this chapter about such claims may shock you, as few people seem to realize just how far from a proven fact evolution and its claims really are, but it is better to learn the truth rather than to remain in the dark about such things.

Some Claims Made By Evolutionists

"It is now generally agreed that, as far as the higher animals are concerned, all evolutionary transformations have had their origin in the chromosomes, and that these bodies which constitute the physical basis of heredity also furnish the material source of evolutionary changes."[19] While this statement made by evolutionist M.J.D. White regarding chromosomes being the physical basis of heredity may be true and something that we can observe in the present, the rest of this statement is pure conjecture, as it encompasses "all evolutionary transformations," which includes the entirety of history, which includes the no longer observable and non-repeatable past. Of course we must remember that all science dealing with origins or past events, whether it is evolutionary biology, geology, creation science, or whatever else it may be, has some level of conjecture involved in it. In historical science the goal is to come to the best possible conclusion *and to base that conclusion on all of the best possible data available.* However, the

---

[19] M.J.D. White, *Animal Cytology and Evolution* (New York: Cambridge University Press, 1954), 1.

point is simply that the above quote by Mr. White is the sort of claim that evolutionists often make, and few people think to question its viability, even though there are good reasons to do so, especially, and including the fact that this is a statement that cannot be proven since it deals with historical science.

Another, more ridiculous claim is the claim made in the March 22, 2012 edition of the infamous scientific journal *Nature*. In an article titled "Raising the Dead," it is said that an evolutionist by the name of Joe Thornton has "resurrected" certain ancient hormones and proteins. The article says that "One deep-frozen vial holds the more-than-600-million-year-old ancestor of the receptors for oestrogen, cortisol, and other hormones, which Thornton brought to life nine years ago. Other tubes house proteins more than 400 million years old, which Thornton resurrected a few years ater."[20] Now, while the ages given for these proteins and hormones may somehow be at least close to accurate,[21] they are nevertheless something that are completely impossible to prove. Now again let me emphasize that all historical science, regardless of the particular discipline and worldview attached to it, has this issue of being unable to prove any statements about things that involve unobservable past events, such as the

---

[20] Helen Pearson, "Raising the Dead," in *Nature* 483 (March 2012): 390.
[21] Although, as a young earth creationist, due to the scientific evidence that I have seen in support of such a position, I am inclined to think that these ages are impossible.

origin or age of a supposed 600-million-year-old-hormone ancestor. I am not trying to say that *only* the evolutionists have this problem to deal with. What I am trying to show is that evolutionists are *included* in those who have these issues regarding their claims, since most people these days seem to think that the evolutionary claims of modern and past scientists that deal with historical, unobservable, and non-repeatable events are somehow proven facts. We must learn to question such assertions, whether they turn out to be true or not. It is a seriously misguided and inappropriate double standard to neglect and deny the assertions of Intelligent Design proponents and creationists with regard to their historical science research and conclusions and yet at the same time accept, many times without question or concern, the assertions made by the evolutionists that are in fact dealing with the exact same historical data and events that are studied by the ID and creationist proponents. This is why it is vitally important to understand that historical science is not ultimately about finding the truth based on empirical data, but rather it is about interpreting the data that is available in the way that best accounts for *all* of the available data.

Let us now return for a moment to the issue of dating rocks. This is another prime example of the evolutionists[22] making blatant assertions that they should

---

[22] Not all geologists are evolutionists, and not all geologists claim the same dates for various rocks and formations, but the vast majority consensus in the modern scientific community is that the earth is

know cannot possibly be validated, and in fact many times they are obviously wrong n dating these rocks. Before we discuss some specific rocks that have been dated by geologists,[23] allow me to first present to you an analogy about rock dating methods that can be found in the book entitled *The Young Earth*. This analogy is called the "Parable of the Potato Basket." This is a very lengthy quote, but it is necessary to give the whole quote so as to fully explain the parable. The analogy is as follows:

> "Suppose that as a scientist you entered a lecture hall to attend a scientific lecture. As you arrived, you saw someone up on the platform with a basket of potatoes on the table in front of him. As you sat down, you noticed that as the second hand of the wall clock reached 12, this man reached into the basket, pulled out a potato, peeled it, and put it back in the basket. You observe him peeling potatoes at the rate of one per minute for ten minutes; and finally, you ask yourself, "I wonder how long this nut's been doing that?"

---

billions of years old and that evolution is a proven fact.
[23] This is not meant to be a scientific or a geological exposition of dating methods and procedures, for this is not the place for that. Rather it is simply an explanation of the basic concept of dating rocks and some inherent problems with the process.

The question you have just asked is exactly the same question as the scientist asks when investigating the age of a rock or system. How old is this rock? How long has this tree been growing? How long has this river delta been building up? How long has this process been going on?

How are you going to determine the length of time the man has been peeling potatoes? Obviously, you would first come up and count the peeled potatoes. Suppose you count 35 peeled potatoes. You have thus observed the present state of the system (the number of peeled potatoes, 35), and you have measured the process rate (the rate of potato peeling, one per minute). Both of these observations are scientific observations, dealing with the present. You would likely conclude that the system has been in operation for 35 minutes.....

Let us step back and think for a moment. In order to derive such a conclusion, you must make certain assumptions about the unobserved past. These assumptions are critical to your conclusion.

The first thing that you must assume about the past is that the rate of potato peeling has been constant throughout the whole history of the potato basket. Scientifically, all you really know is that the man has been peeling potatoes at one per minute for the last ten minutes. You simply do not know what the rate of potato peeling was before you came in. perhaps the man is getting better at it and on y now can peel a potato each minute, whereas before it took him longer. Or perhaps he is getting tired and slowing down. By observing the present rate, you do not necessarily know the rate in the past, and you have no firm basis on which to assume that the rate of potato peeling has been constant. Perhaps your assumption of constant peeling rate is reasonable, but is it correct.

You may recognize this first assumption as the principle of uniformity. Basically, it postulates that things have been uniform throughout the urobserved past, that no process has ever cccurred dramatically different from present processes. It includes at least two parts: the uniformity of processes and uniformity of process rate.......

James Hutton in the late 1790s and Charles Lyell in the 1820s first proposed uniformity in science. Both had a desire to minimize the influence of Scripture in society and tried to marshal evidence for slow and gradual processes acting over immense time, thereby proving Scripture in error. Obviously no one could really know the nature of processes of the past without traveling back in time to observe them. Nevertheless, this assumption of uniformity dominates science, especially the historical sciences......

The next assumption you have to make or the question you must answer is, have any peeled potatoes been added or taken away from the basket throughout its whole history? If so, then your calculation would be misleading. For all you know, someone has sabotaged the experiment by adding several peeled potatoes to the basket, so that some of the peeled potatoes now in the basket did not get there through the observed process of potato peeling. Likewise, you must assume that no one, including the government, has come in and removed some of the hard-earned peeled potatoes. Again, you have absolutely no way of knowing just by looking at the potato basket.

There is another question that you must answer, and that is, were there any peeled potatoes in the basket at the start? Perhaps when the basket was brought in, there were already several peeled potatoes in it, and therefore the time determination is incorrect. Again, you have no certain way of knowing, except by asking the man peeling or another witness who was present at the start, and then you would not really know if you were told accurate information or not.

These three assumptions, (1) regarding the constancy of the process rate, (2) regarding the degree to which the system has been isolated from the environment, and (3) regarding the initial conditions of the system, are inherent in any dating process. Correct assumptions in each area must be made in order to proceed to a correct answer, unless specific, accurate knowledge about the past is known.

We must continually remind ourselves of what is taking place in a dating process – any dating process. Strict scientific observation can only get us started. We are able to observe the present state of things. And we are able to measure the rate of a relevant process. But establishing a date for the unobserved origin of something requires making assumptions regarding unobserved history, to a great degree inaccessible to empirical science. It is legitimate for a scientist to speculate on such things, but it would be better for scientists to approach them with a little more humility. Unfortunately, the results of historic speculations are usually presented as unquestioned fact; and students, or tourists at the national parks, or interested persons watching a TV special or reading the newspaper are sometimes intimidated into accepting a politically correct view of history based on uniformitarian assumptions as if that view were scientific fact."[24]

Now, this author is clearly calling into question the reliability of dating methods of all types, but almost every single person in the world, or at least those in a "civilized" society, accepts the dating methods used by scientists these days to date a wide variety of things, so who is this author to question such methods? Well, first of all, this

---

[24] John Morris, *The Young Earth* (Green Forest: Master Books, 2007), 42-44.

author is Dr. John Morris (mentioned earlier in this book), and while he is a young earth creationist, he has a bachelor of science degree in civil engineering from Virginia Tech, and a Masters and PhD in Geological Engineering from the University of Oklahoma, and he also works with many other scientists from many different fields on a regular basis, so he is more than qualified to talk about such a basic aspect of science, especially one such as this that is within his own field of expertise.

Before we go on let me just say that the reason I am bringing up the issue of dating rocks when the topic of this chapter is macro-evolution is because most scientists use the dates given by geologists and paleontologists of rocks and fossils to support different claims involving macro-evolution, but if the dating methods, or even, as we saw in the lengthy quote by Dr. Morris above, speculation dealing with a combination of present and past events, are less than perfect, then these dates and the claims that they supposedly support must rightfully be called into question, however certain the people making such claims may seem.

Now, in the above quote Dr. Morris says many of the things that we have already established in this chapter, but he also made some other very valid points. However, the main point that I am concerned with here is that since it is impossible to go back in time to see the origin of a rock being formed[25] "millions of years ago," no date of any rock that was not observed as it was being formed can be certain, and the same goes for any fossils that are found, since the same concepts dealing with historical science apply to them as well.

But what about igneous rocks that we know formed at a certain time? Here are some examples of some very recent volcanoes of which we know how long ago they erupted and left the rocks that were dated using various methods. We know this information because these eruptions were so recent that many of us were here when they happened, or they were current enough to have been recorded in recent centuries. These dates are as of 2007: Mt. Etna (erupted 29 years ago; igneous rocks formed from the lava from the eruption dated at 350,000 years old), Mt. Lassen (erupted 85 years ago; igneous rocks from the eruption dated at 110,000 years old), Hualalai (erupted 200 years ago; igneous rocks from the eruption dated between 1.6 million years old and 22.8 million years old), and Mt. Erebus (erupted 17 years ago; igneous rocks from the eruption dated 640,000 years old).[26] Now these dates might not sound alarming to you. However, when you come to realize that when an igneous rock forms from lava its time clock, based on how the dating methods work, should be set to 0, you should begin to see the problem

---

[25] Igneous rocks, rocks formed from former lava, are the only rocks that are possible to date by themselves. Other rocks must be dated based on the layers of rock and fossils that surround them.
[26] Ibid, 52.

with these dates. In essence an igneous rock that formed from an eruption 17 years ago, like the ones from Mt. Erebus mentioned above, should date, by *all* dating methods, to a date of 17 years old, not 640,000 years old like the date given above for this rock, especially since we know for a fact when these rocks formed. So what is the problem? The problem is that the dating methods are flawed for various reasons. Now I do not want to get any deeper into this issue here, but I do want to point out yet again that any assertion about the age of rocks or fossils from the distant past cannot be proven, not "have not," but rather "*CANNOT*," as in it is impossible to prove such dates, since they deal with the unobserved past, and that due to these kinds of dating problems the dates given by various scientists regarding fossils and rocks should be questioned and not just accepted immediately and without quarrel. But the evolutionists, as well as many other people, claim that the many dates for fossils and rocks that date back to millions, billions, or tens of thousands, or hundreds of thousands of years ago are scientifically proven dates that cannot be argued with, when in fact those dates are impossible to prove in the first place, however right or wrong those dates may or may not be.

Another example of a claim that the evolutionists (as well as many Christians who believe that the earth is billions of years old) make relative to geology is that the Grand Canyon in Arizona is millions and millions of years old (some argue as old as 17 million years old). There are a variety of reasons that most geologists claim this sort of age for the Grand Canyon. Now without going into much detail regarding these reasons, I just want to point out that Dr. John Morris (the geo ogical engineer mentioned earlier) and Steven A. Austin (PhD in Geology from Pennsylvania State University) did a thorough study of the eruption of Mt. St. Helens that took place on May 18, 1980, as well as the surrounding events of that eruption. One of the things that they discovered during this study was that a canyon, which has been called "the Little Grand Canyon," approximately one fortieth of the size of the Grand Canyon in Arizona was formed in a single day as a result of the eruptions at Mt. St. Helens. Drs. Morris and Austin recall the event in the following passage taken from the book *Footprints in the Ash: The Explosive Story of Mount St. Helens*:

> "On March 19, 1982, a small summit eruption melted snow within the crater [of Mount St. Helens] and displaced water forming a 20-mile-long mudflow. The mudflow pooled within the big steam explosion pit behind the debris dam. Mud quickly overtopped the west end of the big steam pit and cut back and downward, producing a 140-foot-deep canyon where before there was no canyon. In a single day the new drainage channel of the North Fork

of the Toutle River was established westward through the debris dam by a catastrophic mudflow!

The canyon produced by the mud has been called 'The Little Grand Canyon' because it appears to be a one-fortieth scale model of the Grand Canyon in Arizona. The new canyon, like its famous precursor, has flat areas in highland surfaces on both sides, gully headed side canyons, and enlarged, cup-shaped side canyons."[27]

So, in a single day a canyon approximately one fortieth the scale of the Grand Canyon in Arizona was formed by a massive and rapid mudflow. So who's to say that the Grand Canyon wasn't formed by a massive mudflow caused by, say, a worldwide flood, in a short period of time?[28] Whether or not Noah's Flood recorded in the book of Genesis was a real worldwide event or not is irrelevant here. My point is simply that this canyon produced by a large mudflow near Mount St. Helens was produced in one day, and it is only about forty times smaller than the Grand Canyon, so it is at least possible that the Grand Canyon was produced over a very short period of time by a similar,

[27] Morris and Austin, *Footprints in the Ash*, 75.
[28] This is linked to Mt. St. Helens in that Noah's Flood would have most likely been accompanied by massive volcanic eruptions all over the earth, and there are actually volcanoes right within the area of the Grand Canyon.

albeit much larger, type of event. This means that, yet again, we have another reason to question the scientists when they throw out dates of canyons, rocks, and other things having to do with historical science. Don't just take their word for it! I am not a conspiracy theorist or anything like that. I am just trying to point out that the people in our nation, and people around the world, are being greatly misled by scientists who refuse to qualify their scientific assertions with the proper level of outward expressed humility.

There are also thousands upon thousands of layers of sediment found in this canyon near Mount St. Helens, which geologists generally consider to be one year for each layer, which would at the very least date the canyon to be many thousands of years old. However, we know for a fact that this canyon was created on March 19, 1982, and that the day before that, on March 18, 1982, this canyon did *not* exist, and so we know that this canyon, as of the day that I write this sentence, May 24, 2012, is exactly 30 years, 2 months, and 5 days old, not thousands or millions of years old. But if we had not witnessed the geological event on March 19, 1982 that created this canyon, just like we were not around to witness the forming of the Grand Canyon in Arizona, we would, based on the principle of uniformity and standard geological dating methods, assume that this canyon is in fact much, much older than it really is (and we would be wrong mind you). Why? There are two main reasons for this. One, the geological dating methods used to date such things are flawed, mainly due to the acceptance of the principle of uniformity, for the simple fact that volcanoes erupt all the time, major hurricanes and tornadoes occur yearly, massive floods happen all over the world, and all kinds of other catastrophic events are a regular occurrences in our world should make even the least intelligent of rational individuals aware of the fact that the world that we live in is not "uniform," and that we should be keenly aware of the fact that large areas of land can be greatly manipulated by natural forces in very short periods of time. And two, because we are dealing with historical science and so we are dealing with the aftermath evidence, not observable events, since they occurred in the past and are no longer repeatable, and so unless we use the proper assumptions regarding how things happened, which we cannot be sure of, then we will inevitably, as Dr. Morris pointed out above, come to wrong conclusions regarding the age of the Grand Canyon or any other issue involving historical science.

Now, this is not the place for an argument regarding the age of the earth or over dating methods. No doubt cases have been made elsewhere on both sides of the debate, and I have studied the arguments on both side of this debate mind you. The point here, as we saw earlier, is that these geological claims are often used in direct correlation with claims regarding evolution, such as the age of fossils found in the rocks and so on, and these fossil ages are used to place different fossils on the "evolutionary tree" at different points to try and show that certain things are evolving into other things, since some fossils are slightly, or greatly, different than other fossils, although also similar to those same fossils in certain ways. What we are concerned with at this time is simply the fact that these claims, like all other claims dealing with historical science, cannot be proven, but rather at best are speculation. Of course these issues do matter, and I am certainly not insinuating that all science is pointless since certainty cannot be reached regarding such issues. What I am claiming is that the evolutionists, as well as anyone else making claims dealing with historical science, need to do so with a humble heart and mind, remembering that they could very well be wrong and there is no way to indefinitely prove that they are correct, and therefore they need to present their scientific findings and claims in such a light. This includes school textbooks, as well as statements and claims made by museums, television programs, and other video projects dealing with these issues. I realize that no one wants to look like they are wrong, and that everyone wants to be right, but intellectual integrity is far more important than saving face, and we would all do well to remember that.

Let me take a moment here to say that I am well aware of how unpopular the views that I am presenting in this book, and especially in this chapter, are. One of the main problems with modern society, especially in America, is that if someone is not upholding the status quo, whether it be in politics, religion, science, or whatever the case may be, then that person, and his or her views, opinions, beliefs, etc., are automatically discarded as worthless, and therefore what they have to say essentially does not get any hearing from the public, or the academicians, at all, let alone the time and hearing that it may deserve. This issue w ll be discussed later on in this book in the chapter dealing with the importance of a free-thinking society. For now I just want to make the point that whether a particular view is popular or not is not, or at least should not be the issue. After all, if someone was planning to assassinate our president, and all of that person's friends thought that there was no way he or she would ever do such a thing, would it be wise for our government to ignore the so called rumors that this individual has in fact planned to assassinate the president? Well, to some people I suppose that the answer to that depends on how they feel about the president, but the obvious answer should be that it would most certainly not be wise for our government to ignore the assassination "rumors." The same principle goes for all areas of life and study. We should always be willing to listen to those who are questioning the status quo, whether they are right or wrong, because we never know whether or not the majority may actually have it wrong. Of course, when a certain belief or view is proven to be the correct one, or at least if the available evidence truly supports a particular conclusion better than the other available conclusions, then we should normally accept that conclusion, belief, or view. There is a type of informal fallacy in the realm of logic that our country seems to make on a daily basis. It is the fallacy known as *argumentum ad populum*. According to Dr. Norman Geisler and Ronald Brooks, "This is the fallacy of deciding truth based on opinion polls."[29] This does not require that an actual poll be taken on the topic at hand. It is simply the idea of determining truth based on what the majority thinks about a certain issue. This is of course a very foolish way to determine truth, for what if the whole world believed that circles and squares were the same thing, just with different names? Would that make it true because the whole world believed it? Of course not! That is my point. There is another logical fallacy called *Argumentum ab Annis*, or "Argument because of Age."[30] The mainstream academic, and especially the mainstream scientific, community is often guilty of this fallacy, for they continually claim that the belief in creation, God, and other beliefs are false because they are old and outdated beliefs, but think about it. I bet you everything I have that four thousand years ago humans in general believed that some humans could walk. So should we not believe that some humans can walk anymore since that is a very old belief? Absolutely not!

---

[29] Norman L. Geisler and Ronald M. Brooks, *Come, Let Us Reason: An Introduction to Logical Thinking* (Grand Rapids: Baker Book House, 1990), 97.
[30] Ibid, 99.

That is obviously foolish. This is a simple and seemingly ridiculous example, but it nevertheless makes my point, and it shows that beliefs should not necessarily be abandoned, and cannot automatically be false simply because of how long they have been around. So, just because the views set forth in this book are not popular views, especially among the secular scientific community, that does not in any way mean that the views in this book are wrong. Also, the same goes for the fact that the creationist views set forth in this book are very old views in general. They are not false simply because they have been around for thousands of years. We should make our choices as to what we choose to believe based on what makes the most sense based on *all* of the available evidence, but we cannot do that without being aware of the available evidence. That is why I have written this book, to try and make the public aware of many pieces of available evidence (not necessarily scientific evidence) that the mainstream scientists are purposefully refusing to tell you because if you knew about these things then you might question them and their assertions, and that of course would make the scientists uncomfortable.

So, we have looked at some specific examples of some claims that evolutionists, and historical scientists in general, make, and how all claims dealing with historical science are impossible to prove. We are now going to take a look at why claims regarding macro-evolution, as well as other similar claims regarding historical science, are either untrue claims or claims that cannot be proven. After that we will close this chapter with some concluding remarks.

Why Macro-Evolutionary and Similar Claims are Either Untrue or Un-provable Claims

We have already discussed this issue to some extent in the previous sections of this chapter, but now I want to take a closer look at some specific statements made by a philosopher that essentially says the same things that we have been saying throughout this chapter so far, and then we will briefly discuss a quote regarding evolution in the early twentieth century made by another evolutionist.

Philosopher of science Derek Turner says this:

"One of the central problems of the scientific realism debate is an epistemological problem, or a problem having to do with scientific knowledge: Virtually all scientists and philosophers of science are empiricists, in the sense that they think that all claims to scientific knowledge must be based on evidence, and that our evidence comes from observation and experimentation. Can observational evidence ever support our claims to have scientific knowledge of entities and mechanisms that we cannot, and probably never will observe? Does science deliver knowledge of unobservables?"[31]

Now, scientific realism is "a positive epistemic attitude towards the content of our best theories and models, recommending belief in both observable and unobservable aspects of the world described by the sciences."[32] In other words, scientific realists are confident that we *can* know things by way of various scientific theories, whether they deal with observable *or* unobservable data. To some extent there is no problem with this, but many people take it too far by claiming that we can have *certain* knowledge regarding such unobservable data. It is one thing to be justified in believing a proposition because there seems to be a wide body of evidence supporting it. It is quite another to be absolutely certain of the truth of a proposition that you have no way of verifying completely. This second camp is the one that the modern evolutionists fall into, for they claim that they have indubitable knowledge of evolution and its truth, when in fact that is impossible, since it deals with past, un-repeatable, and unverifiable events and propositions, not to mention the fact that, as we have shown in this book already, evolution as it is presented

---

[31] Derek Turner, *Making Prehistory: Historical Science and the Scientific Realism Debate* (New York: Cambridge University Press, 2007), 28.

[32] _____, Stanford Encyclopedia of Philosophy, "Scientific Realism," Stanford University, http://plato.stanford.edu/entries/scientific-realism/ (accessed May 23, 2012).

today by naturalistic scientists is one 100% impossible. One cannot have knowledge about something that is impossible (other than to know *that* it is impossible), for as we saw earlier *truth* is a necessary component for knowledge, and a proposition that something that is impossible is actually possible and true is necessarily a false statement, thereby making knowledge of it impossible! And so the scientific realists who take their realism to such a level are foolhardy and need to exercise far more caution and humility in their scientific endeavors and assertions.

The above quote by Derek Turner also makes it clear that "virtually all scientists and philosophers are empiricists." An empiricist is someone who "bases our knowledge, or the materials from which it is constructed, on experience through the traditional five senses,"[33] as we saw earlier. The problem with this, relative to the study of origins and other historical science topics, as this quote suggests,[34] is that it is impossible for us to come to any solid conclusions about such events, since they are "unobservables," or events in the past that cannot be

---

[33] Ted Honderich, ed., *Philosophy: The Oxford Guide* (New York: Oxford University Press, 2005), 242.

[34] I am not insinuating that Derek Turner necessarily agrees with my conclusions in this quote, for the quote ends before the answers are given to the questions. I am merely stating that these questions are good questions, and they are suggestive in and of themselves of my assertions. The conclusions that I draw from them and the answers that I provide for them are mine, not Derek Turners.

observed in the present, because, quite simply, they happened in the past.

Turner also says, "Scientists who work on problems in geology and paleontology often experience these limits [to our knowledge of the distant past] in the following way: Everything up to a certain point has the feel of good, solid research. But everything beyond that point has the feel of speculation, educated guesswork, or (at worst) mere storytelling."[35] The point here is plain to see. Historical scientists, as already stated, deal with aftermath evidence, not observable events, and so it is inevitable that there will always be a level of doubt regarding the conclusions that they come to regarding such data.

One more quote by Turner is necessary here, and then we will move on to a final statement by an evolutionist regarding the level of perceived "health" within evolutionary theory and the evolutionary scientific community. Turner says, in the same book that the above quotes were taken from,

> "...historical processes – such as the movement of tectonic plates, or macroevolutionary processes, occur very slowly, relative to our lifespans. This means that although we might be able to make predictions based on observed trends about

---

[35] Turner, *Making Prehistory*, 11.

where those processes will go in the future, we will not be around long enough to check to see if those predictions are born out.............(also) A great many predictions in experimental science have the form: 'If we do thus-and-such, under these conditions, and if this theory is correct, then that is the effect we should observe.' That is, scientists pred ct what will happen as a result of certain experimental manipulations. But since we cannot manipulate the past..... our powers of testing predictions derived from claims about the past are limited."[36]

This quote shows us two things, among others. One, that macro-evolutionary and other historical science predictions regarding such large scale issues as the movement of tectonic plates cannot really be validated in the scientist who makes such predictions' lifetime, due to the nature of the supposed speed of such issues and events. This is one of the reasons that evolutionists are so arrogant, open, and willing to assert the "reality" of evolution, because they think they can simply claim that somewhere and at some time in the future it will be proven beyond a doubt that evolution is true, knowing good and well that they will not be around to be ridiculed

---

[36] Ibid, 114-115.

if they turn out to be wrong, but there are two problems with this. One, they have nothing legitimate to base their presumptions off of in the first place (regarding macro-evolutionary claims), and two, this is another logical fallacy known as *Argumentum ad Futuris*, or an argument to the future. It says, in essence, "Accept this because future evidence will support it."[37] This is what Darwin did in his days, for since he knew that the fossil record did not support his theory of evolution at the time he was alive, he claimed that it would do so in the future once more fossils were discovered. However, at least he was honest enough to admit that the fossil record did not support his beliefs in evolution during his time. Unfortunately today many evolutionists are no longer as honest as Darwin was and they tend to claim that the fossil evidence is now adequate enough to support the "fact of evolution," but as we have already seen, no such fossil evidence actually exists, no matter what Richard Dawkins (see his book *The Greatest Show on Earth*) and others like him claim.[38]

---

[37] Geisler and Brooks, *Come, Let Us Reason*, 99.

[38] Let me also say here that one does not need a PhD, or any other type of degree, in a scientific field to be able to understand evolution and its supposed evidence, but rather one need only to study the issues for a short time under the right conditions. After all, the actual information on evolution and the basics of how it works is minimal, and even the supposed evidence supporting it is considerably lacking. I have viewed enough science textbooks, read enough other books about science and evolution, taken enough science classes, and studied the issues more than enough to know that what I am telling you is accurate. If I hadn't I certainly would not have written this book. Nevertheless, I beg of you not to take my word for it, but to utilize the additional reading section in the back of this book, along with the

The second thing that this quote shows is that, just as we have already seen, there are limits to the level of knowledge that can be attained whenever one is dealing with historical science.

Now, G.S. Carter, an evolutionist, in 1951 said this in his book *Animal Evolution*, which was also quoted from earlier in this chapter. He said,

> "Thirty or forty years ago interest in the study of evolution was decreasing, and it seemed likely that it would decrease further as time went on. The opinions of paleontologists and geneticists were opposed, and investigation of evolutionary problems on the lines followed since the middle of the nineteenth century seemed to have reached a dead end. The result of this unsatisfactory state of affairs was that many zoologists, having lost interest in the problems of evolution, hastily concluded that it was questionable whether the Darwinian theory was at all generally true."[39]

Carter here is referring to the 1910s and the 1920s. Apparently zoologists, and other members of various scientific disciplines most likely, had "lost interest in the

---

bibliography, and check these things out for yourself.
[39] G.S. Carter, *Animal Evolution*, v.

problems of evolution," since there seemed to be a lack of evidence supporting the theory. Why this was a "hasty" conclusion according to Carter we can only guess at, but the fact is that there has since been a very hefty revival of a widespread belief in evolution, macro-evolution, since that time. Of course there are more reasons today than ever before to doubt the theory of evolution, which can easily be seen by reading books like Biochemist Michael Behe's *Darwin's Black Box*; retired law professor Phillip E. Johnson's book *Darwin on Trial*; medical doctor Geoffrey Simmons' book *Billions of Missing Links* mentioned earlier in this chapter, and, honestly, even by reading Richard Dawkins' painfully unsuccessful attempt to validate the evolutionary worldview in his book *The Greatest Show on Earth*, also mentioned earlier in this chapter, for if you understand even basic science and how the world works, you can easily see how none of his supposed evidence is legitimate. Of course you must know something about the fossils that he claims are proven intermediates, but that just takes a little research On the whole though if you read his five hundred plus page book on the "evidence for evolution" you will see, if you are looking for the truth with an open and critical mind, that even Richard Dawkins', poster boy for macro-evolution, best attempt to prove the reality of evolution comes up far short of anything even remotely close to something that could be considered worthy of being classified as proof. Even the concept of artificial selection (which Dawkins uses to try to support evolution in his book), such as humans breading various animals to accentuate specific traits in them, and human genetic manipulation, do not support the idea of macro-evolution, for all of them directly involve an intelligence, namely humans, to go about such business. If you take away the intelligent entity doing the selecting and the manipulation, then those types of things simply do not happen anymore, especially not in the way that they do when the intelligence is present. Just like micro-evolution cannot be used to support macro-evolution, so neither can artificial selection be used to prove that natural selection can accomplish similar ends, and as we saw earlier, the whole concept of natural selection is incoherent anyway.

Nevertheless, some of this revival in a belief in evolution was no doubt due to the many hoaxes of nineteenth and twentieth century evolutionists, such as Piltdown Man. The fact that most people in our part of the world seem to believe the scientists when they tell the public that evolution is a proven fact, makes arguments like the ones I am making in this book hard to stomach, but the *fact* of the matter is, as we have seen in this chapter many times already, macro-evolutionary theory and the idea of universal common descent of all life on earth cannot be proven. Not "are not yet proven," but *CANNOT* BE PROVEN, as they necessarily deal with historical science, and historical science requires that those who deal with it can at best make educated guesses on what happened in the past. Hence, any claim that macro-evolution is a proven fact is not only unrealistic, but it is, quite simply, untrue. To put it more bluntly, it is a bold faced lie for anyone, especially an educated person of science, to claim that macro-evolution or any other theory dealing with historical science is a proven fact, since it is impossible to prove such things.

Conclusion

So, we have seen what historical science is, what empirical science is, and how they differ. We have also looked at some claims made by evolutionists in relation to historical science. Finally, we looked at why claims regarding macro-evolution, as well as all other claims about historical science, must be viewed in light of the fact that only a certain level of assuredness can be gained and maintained when dealing with past events.

Well, that concludes our discussion of evolution for now. Although we will refer to and discuss evolution from time to time throughout the remainder of this book, it will not be our main focus. We are now going to discuss a couple of other concepts regarding science and worldviews. One of these concepts is actually a type of science, as we will see, called Intelligent Design. The other is a religiously based worldview known as Young Earth Creationism. After we discuss these concepts and how they differ we will move on to discuss the importance of a free thinking society, and also why it is not appropriate, especially in the "Land of the Free" to censure science as much as our nation is currently doing. We will then end the book with a brief discussion on what we should all, as a nation and society, do about the issues discussed in this book, and then finally we will be discussing, in the appendix, the ridiculous problem between young and old earth creationists. This will not be a debate about who is right, but rather it will be a biblical rebuke to all those involved in the vehement disrespect that is being thrown from one side of the debate to the other. If you do not care what the Bible says or if you are not a Christian then feel free not to read the appendix if you so choose. If you are a Christian, and most especially if you are involved in the debate between the old and young earth creationists, then I strongly urge you to read the appendix in this book, and to read it carefully. However whoever you are and whatever your beliefs are, please, I beg of you, read my short note to you, the reader, after the appendix. It will only take a few minutes of your time, and it is by far the most important information that you will ever come into contact with, that much I can promise you. So, let us now move on to part 2 of this book.

Part 2

Intelligent Design, Young Earth Creationism, A Free Thinking Society, and What Needs To Be Done

8

What Exactly Is Intelligent Design?

"You look at the incredible diversity and complexity of life, and inevitably the question arises, 'What brought all this into existence?' Was it simply chance and necessity, undirected natural forces, or is there something else going on? Is there a purpose, a plan, a design; a design due to an intelligent cause? I think that is the fundamental question."[1]

- Dr. Paul Nelson (Philosopher of Science)

This statement, made by philosopher of science Paul Nelson, is a prime example of the type of thinking that goes on within the ranks of the Intelligent Design movement. But what exactly is Intelligent Design? Is it merely Creationism masquerading around with a different name? Is it science? Is it religion? Well, we are going to look at the second one of these questions in more detail in a later chapter regarding the differences between ID (Intelligent Design) and YEC (Young Earth Creationism), although we will briefly address the issue in this chapter as well. As for the other two questions, we will be discussing those below later on in this chapter, along with some

---

[1] _____, *Unlocking The Mystery Of Life* (Illustra Media: 2002), DVD.

other aspects of ID. Ordinarily I would begin a chapter like this with a discussion of what exactly Intelligent Design is, i.e. by defining it. However, due to the fact that there is a great deal of disrespect within the modern mainstream scientific community regarding ID and its proponents, and since those who deny that ID is science essentially call the credentials of the proponents of ID into question, I think it more appropriate, and that it will serve us better here, if we begin with a brief look at some of the proponents of ID and their credentials. We will then proceed to define and discuss what exactly ID is, followed by a brief discussion of some of the basic ideas that ID deals with. We will then discuss what it is that the proponents of the ID movement are seeking to accomplish with such seemingly provocative claims about the universe and the things in it.

Who Are Some Proponents of Intelligent Design, and Are They Credible?

So who are some of the people that support the ID movement, and what exactly are their credentials? Well, there are actually a wide range of people in various areas of expertise who support the movement. Wikipedia[2] lists 91 supporters of the ID movement.[3] Now of course there

---

[2] I usually would not cite a source like this, but this is a broad topic and the information here is basic and can be checked many different places, as these are all public figures, or at least people who have bios about them online that are easily accessible.

[3] _____, "Intelligent Design Advocates," Wikipedia, http://en.wikipedia.org/wiki/Category:Intelligent_design_advocates (accessed May 31, 2012).

are many more advocates of Intelligent Design than that, but these are just some of the more well-known proponents of ID. Now remember that one does not need to be a scientist to support or understand ID, just like one does not need to be a biologist to support or understand the study of biology, or be a preacher to understand religion. What matters for our purposes is whether or not there are credible, intelligent people that support this movement. Here are a few of the examples of people (and some of their credentials) who support ID given on the Wikipedia site:

- Michele Bachmann (United States congresswoman, B.A., J.D., LL.M.)
- John R. Baumgardner (PhD in Geophysics and Space Science from the University of California at Los Angeles)
- Michael Behe (B.S. in Chemistry from Drexel University; PhD in Bochemistry from the University of Pennsylvania)
- John Andrew Boehner (Speaker of the United States House of Representatives)
- Walter Bradley (retired professor of engineering of Baylor University and Texas A&M University)
- Michael Egnor (M.D. and a neurosurgeon)
- William Harrison Frist (former United States Senator, graduate of Princeton University with a degree in Health Care Policy, and also a graduate of

Harvard Medical School with a Doctor of Medicine degree (with honors))
- Scott A. Minnich (PhD from Iowa State University and associate professor of microbiology at the University of Idaho)
- Paul A. Nelson (PhD in Philosophy from the University of Chicago)
- Rick Santorum (former United States Senator, 2012 United States presidential nomination candidate, and he also holds an MBA and a J.D. (with honors))
- Roy Spencer (B.S. in Atmospheric Sciences from the University of Michigan, M.S. and PhD in Meteorology from the University of Wisconson-Madison, and a climatologist and Principal Research Scientist for the University of Alabama in Huntsville, as well as the U.S. Science Team Leader for the Advance Microwave Scanning Radiometer on NASA's Aqua satellite)
- William Dembski (Bachelor's degree in Psychology, Master's degrees in Statistics, Mathematics (University of Chicago), and Philosophy, MDiv (Princeton Theological Seminary), PhD in Mathematics (University of Chicago), and a PhD in Philosophy)
- Guillermo Gonzalez (B.S. in Physics and Astronomy from the University of Arizona, PhD in Astronomy from the University of Washington. He has received fellowships, grants and awards from NASA, the

University of Washington, Sigma Xi, and the
National Science Foundation)
- Geoffrey Simmons (B.S. in Biology, M.D. from the
University of Illinois Medical School)
- Lee Strobel (Bachelor's degree in Journalism, M.S.L.
from Yale Law School)
- Caroline Crocker [A.A., B.Sc. in Microbiology, M.Sc.
in Medical Microbiology, PhD in
immunopharmacology)
- Ernie Fletcher (former United States congressman,
former governor of Kentucky, B.S. in Mechanical
Engineering (with top honors), M.D. from the
University of Kentucky College of Medicine)
- Ann Coulter (B.A. in History from Cornell University
(cum laude), J.D. from the University of Michigan
Law School)

I hope that this is enough of a list to show you that not
only are the proponents of ID diverse in their educational
backgrounds, but many of them graduated from the top
schools, and many of them even graduated with honors. I
myself graduated *summa cum laude* from Liberty
University with a B.S. in Religion (Bible and Theology),
magna cum laude from North East Kansas Technical
College with a diploma in Electrical Technology, and also
from Pinnacle Career Institute with a diploma in Personal
Training (where we studied a good deal of science
regarding the human body and mind relative to exercise),
magna cum laude from Temple Baptist Seminary with an

M.A. in Theology, and I have also done graduate work in law, bioethics and leadership, and I am also a supporter of Intelligent Design. I also know firsthand, due to my years as an electrician, that complex things, such as electricity running through a house or car, do not get there on their own.[4] Who has ever had a house built without someone putting in the wires and fuses necessary for the electricity to work in it, and still somehow ended up with electricity in their house? I mean sure you can buy battery operated lights and things like that, but electricity, harnessed electricity, does not exist unless there is first someone to harness it, and with the exception of lightning and some forms of electricity seen in certain animals, electricity must be generated using means that only intelligent entities can utilize. And just like electricity keeps electronic things running, where did life come from? Why is anything alive? After all, science, whether they want to admit it or not, has a principle known as "life from life," meaning that only life can bring forth life. For instance, a rabbit that has been dead for a month cannot naturally give birth to a live rabbit, nor can a piece of house dust (dead skin cells) divide into new living cells. Unfortunately they ignore their own principle when they, the modern mainstream scientists, assert that life came from nonlife, also known as abiogenesis (which we briefly discussed in an earlier chapter), while knowing full well that that is absolutely

---

[4] Barring any lightning strikes or static electricity of course. I am referring here to harnessed electricity.

impossible based on their very own principle and knowledge of how the world works. We have a life force flowing through us that science cannot explain, regardless of how hard it tries. Just like the electricity in a building has to be put in by the electrician[5] to make the house light up or the electrical receptacles work (there are no possible exceptions to this rule with regard to harnessed electricity), so there must be a life giver for there to be life.

There are many, many different people in many different disciplinary fields that are supporters of ID. One thing that is incredibly important to remember is that the majority of the major Intelligent Design proponents went to the same types of schools as the people who hate ID. They did not necessarily go to Christian universities that teach Creationism (this would not necessarily make them un-credible anyway) and have anti-science classes (as if there is such a thing), but rather they went to the same kinds of schools that almost everyone else who goes to college goes to. So we cannot say that these people somehow had a tainted education or that they were brainwashed by their Christian professors, or whatever else it is that the antagonists of ID are saying. The proponents of ID, in general, are just as credible as those people that disagree with them, and some more so, like

---

[5] I am not saying that the one putting in the electricity does not have to be an electrician by trade, but if he or she is installing electricity, during that time he or she can rightly be called an electrician, at least to some extent.

William Dembski, who, as we saw above has a bachelor's degree, four master's degrees, and two PhDs, several from top schools like the University of Chicago and Princeton. Now although I disagree with some of Dr. Dembski's scientific conclusions, mostly regarding the age of the earth (as I have told him in person), he is nevertheless an extremely intelligent individual, and people like him should not merely be brushed off to the side like they don't know what they are talking about, for he is no doubt one of the most educated people in our country, and possibly on the planet. Of course that doesn't necessarily mean that he is right either, but it does mean that we should at least listen to what he has to say on matters that he has studied. We will look at some of Dembski's statements regarding ID below, as he is one of the most avid supporters of ID and, dare I say one of its leading giants. The main point, again, that I want you to grasp here is that advocates of ID are not idiots simply because they support ID. They are not foolish or mistaken just because they disagree with what the modern mainstream scientists are saying. After all, we saw in the beginning of this book that such a claim, namely that ID proponents are dumb or wrong simply because of the fact that they support ID is a logical fallacy known as the genetic fallacy, for this is essentially claiming that their scientific conclusions and assertions are false because those conclusions and assertions are coming from those who support ID, and so therefore those who support ID are wrong because, quite simply, they support ID; or in other words their conclusions are wrong because of the source that they are coming from, namely supporters of ID. This is ridiculous. If someone, anyone, is wrong about what they purport, it is because what they purport is inherently false due to the fact that it does not line up with reality. What someone does or does not believe or support has no bearing on whether or not it is false, but rather only the facts do. What we should all be doing, instead of simply claiming that the ID and YEC proponents are wrong because they differ in what they believe from what modern science teaches, is determining, based on the available evidence (all of it), who is right and who is wrong, or who is most likely to be right and who is most likely to be wrong, while throwing out any and all preconceived notions as to what can or cannot be the case.

So, we have seen that there are a wide variety of very educated individuals who support ID. We have also seen that just because someone supports ID that does not make them wrong or a fool, regardless of what the modern mainstream scientists are saying. Now, let us take a look at what exactly ID is and how to define it.

What is Intelligent Design?

Before we get started with our discussion of what exactly ID is, which is the main purpose of this chapter, I first need to mention what this chapter is not intended to be about. This chapter is not at all intended to be a scientific defense of ID, although at times it might seem that way. For that I encourage you, the reader, to examine the additional information section in the back of this book regarding the resources mentioned for more information on ID. I am not a scientist, and although I know a lot about science and many different areas of it, this book is not meant to be a scientific expose of ID, evolution, or YEC, but rather it is meant to be a book that distinguishes between and defines certain terms, such as evolution, religion, science, Intelligent Design, and so on, and discusses the specific issues that are facing our nation (and the world) regarding some of these terms. There are many other highly qualified people who have already legitimately defended ID scientifically, such as those who participated in the making of the video *Unlocking The Mystery Of Life* (2002, produced by Illustra Media), and Dr. Jobe Martin with his video series *Incredible Creatures That Defy Evolution 1, 2, and 3* (2000, 2002, and 2004 respectively, produced by Steve Greisen) in which he goes to great lengths to show the concept of irreducible complexity, which we will discuss below; as well as Geoffrey Simmons in his book *Billions of Missing Links*. Hence, we will try to avoid getting too deep into the arguments of the various ID proponents, although we will need to use one or two of them as examples of what kinds of arguments the ID proponents are making, so as to better define the concept as a whole.

In a detailed pamphlet put out by Rose Publishers titled *Intelligent Design*, written by Dr. William Dembski and Sean McDowell, Intelligent Design is defined as follows: "Intelligent Design is the study of patterns in nature that are best explained as the result of intelligence."[6] So we can see here that ID is really nothing more than a particular type of scientific inquiry, namely that of seeking to understand patterns in nature. If you think back to the chapter earlier in this book when we defined science you will remember that we defined science as: *the use of the scientific method to study anything and everything that exists in nature*. So when we say that ID is the study of patterns in nature, "patterns" are obviously part of "anything and everything that exists in nature." Now of course patterns do not *exist* in the normal sense of the word (exist), but they are nevertheless part of our natural reality,[7] and as long as we use some form of the scientific method to study those patterns then ID, as defined above, fits into what we have defined as science in this book, and remember that we got our definition of science from secular science textbooks that are used in state universities across the country. So, before we go any further it needs to be stated that, by the modern mainstream scientific community's own definition of science, ID, as defined by Dembski and McDowell, is *rightfully classified as science*. But wait! We determined

---

[6] William Dembski and Sean McDowell, *Intelligent Design* (Torrance: Rose Publishing, 2009), no page numbers.

[7] This of course would not square with a materialistic view of reality, but as we have already seen materialism is a self-refuting and therefore false view of reality, and so we need not worry about it.

earlier that we cannot even rightfully classify evolution as science, right? Yes, we did! So sit back and think for a minute about what that means about what we should or should not allow to be taught in our science classrooms. Evolution is certainly a scientific idea (an idea that deals with science), and so it may very well have its place in the science classroom, but ID, as we have seen above, can actually rightfully be classified as science itself, not just a scientific idea, and this, namely science, is a classification that even evolution lacks, and yet in 2005 at the Dover case, a U.S. Court case, the United States Court Judge John Jones III decided that ID is not science and so it cannot be taught in the science classrooms in our country.[8] This should outrage any earnest seeker of truth! But I digress, for we will discuss the implications of this book more in a later chapter. For now we are discussing what ID is, but first let us look at one more statement made by Dembski and McDowell in the opening remarks of this pamphlet titled *Intelligent Design*. After the above statement they go on to say:

> "Intelligent Design (abbreviated ID) shouldn't be controversial. Archeologists, forensic scientists, and SETI researchers (scientists looking for signs of intelligence from outer space), are all doing Intelligent

---

[8] Norman Geisler *Creation & the Courts: Eighty Years of Conflict in the Classroom and the Courtroom* (Wheaton: Crossway Books, 2007), 29-30.

Design research. ID is controversial because
it claims to find signs of intelligence in
biology. This raises the question of who the
designer could be."[9]

Now before we discuss this particular quote I would like to
go back for a moment to the previous quote. If you read
the definition of ID given earlier by Dembski and McDowell
carefully you would have noticed that it includes the
phrase "patterns in nature that are best explained as the
result of intelligence." You see, it is not the idea of
whether ID is or is not science that is really bugging the
mainstream scientists, but rather it is the implications of
such science. It is the obvious philosophical and religious
implications that make them uncomfortable, and instead
of admitting that they simply purport that ID is not science
but rather religion. However, last time I checked the
implications of something does not determine what that
something *is*, or, put differently, the *implications* of
something has no bearing on its *definition* or *classification*.
For instance, if I said to you, "I don't like you," that might
very well imply that I don't want to spend very much time
around you, but the fact is that what I told you was a
statement, plain and simp e. The implication that I don't
want to spend time with you does not change the fact that
the statement itself, "I don't like you," is in fact just that, a
statement. In the same way, just because the science of ID

---

[9] Dembski and McDowell, *Intelligent Design*.

includes possible, or even definite religious implications, that does not in any way mean that ID is religion, and besides, we have already shown that ID is science, not religion, above. Again, the implications of something do not determine what that something is, for the implications are external and secondary to that something. What a thing is must be defined based on all that is intrinsic to it, before anything is added to or taken away from it, and so the purest definition of ID, namely "the study of patterns in nature," fits squarely with what we, and the mainstream scientific community, have defined as *SCIENCE*, not religion.

Going back to the above quote by Dembski and McDowell we see that if the mainstream scientists are allowed to look for intelligence in the universe and call it science, then it naturally and logically follows that all scientists should be able to look for intelligence in the universe and call it science,[10] for no one has an inherent right to a monopoly on such a thing, or on anything for that matter. But ID itself does not go as far as to define what or where that intelligence is, nor is it even necessarily looking for intelligence, but rather it is merely the study of patterns in nature that seem to be best explained by positing some form of intelligence. Sure, when you start discussing what or who this intelligence could be you enter the realm of philosophy, and possibly

---

[10] Although the fact that the mainstream scientists are doing it does not necessarily make it right or wrong. I am not a pragmatist.

religion, but as far as the studying of the patterns themselves go, which is what ID consists of, it is, was, and always will be science.

Six hundred years ago it was considered common knowledge that the universe and all that is in it was designed, but since then a whole bunch of "smart people" have taken it upon themselves to decide that the previous multi millennia generations of the west, and some of the east, were in fact wrong about that, without proving them wrong mind you. One thing that needs to be mentioned here is that it is *impossible* to prove that God, gods, spirits, or anything supernatural does not exist, because of its very nature of being non-natural and therefore, at least ordinarily, non-material, or invisible. There are millions of people around the world that seem to think that anyone who believes in the supernatural is necessarily foolish because the supernatural has been proven not to exist. That is, quite simply, as I just stated, not the case, for it is in fact impossible to prove the non-existence of the supernatural. We must remain rational and understand what can and cannot be proven, and we mustn't be dogmatic about what cannot be proven, for to do so is to become irrational, and if we deny rationality then we are to be but fools. And so the hostility towards Christians, as well as the billions of other people on planet earth who believe that some supernatural entity or entities do exist needs to cease, because just like we cannot prove that the supernatural does exist, those who oppose supernaturalism cannot prove that the supernatural does not exist, and so we should be equally gracious to one another with regards to such an issue, for after all we are all people with feelings, beliefs, wants, needs, goals, dreams, and so on and so forth, and no one is inherently more valuable than anyone else, regardless of what the evolutionists' teachings imply.[11] And so while ID may have supernatural implications, that should not and does not make it, or its proponents, automatically wrong or foolish.

We must also remember that ID is not a completely new concept. After all, William Paley, in the early 1800s, before Darwin's time, made the argument that if someone were to find a watch lying in a field, it would make far more sense to assume that the watch had a watchmaker who put the watch together in working order, rather than to simply assume that the watch just randomly came together on its own somehow.[12]

So, let me recap what we have said so far. ID is in fact science based on the definition: *the study of patterns in nature*, which is a legitimate definition of ID given by

---

[11] Having said that, I am of the persuasion that there is far more evidence supporting the idea that supernaturalism is true than there is supporting the idea that it is false, and so it seems more coherent and intelligent to me to uphold supernaturalism as more likely to be true than anti-supernaturalism.

[12] William Paley, *Natural Theology: Or Evidences of the Existence and Attributes of the Deity Collected from the Appearances of Nature*, reprinted (Boston: Gould and Lincoln, 1852 [1802]), quoted by Dembski and McDowell, *Intelligent Design*.

two of its most prominent proponents. Also, while the implications of ID and the explanations regarding what is discovered by the ID scientists may entail philosophical and religious concepts, those implications and explanations are secondary and external to ID and therefore cannot rightfully be used in determining whether or not ID is science or religion, because ID must be defined on its own internal, primary terms.

Now, remember a little while ago when we said that as long as the ID proponents are using some form of the scientific method while studying the patterns in nature then ID is in fact science? Well, now we are going to talk a little about just that, namely the form of the scientific method used by ID proponents. This form of the scientific method is known as *specified complexity*, or rather looking for specified complexity is the method that they use.

What is Specified Complexity?

Dembski and McDowell say this about specified complexity:

> "Specified complexity is the fingerprint of design. For something to exhibit specified complexity it must be hard to reproduce by chance (complex) and it must match an independently given pattern (specified). Any mountain you see is complex. It would be highly unlikely for the forces of nature to

reproduce its exact shape anywhere else. But Mt. Rushmore isn't just complex. It's also specified — it matches the faces of four U.S. presidents. Because Mt. Rushmore is complex and specified, we know it's designed."[13]

We see here an example of specified complexity in Mt. Rushmore. As Dembski and McDowell point out in the above quote, while all mountains are complex, not all mountains look like the faces of American presidents. Mt. Rushmore is a great example of something that screams *design* at us, for who in their right mind would assume that the faces of the presidents on it were made simply by erosion or any other natural force? Remember that we must remind ourselves to remain true to the evidence that is before us, even if it goes against what we have believed our whole lives, for if we are not willing to be honest with ourselves and others then I will gladly be the one to say that we have at that point become worthless in the grand scheme of things, for if we are not going to live, act, and think realistically, no matter what, then we lack the integrity required to be rightfully taken seriously, and if we cannot be taken seriously then what good are we? So if the evidence points to a designer, then no matter how uncomfortable we are with that implication, we should look into it with an open mind.

---

[13] Ibid.

Dembski also says this about specified complexity in his book *The Design Revolution*:

> "Intelligence leaves behind a characteristic trademark or signature – what I call *specified complexity*. An event exhibits specified complexity if it is contingent and therefore not necessary; if it is complex and therefore not readily repeatable by chance; and if it is specified in the sense of exhibiting an independently given pattern.....In determining whether biological organisms exhibit specified complexity, design theorists focus on identifiable systems – such as individual enzymes, metabolic pathways, molecular machines and the like. These systems are specified in virtue of their independent functional requirements, and they exhibit a high degree of complexity (emphasis original)."[14]

Dembski here gives another example of specified complexity using biological organisms. An example of what Dembski is referring to here would be, on a larger scale, a human heart. An independent functional requirement of the human heart would be something like the need for all of the valves to be able to open and close appropriately.

---

[14] William Dembski, *The Design Revolution* (Downers Grove: InterVarsity Press, 2004), 35.

My older brother, about eight years or so ago, had to have heart surgery because two of his heart valves were fused together and so the blood was going into his heart at a rate much higher than it was leaving his heart. When the doctors found the problem they gave him one week before he would have had to have a full heart transplant because his heart was literally three times the size that it was supposed to be. He could not even walk across the room without getting dizzy, and several times he even passed out just by taking a few steps. Fortunately for him they did surgery within the week and replaced the fused valves with two valves made of a mixture of animal tissue and plastic and he is doing well now, although he will have to have those valves replaced every ten to fifteen years for the rest of his life, and he is only 30 years old now. The point here is that if the valves of the heart are not working properly, then the heart cannot function appropriately. This is what Dembski means by independent functional requirements, namely the things that the organism must have in order to function properly, or at all, in and of itself. These requirements make each organism specific. And it is not hard to see that biological organisms, even single celled organisms, are incredibly complex. Just look at one of them under a powerful microscope or find a diagram of one in a science textbook. This is another great example of specified complexity.

Again, specified complexity is the idea that something must be both hard to reproduce by chance (complex) and it must exhibit some form of independently given pattern. Dembski, in the above quote, added the third criteria that it must also be contingent. This just means that whatever it is cannot be necessary, or put another way, something that is contingent necessarily depends on something else for its existence (hence the need for a designer). Everything in the natural world is contingent, whether we want to admit it or not, so that is probably why Dembski and McDowell left that characteristic out of their description of specified complexity in the earlier quote that we looked at. Looking for specified complexity is the particular method that the ID proponents use to study the patterns in nature, or in other words the ID scientists are looking for specified complexity in nature. This is classified as a scientific method because they can continually (repeatedly) look for these attributes in the things that they are looking at, which means that looking for specified complexity entails repeatable experimentation on a given "population" to determine whether or not the hypothesis (that something is designed) is most likely true. This is, according to our definition of the scientific method that we established earlier in this book, an adequate type, or use of, the scientific method, and so, like we said, ID is rightfully classified as science. Now we are going to look briefly at another component of ID that was mentioned earlier in this chapter known as *irreducible complexity*.

What is Irreducible Complexity?

Now that we have discussed specified complexity, let us move on to discuss something that, whether the evolutionists like it or not, even Darwin himself said would be a fatal flaw to his theory of evolution by natural selection. Remember though that this chapter is not intended to be a scientific defense of ID, but rather we are simply looking at what ID is and a few of the major scientific contributions that it has to offer.

The following is a quote taken from Darwin's infamous *Origin of Species*: "If it could be shown that any complex organ existed which could not possibly have been formed by numerous, successive, slight modifications, my theory would absolutely break down."[15] Again, like the quote by Darwin that we saw at the beginning of the previous chapter in this book, this quote makes it clear that even Darwin himself was aware of some possible major flaws in his theory of evolution. Unfortunately over the last century or so the mainstream scientific community has idolized the theory of evolution and Darwin so much that the scientists do not even seem to care whether or not there are actual, or even possible, flaws in the theory of evolution anymore. Instead they just act like everything is fine with it and, like we also saw in earlier chapters of this book, that macro-evolutionary theory is no longer a

---

[15] Charles Darwin, *Origin of Species: 6th edition* (New York: New York University Press, 1988), 154, quoted by Michael J. Behe, *Darwin's Black Box: A Biochemical Challenge to Evolution* (New York: The Free Press, 1996), 39.

theory but rather a proven fact. But we also saw in the last chapter that it is impossible to prove macro-evolution, did we not? We most certainly did!

So what does this quote by Darwin have to do with ID? Well, put plainly this quote is directly addressed by one of ID's leading proponents, Michael Behe. In his book *Darwin's Black Box: A Biochemical Challenge to Evolution*, Behe discusses a concept known as irreducible complexity. This is how Dr. Behe defines irreducible complexity:

> "By *irreducibly complex* I mean a system composed of several well-matched, interacting parts that contribute to the basic function, wherein the removal of any one of the parts causes the system to effectively cease functioning. An irreducibly complex system cannot be produced directly (that is, by continuously improving the initial function, which continues to work by the same mechanism) by slight, successive modifications of a precursor system, because any precursor to an irreducibly complex system that is missing a part is by definition nonfunctional. An irreducibly complex biological system, if there is such a thing, would be a powerful challenge to Darwinian evolution."[16]

---

[16] Behe, *Darwin's Black Box*, 39.

Behe goes on to discuss a biochemical organelle known as a bacterial flagellum as evidence of such an irreducibly complex system. Now since we want to avoid getting too scientifically technical here I encourage you to do some research of your own on the bacterial flagellum, perhaps by watching the video mentioned earlier titled *Unlocking the Mystery of Life* or by reading Behe's book that the above quote is from, *Darwin's Black Box*. Personally I think that the bacterial flagellum is absolutely fascinating and a great, albeit microscopic example of irreducible complexity.

Dr. Jobe Martin, in his video series mentioned earlier in this chapter entitled *Incredible Creatures That Defy Evolution*, also gives many, much larger examples of irreducible complexity.[17] For instance, in the first video of the series Dr. Martin discusses the giraffe, the world's tallest animal, and how evolution cannot possibly explain this magnificent creature due to the nature of the length of its neck and how tall it is, because the height of this animal and the length of its neck would cause the animal to die the first time it tried to get a drink from a river or lake, since its heart is so big and powerful that once the head got below the heart the amount of blood that would

---

[17] However, the examples that Dr. Martin gives are various types of animals. I am not insinuating that these animals cannot survive without every single one of their natural parts. What I am arguing here on behalf of irreducible complexity is that these animals have certain basic anatomical and functional requirements that are absolutely necessary for them to function, and to reproduce.

be pumped to the brain would cause the giraffe's brain to explode almost instantly. And so the giraffe would have had to have the many different types of biological features that it currently has that prevent that from happening right from the start, without the possibility of a progression of genetic stages over long periods of time leading up to how its whole system now functions, since if the giraffe's system did not initially accommodate such an issue then giraffes would never have survived so as to be able to evolve to be more functional, for dead giraffes do not evolve.[18] His main argument as a whole for the series is conducive of the nature of irreducible complexity though, for he essentially argues that animals could not have evolved by slow, successive steps, because you have to have a complete animal, including lungs, heart, brain, and so on, all fully functional, all at once, or else you cannot have a living animal, and if the animal is not living then it cannot evolve in the successive steps that are purported by the evolutionists to take place to eventually come up with more evolved living animals, and dead animals cannot produce offspring with new, more beneficial traits either.[19] And so animals are an excellent example, believe it or not, of irreducible complexity, because if the animal, any animal, is not fully intact, at

---

[18] Jobe Martin, *Incredible Creatures That Defy Evolution 1* (Real Productions: 2000), DVD.
[19] I realize that an animal could be born with certain biological defects and still function somewhat, but it still has to have all of the necessary organs and such if it is to live, let alone reproduce.

least to the extent that it can possess life and reproduce, then it not only will not live, but it cannot evolve and pass on its genes to successive generations so that they can evolve. And so this idea of irreducible complexity really is an incredibly powerful concept in the conceptual arsenal of ID proponents.

Something we need to briefly discuss in passing here is the evolutionary concept known as punctuated equilibrium. This is the idea that evolution sometimes, or possibly always, happens in large steps rather than slow successive steps. For example, an animal may evolve into a new species over a few months, years, or a thousand years, instead of over millions of years, albeit with long periods of minimal or no evolving in between. Evolutionists may use this to try and refute the idea of irreducible complexity and simply claim that the parts necessary for the organism to initially survive came about all at once, and then after that the steps were gradual, but this would have to include every type of animal that we currently have, with the exception of variations within species, or within orders. But wait! How is that any different than what the creationists believe, namely that all of the animals appeared fully in-tact from the beginning of their existence? That is a very good question, and one that needs to be addressed (and also one that evolutionists would probably refuse to answer, or at least do their best to avoid), but here is not the place for such questions. The point I want to make clear here is that positing punctuated equilibrium for the evolutionist to the extent necessary to account for the magnitude of irreducible complexity necessary for animal life to exist ultimately puts the evolutionist out of business and puts them on the same plane as those who believe that all major forms of life on earth appeared at essentially the same time, something that scientists generally call the *Cambrian Explosion*.

And so we see that the concept of irreducible complexity not only is a valid scientific concept, but also that it raises serious and at least seemingly insurmountable difficulties for the evolutionist.[20] This shows that ID is not only scientifically valid as a branch of science, but also that it actually has some substantial contributions to give to science in general, and probably most especially biology. Now we are going to look at one more issue regarding ID, namely the widespread study of life systems to enhance our understanding of nanotechnology. After that we will close this chapter with a brief discussion about what the ID proponents are ultimately seeking to accomplish with their innovative concepts, such as specified complexity and irreducible complexity.

Nanotechnology

---

[20] Remember though that even if the evolutionist can somehow overcome this objection, the other objections in this book that have already been made against evolution ultimately make it completely untenable no matter what the evolutionist decides to say or claim.

It should not surprise us, considering how incredibly efficient living cells and microorganisms are, that many of America's top government agencies are continually studying such things to learn how to develop more advanced nanotechnology. Nanotechnology is really just a fancy word for mini-technology, and when I say mini I mean at a molecular and atomic level. This is what ID advocate Ralph Muncaster has to say about the issue:

> "Top Scientists and engineers in the world are now looking at what *works*. They're digging into biochemistry for secrets to design. Yes, *design*.....How serious is the twenty-first century about nanotechnology design? Well, apparently the United States government takes it *very* seriously.
>
> The National Nanotechnology Initiative has set up special agencies to analyze and take advantage of what we're beginning to learn. Included in the governmental groups appointed to analyze nanotechnology are the following:

- The Department of Agriculture
- The Department of Commerce
- The National Institute of Standards and Technology
- The Department of Defense
- The Department of Energy

- The Department of Justice
- The Central Intelligence Agency
- The Department of Transportation
- The Department of the Treasury
- The Department of State
- The Environmental Protection Agency
- The National Aeronautics and Space Administration
- The National Institutes of Health
- The National Regulatory Commission
- The National Science Foundation

> Clearly, the U.S. government takes the design that is exhibited in life systems extremely seriously and is investigating its application (emphasis original)."[21]

We can see here, thanks to Muncaster, that a wide variety of American government agencies take life design very seriously. While this may not necessarily be looking for specified complexity, it nevertheless is an attempt to understand natural design better, and in a way that will further benefit (or inhibit, depending on how it is used) humanity. So why, if our very own government is so seemingly obsessed (due to the nature of how many different agencies are studying these things) with natural design, and by implication Intelligent Design, are they also

---

21 Ralph O. Muncaster, *Dismantling Evolution: Building the Case for Intelligent Design* (Eugene: Harvest House Publishers, 2003), 177-178.

so quick to deny Intelligent Design the right to be taught in our schools? Is that not extremely hypocritical? Indeed it is, and we will talk more about similar issues in the last couple of chapters in this book. For now just note that the study of *natural design* is not something that only the ID proponents are doing, but rather it is being done by many different organizations across America, and presumably in many other countries as well.

So What Exactly Are the ID Proponents Trying To Accomplish?

So what is it that the advocates of and scientists practicing ID are trying to accomplish by making such a big "fuss" about things like specified complexity and irreducible complexity? Well, first off, contrary to what most of the evolutionists are claiming, the ID proponents are not trying to get Creationism taught in the schools again. Geoffrey Simmons says, "Intelligent Design is not synonymous with Creationism."[22] Sure some of the ID advocates are creationists also, but it is the also in that statement that matters here. Some evolutionists are also shameless adulterers no doubt, so should we say that all evolutionists are trying to convince everyone to commit adultery or that it is okay to cheat on your significant other? Absolutely not! Some evolutionists are murderers

---

[22] Geoffrey Simmons, *Billions of Missing Links: A Rational Look at the Mysteries Evolution Can't Explain* (Eugene: Harvest House Publishers, 2007), 21.

also, so should we claim that all evolutionists are trying to make murder legal? Absolutely not! That is absurd. The main issue should remain the main issue, always. The issue that the ID proponents are fighting for is ID first and foremost. That is why we are calling them ID proponents to begin with. Whatever else some of them may be seeking to accomplish is irrelevant with regard to whether or not ID is science, and a so to the issue of whether or not ID should be taught in our schools. The issue most certainly should not be, as we have already discussed, "What is the popular and prevailing opinion of current scientists?" but rather what is the truth, and do we want our children and our citizens to know it, relative to basic scientific inquiry. I think the answer to the latter question should definitely be "yes," for no good parent or citizen thinks it noble or just to be a liar or to hide the truth from those with a right to know it. Of course some might argue that the people in our country do not have a right to know the truth about basic scientific inquiry, and if so I would like to ask those individuals what exactly makes them think that they have a right to decide such a thing, for something like that is akin to being dictatorial, like Stalin, Hitler, and Kim Jung III, and no decent person can honestly say that acting like that is appropriate on any level!

Now although I obviously do not know all, or even most of the ID proponents. I nevertheless am aware of their main intent. Bruce Bickel and Stan Jantz say it best in their book *World Religions and Cults 101* in their chapter discussing the religion of Darwinism (note that this book is NOT in any way calling ID religion): "It is important to note that the scientists supporting Intelligent Design do not oppose Darwinism because it contradicts the Bible or challenges notions of Christianity. For these scientists, it is not about religion (some of them describe themselves as agnostics); it is about the integrity of scientific investigation."[23]

You see, ID proponents ultimately just want people to know that Darwinism does not have all the answers that it claims to have, and that there are other things, such as patterns in nature and irreducibly complex organisms, to be studied also that can lead us to a better, fuller understanding of the world that we live in. It is *NOT* about religion. It *IS* about science, plain and simple.

Conclusion

In conclusion, we have seen in this chapter a list, although certainly not exhaustive, of many of the proponents of ID and their credentials. We have seen that these individuals have the same types of degrees from the same types of universities as the evolutionists, and so we cannot rightfully say that all of these people and what they have to say about science is somehow less credible and not worth listening to. We have also noted that regardless

---

[23] Bruce Bickel and Stan Jantz, *World Religions and Cults 101* (Eugene: Harvest House Publishers, 2002), 246, 248.

of where someone gets their education, the truth is the truth, and that is what we should be concerned with, because that is what matters; and that you do not have to be a scientist to understand science. We also briefly discussed the concepts of specified complexity, irreducible complexity, and we took a quick look at how many different agencies across our nation study life systems and natural design to better understand nanotechnology. Finally, we saw that ID proponents are not looking to push their religious views on anyone, but rather they are simply asserting that Darwinism does not have all the answers, and that there are other methods of doing science that are also beneficial for a better understanding of nature. We must remember what we discussed earlier, that the implications of ID and the explanations regarding what ID proponents discover when doing ID science are irrelevant to what ID actually is, and that ID, fundamentally, can rightfully be classified as *science*. Every major issue has implications that are unsavory for some people, for we saw this very concept at play in our earlier discussion of why the prominence of evolution matters so much. However, you don't see the government banning evolution from the school science classrooms because it implies that there is no god, or that white people are better than black people, or that there is no objective morality and that we should therefore be able to do whatever we want, do you? Of course not! Then why should the fact that ID implies that there may be a designer to our universe and the things in it matter regarding whether or not it should be taught in our schools? Science is science. Everything else is only secondary in relation to the issue. Let us remain, or should I say regain, focus on what matters here, namely that integrity be used and upheld at all levels and areas of academia, *including* science.

Now that we have discussed what ID is we are going to move on to discuss what exactly Young Earth Creationism is and whether or not good science can be done within such a framework of belief. Remember that Darwinism is also a framework of belief, and good science is done within it all the time.

9

What Exactly Is Young Earth Creationism, and Can Young Earth Creationists Do Good Science?

"For the past five years, I have closely followed creationists' literature and have attended lectures and debates on related issues....Based solely on the scientific arguments pro and con, I have been forced to conclude that scientific creationism is not only a viable theory, but that it has achieved parity with (if not superiority over) the normative theory of biological evolution. That this should now be the case is somewhat surprising particularly in view of what most of us were taught in primary and secondary school. In practical terms, the past decade of intense activity by scientific creationists has left most evolutionist professors unwilling to debate the creationist professors. Too many of the evolutionists have been publicly humiliated in such debates by their own lack of erudition and by the weakness of their theory."[1]

- Roger F. Smith (a member of the Western Missouri Affiliate of the American Civil Liberties Union at the time he made this statement in 1980)

The above quotation is from 1980 and it is referring to Young Earth Creationism, which then was synonymous with "scientific Creationism." This quote clearly shows that

---

[1] Paul D. Ackerman's book, *It's A Young World After All: Exciting Evidences for Recent Creation* (Grand Rapids: Baker Book House, 1986), 11-12.

even as far back as over thirty years ago Young Earth Creationism had already become an incredibly viable position to hold in the realm of science, regardless of what the evolutionists were saying.

Now that we have looked at what Intelligent Design is we are going to move on to discuss what exactly Young Earth Creationism (YEC) is, and whether or not YEC proponents can do good science. There are actually an incredible amount of people in America that, according to a number of national polls, still believe the basics of what YEC teaches.[2] There are also, however, an extremely limited number of professional scientists who agree with YEC, let alone that will even admit that YEC proponents are sane in light of their "ridiculous" beliefs about science and the age of the earth and universe. So what are we to do with this dilemma? Well, we already saw an example of what the young earth creationists teach in terms of science in our earlier chapter on the issue of whether or not macro-evolution can be proven, namely that general dating methods for rocks and fossils are flawed. But what are some of the other things that YEC proponents use to base their conclusions about the age of the earth and the universe on? Again, just like the last chapter was not intended to be a scientific defense of ID, this chapter is not intended to be a scientific defense of YEC, although we will

---

[2] The evolutionists do not generally deny this, but rather they simply claim that it is very sad and distressing that people are not more "up to date with the facts."

have to consider a few of the arguments used by the YEC advocates to get a better understanding of what exactly they believe and where they are coming from. We are again, like we did in the last chapter, going to start off by taking a look at some of the more well-known proponents of YEC and their credentials, since there is in general even more hostility toward the YEC view than there is toward ID, and unfortunately much of this hostility comes from within the Christian creationist community.[3] After that we will then move on to discuss some of the major arguments used by the YEC proponents that lead them to their conclusions about the age of the earth and the universe, although we will try to avoid getting too technical for the sake of simplicity, and then we will close the chapter with a brief discussion regarding whether or not young earth creationists can do good science. Along the way we will also be discussing a few prominent issues within the YEC camp that need to be addressed for the sake of the YEC proponents own credibility.

Who Are Some Proponents of Young Earth Creationism, and Are They Credible?

So who are some of the people that espouse the views of YEC, and are they credible? Well, here is a list of some of the more prominent exponents of YEC:[4]

---

[3] This issue will be addressed in the appendix at the end of this book.
[4] This information can also be found on various pages on Wikipedia and other sites and bios on the internet.

- Paul Nelson (mentioned in previous chapter, PhD in Philosophy from the University of Chicago)
- Jeffrey Tomkins (PhD in Genetics from Clemson University)
- James J.S. Johnson (J.D. from the University of North Carolina, which included studies at Duke University, and he has a Th.D.)
- Larry Vardiman (PhD in Atmospheric Science from Colorado State University)
- John D. Morris (B.S. in Civil Engineering from Virginia Tech, PhD in Geological Engineering from the University of Oklahoma)
- Steven A. Austin (PhD in Sedimentary Geology from Penn State University)
- Frank Sherwin (B.A. in biology from Western State College, M.A. in Zoology from the University of Northern Colorado)
- Brian Thomas (B.S. in Biology and M.S. in biotechnology from Steven F. Austin State University)
- Jason Lisle (Bachelor's degree double major in physics and astronomy and a minor in mathematics from Ohio Wesleyan University (summa cum laude), Master's degree and PhD in astrophysics from the University of Colorado)
- Nathaniel Jeanson (PhD from Harvard Medical School in cell and developmental biology)

- Randy J. Guliuzza [B.S. in Engineering from the South Dakota School of Mines and Technology, B.A. in Theology from Moody Bible Institute, M.D. from the University of Minnesota, and a Master's degree in Public Health from Harvard University, and he is also a registered Professional Engineer and a retired Lt. Col. from the U.S. Air Force)
- Jerry Bergman (A.A. in Biology and Behavioral Science from Oakland Community College, Bachelor's degrees from Wayne State University in Sociology, Biology, and Psychology, M.Ed. in Counseling and Psychology. He also studied for a PhD in Measurement and Evaluation with a minor in Psychology from Wayne State. He has an M.A. in Social Psychology from Bowling Green State University, a PhD in Human Biology from Columbia Pacific University (before they lost their accreditation), an M.S. in Biomedical Science from the Medical College of Ohio, a Masters of Public Health degree from the Northwest Ohio Consortium for Public Health, and another M.A. from the Medical College of Ohio. He has also done at least 33 semester hours toward another doctorate through a number of other state approved Universities, and he has over 700 publications in a variety of scientific and popular journals, plus 20 books and monographs. He has also been listed in a number of Who's Who lists in a

number of different fields and subjects, and he is a Member of MENSA (an organization for only the smartest people in the world, namely people with IQ's in the 98th percentile and above)).

I am sure that some of you who read the above list of supporters of YEC were quite stunned by the credentials of these individuals. Some of you probably thought that only theologians and "Bible Thumpers" were YEC proponents, right? Well, unfortunately for the overzealous and incredibly dogmatic individuals who so vehemently oppose YEC, both Christians and non-Christians alike, these individuals and many other YEC advocates just like them are in fact just as qualified to take a scientific stance on such matters as the age of the earth as the mainstream community that believes that the earth is billions of years old. But I digress, as my point here is simply to show that the YEC advocates are just as credible as the old earth creationists and the evolutionists are, and some, like Dr. Bergman, listed above, are even more credentialed than almost all of those who oppose the YEC view. Of course I am not certain that Dr. Bergman would classify himself as a young earth creationist, for when I asked him if he was a young earth creationist he responded that he is a "mature creationist," although he also said that he is certainly not opposed to YEC either. I bet you never thought you'd see a member of MENSA not being opposed to YEC, did you? Truth be told, I qualified to become a member of the

Prometheus Society (top 99.997th percentile of IQs in the world) when I was in elementary school with my IQ test scores, but my parents did not care about that kind of stuff (or maybe they just didn't know about IQ societies), and I was also offered the chance to spend the summer at Duke University and take my SATs during that summer, and possibly start college shortly after that (depending on how I would have done on my SATs) when I was *eleven* years old (in the sixth grade), but my parents said no to that as well. Now please do not misunderstand me here. As I said before, I am not trying to brag on how intelligent I am, for that would be arrogant, and I despise arrogance, even though I at times, like everyone else, fall prey to it. My point here is simply that even people like me, who are smarter than almost everyone on the planet (based on IQ scores) are ID and YEC proponents. That is why I get so disgusted and peeved when evolutionists and other individuals who oppose YEC act like all YEC proponents are idiots. I don't claim to be perfect, but I am most certainly not an idiot, nor are any of the other people listed above who also support the ideas of YEC, and so while it may not be a popular view, it is also not something that is *necessarily* nonsense or unintelligent to believe in and therefore should at least be given a fair shake in the grand scheme of things. We also need to mention here that the proponents of YEC mentioned above, for the most part, got their degrees from the same types of universities as those who oppose YEC, just like with the ID proponents.

Now ultimately it does not matter what school someone gets their degree from in terms of how credible they are, as we saw in the previous chapter on ID. After all I have attended both secular and Christian schools of higher education, but I also had good teachers who taught me to think for myself, and I read constantly on my own time. Anyone can learn anything when presented with the right information in the right way, assuming of course that they have the aptitude for the subject matter at hand, and as we will discuss more later on, the government should not have a right to determine what is the "right information" when it comes to matters of mere opinion and un-provable theories, unless of course such theories can actually (not presumably) be shown to be so unviable that they are simply absurd to even consider, like macro-evolution!

So, we can see that YEC advocates are often just as credentialed as those who oppose their young earth views. Now we are going to take a look at a few of the major arguments that the YEC proponents use in support of their conclusions regarding the age of the earth. While some of their arguments are biblical, of which we will look at only one, many of their arguments are legitimate scientific arguments also. Let us now turn to some of these arguments.

What is the Main Driving Presupposition of YEC?

What is the major presupposition that YEC uses to support its position? To be sure, the major premise used by most young earth creationists to support the idea that the earth is only six to ten thousand years old is that the genealogies in the Bible, depending on which ancient manuscripts are used, if you add up the ages of each successive individual in these genealogies, come out to a sum of between six and ten thousand years from Adam, the first man, to present day when taking into consideration all of the years since the Bible was written and also the most probable life expectancies of each individual mentioned, since there are various ages mentioned in the different ancient texts.[5] Dr. David Dewitt states it this way:

> "Young earth creationists generally insist that the earth is about 6000 years old. This date is derived by using the…..assumptions….
>
> 1. The creation week of Genesis 1 is seven normal – 24 hour days.

---

[5] There are also Muslims who are YEC proponents, and while some of them may base their young earth beliefs on the Bible, it needs to be mentioned here that the Qur'an also makes statements that would lead one to similar conclusions, depending on one's method of interpretation. As for YEC proponents who are neither Christian nor Muslim, I do not know of any of these, but if there are any I would presume that they either base their beliefs on the Bible, the Qur'an, or the scientific evidence that is currently available, some of which we will look at below.

2. The ages of the patriarchs given in Genesis 5 and 11 are reasonably accurate.
3. There are no significant gaps in the genealogies of Genesis 5 and 11."[6]

However, Dr. Dewitt, as a scientist by profession, rather than a theologian, _may_ be unaware of the reality that the genealogies in the Old Testament, were not always or necessarily meant to be taken in a literal chronological progressive sense, for often times only the head of a group or household would be mentioned, and sometimes entire generations would be left out as unimportant, which leaves the possibility that there may very well be significant gaps in the genealogical records of Genesis 5 and 11. Of course Dr. Dewitt may know that already and simply be ignoring or discarding the issue, but as one who studies the Bible, as well as many other things, on a regular basis I cannot in good conscience discard such information. In the words of theologian John J. Davis in his commentary on the book of Genesis,

> ".....at the present time a specific date for the origin of either the earth or man cannot be fixed with certainty. The only way it could, would be to agree, without

---

[6] David Dewitt, _Unraveling The Origins Controversy_ (Lynchburg: Creation Curriculum L.L.C., 2007), 121.

qualification, to one of two rather arbitrary presuppositions. The first is that on which uniformitarian geology is based, that all natural processes have remained essentially unchanged. If this is not granted, then all modern chemical and radiological dating techniques are suspect, and the scientist must seek other means of establishing a time sequence for earth history. The second presupposition is that the genealogies of Genesis 5 and 11 are sequential and unbroken, providing a fully dependable basis for a chronclogical scheme. This writer's view is that, given the objective data currently available, neither presupposition can be granted. The geological record of earth history points to major catastrophes which have sufficiently interrupted natural processes to render any general, unbroken uniformitarianism untenable. And because genealogies in Scripture are notorious for their schematic arrangement and omissions, the second presupposition is equally untenable."[7]

[7] John J. Davis, *Paradise to Prison: Studies in Genesis* (Salem: Sheffield Publishing Company, 1998), 31-32.

I wholeheartedly concur with everything in the above quote, both scientifically and biblically speaking. I couldn't have said it better myse f!

Now although this is not the place for a discussion on the reliability of the Old Testament, it needs to be noted here that some of these manuscripts with varying ages for the individuals in these genealogies are far more reliable than others, and the ones that are most reliable are the ones that are, in general, used for Bible translation. The others are used more for textual criticism purposes, and possibly for historical research purposes.[8]

The main point that needs to be made here is that there is the basic presupposition in YEC that the earth is young because the Bible seems to indicate that it is young (relative to the dates given by modern mainstream scientists), and that this supposition does not come strictly from science. But this should not really be an issue at all anyway since the naturalistic evolutionists also have presuppositions about the earth and the universe that are not based on science, such as that only the natural exists and that the supernatural does not, or that the principle of uniformity has been true throughout all of history.[9] It also

---

[8] For more information on this issue see Dr. Norman Geisler's article, "Old Testament Manuscripts," in his book *Baker Encyclopedia of Christian Apologetics* (Grand Rapids: Baker Academic, 1999), 548-553.
[9] Many, if not all old earth creationists who openly deny evolution also hold to this last presupposition regarding the principle of uniformity being true throughout history

needs to be noted here that while the young earth creationists start with a presupposition that entails a particular view of the Bible, that view does not influence *how* they do science necessarily, but rather it merely influences the types of hypotheses that they make and the outcomes that they expect from their scientific experiments. For instance, if one believes that the earth is only 6,000 years old (regardless of why they believe that), they will naturally expect to find indications in their scientific endeavors that support such a thesis, but they would also, assuming they have integrity, be open to changing their position if they come to find that their thesis, or their presupposition, that the earth is only 6,000 years old, is not supported by the evidence that they are presented with. Now there is a difference between actual evidence that supports an opposing thesis and supposed evidence that someone claims supports an opposing thesis. I have not come in contact with any information from any branch of study so far that demands that I abscond my young earth beliefs, and so I maintain such a position, but not simply because the Bible seems to indicate that the earth is young, but rather also because there is good, solid scientific evidence that supports the belief that the earth is fairly young. There is also a difference between interpreting the Bible through the eyes of science, which I do not condone, and realizing that if something is found to be most likely true that it must necessarily mesh with what the Bible says (if it is actually true), because all truth is God's truth as they say, and none of it, by definition, can contradict, and so if at some point there is evidence available that *actually* shows that the earth is most likely very old, assuming that is even possible at this point,[10] then one would need to possibly rethink his view of the opening chapters of Genesis. That is not to say that one's hermeneutical approach to Scripture should entail an integration of scientific findings per se,[11] for to be

---

[10] The fact that there is a legitimate young earth response to every old earth claim at this point, to my knowledge based on the claims that I have seen and studied, makes this unlikely, although not impossible. However, there is abundant *proof* that the principle of uniformity and most, if not all modern mainstream dating methods, since they all rely on the principle of uniformity, are faulty and unreliable at best, and downright ridiculous at worst, and so, due to that proof, and due to the nature of proof, seeing as how it cannot be falsified since it is by nature a fact and truth, it is, quite frankly, nearly, if not impossible that the current dating methods and the principle of uniformity will ever be truly shown to be reliable, since they have already been proven to be unreliable (there is of course the exception of Carbon 14 dating, but even according to the principle of uniformity Carbon 14 dating is essentially useless after about 57,300 years or so, since at that point, according to the principle of uniformity, there should be essentially no Carbon 14 left in whatever is being dated. See John Morris' *The Young Earth* on page 63). Of course we may find new dating methods, but they must rely on something other than the principle of uniformity, and that also seems highly unlikely to be possible if the method is intended to be precise. Ultimately though, even the dating methods that do not rely on geological uniformity but rather a more general principle of uniformity also cannot be proven, and so they should be utilized with caution and humility. (While science, as we have seen, cannot prove anything to be 100% true due to its inductive nature, it can prove things to be false, such as the modern dating methods and the principle of uniformity discussed above in this footnote).

[11] Robert L. Thomas, *Evangelical Hermeneutics: The Old Versus the*

sure not all truth is equal in either its value or its scope, and we must not allow our interpretive measures to be hindered or affected by secular disciplines. I am simply trying to say that if the earth really is old (purely hypothetically speaking, then the Bible, being the ultimate source of absolute truth, would necessarily have to support such a truth. But like I said, there is good reason to believe that the earth is not old, both on biblical and on scientific grounds, and so I personally choose to believe that it is more on the younger side.

The naturalistic and uniformitarian presuppositions held by the evolutionists mentioned above are founded on faith, and as such they are not extrapolated from science of any type. So the fact that YEC is also founded on certain premises that stem from faith should not be an issue, unless we are going to make it an equally valid issue that the naturalistic evolutionists also base their science beliefs largely on faith, but even then I would argue that the presuppositions in question are ultimately irrelevant to the overall issue of doing science, for everyone has presuppositions, as presuppositions cannot be avoided completely. The proper question is whether or not the presuppositions being used are arbitrary, unfounded presuppositions, such as that Naturalism and Materialism are true, or whether they are founded on some form of evidence.

New (Grand Rapids: Kregel Publications, 2002), 113.

A Recent Global Flood

There is one argument that the YEC advocates tend to use above all the others, at least historically speaking, and that is the appeal to Noah's Flood in the book of Genesis as a worldwide, global flood that literally covered the entire earth. Now many people these days, including many Christians, do not believe that there was ever a global flood, but rather they believe that either the story in the Bible is a myth or that the flood was merely local and not global. However, several things can be said in support of the position that there was a global flood some years back.

Dr. David Dewitt, head of the biology department at Liberty University (mentioned above) says this about Noah's Flood: "...a world-wide global flood would have certainly left *geological*, *biological*, and *historical* evidence (emphasis original)."[12] So what is some of this evidence? I was once watching a lecture by Ken Ham, the President of a YEC organization, *Answers in Genesis*, in which he said that if there was a global flood then one of the things that we would see is billions of dead things buried in rock layers all over the earth. He then proceeded to ask the questions, "and what do we find?" His response was not at all surprising, which was that what we find is billions of dead things buried in rock layers all over the earth. Now of course this is not a sure indication of a global flood, but it

---

[12] Ibid, 83.

is nevertheless something that would certainly be expected if there ever was such a flood, and it just happens to be exactly what we find, as Mr. Ham pointed out in that lecture. Some of this evidence includes fully formed fossils found high up in the mountains of animals and fish that would have lived at either low altitude generally or even in the water, far below the mountain tops. This is an indication that water at some point covered these mountains, which is exactly what the Bible says happened in Noah's Flood.

There have also been many types of animals and fish found that were fossilized while in the process of eating, which is shown by pictures like the one on page 82 of *The Fossil Record*, written by Dr. John Morris and Frank Sherwin, where a fossilized fish is shown with another smaller fish, also fossilized, in the process of being swallowed by the bigger fossilized fish.[13] Other fossils have also been found with similar implications, such as rocks with fossils on them indicating mass burials of fish and/or trilobites, like the one seen on page 54 of the same book, *The Fossil Record*. These and other types of fossils indicate an extremely rapid burial, something that can only be explained by a major catastrophe, such as a global flood. Some might argue that a volcanic eruption could cause such rapid burials in ash or other forms of sediment, but

---

[13] John D. Morris and Frank J. Sherwin, *The Fossil Record: Unearthing Nature's History of Life* (Dallas: Institute of Creation Research, 2010), 82.

remember that the global flood of Noah's day would have almost certainly included massive volcanic eruptions all over the world, as indicated in the opening pages of the book *Footprints in the Ash* by Drs. John Morris and Steven A. Austin.[14]

Another geological/biological evidence in support of a global flood is the Petrified Forest at Yellowstone National Park that we mentioned in our earlier chapter on macro-evolution. This forest is interesting relative to a global flood in that there is evidence that the trees, even though they are in several different layers of rock strata buried on top of each other, are the same age and that they were alive at the same time, which goes against what modern geologists teach regarding different rock strata. Mainstream geologists teach that the rock stratum closest to the bottom was laid first, and that the fossils in it are the oldest, relative to the strata above it. They also teach that each layer of strata represents a different period of time, often separated by many thousands or millions of years per stratum. The mainstream scientists also teach that the Petrified Forest is actually many successive forests that were buried by many successive volcanic eruptions. However, this is what Drs. Morris and Austin[15] have to say

---

[14] John Morris and Steven A. Austin, *Footprints in the Ash: The Explosive Story of Mount St. Helens* (Green Forest: Master Books, 2003), 10-17.
[15] John Morris is a Geological Engineer and Steven A. Austin is a Geologist and Biologist.

about the trees found in the different strata in the Petrified Forest in their book *Footprints in the Ash*:

> "The tree rings of trees found in several consecutive layers at Yellowstone Park were compared. If the trees lived at different times, their tree rings would show entirely different yearly patterns. If the trees lived at the same time and died in the same catastrophic volcanic event, they would retain similar patterns in their tree rings since they lived at the same time. They would record the same history of environment throughout their lives, even if they were eventually buried in different layers.
>
> A recent study of Yellowstone petrified wood did indeed find that the trees retained matching signature patterns in the tree rings. Thus, they lived at the same time and were transported and deposited within different strata by successive mudflows. They did not live in successive forests."[16]

Now the tree rings that are being referred to here in this quote are simply the rings on a tree stump that you see after you cut the tree down. These rings are inside the tree

---

[16] Ibid, 102-103.

and each ring represents a year of growth. Drier weather years will be shown by rings that are thinner, while years that have moister weather are indicated by rings that are thicker.[17] What Morris and Austin are saying here is that trees in several different strata in the Petrified Forest, which the mainstream scientists claim lived at different times in different, successive forests, were found to indicate the same yearly weather patterns by their tree rings, indicating that they lived at the same time. Using tree rings in this way is a widely accepted scientific method of dating trees, even in the mainstream scientific community. The issue here is that if the trees did in fact live at different times in different successive forests, the likelihood that their tree rings would match up so well is very low, making it almost certain that these trees lived at the same time.

How does this relate to a global flood? Well, in the same book, *Footprints in the Ash*, Morris and Austin point out that in Spirit Lake, just North of Mt. St. Helens, trees were deposited in the same way as they are seen in the different strata in the Petrified Forest, namely both horizontal and upright, in various layers of sediment on the bottom of the lake in *just a few years' time*. This was due to the massive amounts of trees that were uprooted in the eruptions of Mt. St. Helens in the early 1980's and that ended up in Spirit Lake. As the sediment (volcanic ash

---

[17] Ibid, 103.

and so on) settled at the bottom of the lake and the trees became water logged and sunk to the bottom they were buried in the sediment at the bottom of the lake.[18] This is an indication that when in a body of water, and when large amounts of sediment are present in the water (which would have been the case in a global flood) trees can be quickly buried in different successive layers of sediment, without the need for long periods of time in between. The idea is that if you take what happened at Mt. St. Helens and you multiply it many, many times over, you would expect the same types of things to take place on a much greater scale in a global flood. This is exactly what we find in the Petrified Forest of Yellowstone, namely what happened at Mt. St. Helens in Spirit Lake on a much greater scale.

Now, one thing that needs to be mentioned here before we continue is that everything we just talked about regarding the dating of the trees, strata, Spirit Lake, and so on, was all *scientific*, and that none of it had anything necessarily to do with the Bible. That is essentially what the YEC scientists do. They look at the Bible and try to figure out what they would expect to find scientifically if it is true, like we explained earlier, and then they go out into the world and see if they actually find such things through *scientific experimentation and observation*. They DO NOT simply look at the Bible and say, "this is what the Bible

---

[18] Ibid, 99.

says, so this is how old the earth is" and then leave it at that,[19] or at least they shouldn't do that, because as we will see later on in this chapter it is not that simple. Yes their basis for their belief that the earth is not very old is based on what the Bible seems to indicate, and the flood is evidence of a recent earth to them because the Bible seems to indicate that the flood was around four or five thousand years ago based on how long after the flood we think Abraham lived (most scholars and archeologists agree that Abraham lived about 2000 BC or so), along with the idea that Adam only lived a few thousand years before the flood, and that the earth only existed for a few days before Adam was created.[20] All of this ties in, in their minds, to their literal interpretation of the first chapter of Genesis, which indicates that the universe and everything in it was created in six literal days. Now of course there are various other ways of interpreting Genesis 1, and the old earth creationists, who are to my knowledge in the majority in the age of creation debate, certainly do not interpret Genesis 1 in a literal way. But that is not the issue here. I am simply trying to point out that the global flood is used to support a young earth by connecting it with a literal interpretation of Genesis 1, the genealogies in the Old Testament, and the date commonly accepted for the life of Abraham, but the science that is done to

---

[19] I am here referring strictly to YEC scientists, not YEC proponents in general.
[20] Remember though that all of these presuppositions are not necessarily true do to the nature of the genealogies in the Bible.

corroborate this information is not the same thing as "Bible thumping" or whatever the mainstream scientists would like to call it. The science, whether it be geology, biology, archeology, or whatever, is still *science*. Again we must remember that the mainstream evolutionists start with the supposition that Naturalism and Materialism are true and then go from there to do their science, which is bad science, since you should actually start with no *predetermining* presuppositions when you do science, but rather, even though you may have certain presuppositions when you start, if the evidence indicates that your presuppositions are wrong then you must abandon them, especially if you are to remain a person of integrity, and we saw in earlier chapters of this book that the naturalistic materialistic evolutionists have an a priori commitment to Naturalism and Materialism, meaning that regardless of where the evidence seems to lead them they will at all costs maintain that no evidence really contradicts their naturalistic, materialistic, or evolutionary beliefs, and so they will by nature (pun intended) throw out any conclusions that do not fit their naturalistic materialistic views. Technically even the young earth creationist is not bound to this problem as the typical evolutionist is. For instance, while some YEC proponents would no doubt refuse to abandon their young earth beliefs even if there was a large body of *legitimate* evidence supporting the idea of a much older earth, I am not one of those people. I do not have an a priori commitment to the idea of a young earth, and the evolutionists are not required to have any a priori commitments either, but many of them do as we have seen. This is why those evolutionists are doing bad science, because they have predetermined sets of boundaries for their conclusions regarding their scientific experimentation, and so often times they end up making conclusions that, while they fit their own personal presuppositional commitments, they are nevertheless incoherent and inappropriate relative to the available facts, such as the conclusions and arguments of Stephen Hawking that we saw in chapter 5 of this book.

It is not the *young earth* that should ultimately be important to the YEC proponents anyway, because the fact of the matter is, while Genesis 1 does *seem* to indicate that it is meant to be taken literally, and while the genealogies in the Old Testament do *seem* to indicate that Adam did not live all that long ago, the Bible does not say how long ago Adam lived, nor is there specific enough information in the Bible to infer such a thing, as we saw earlier in this chapter, and Genesis 1 *can* be translated and interpreted in ways that allow for the earth to be much older than six to ten thousand years, and so we must not be dogmatic about such things, especially to the point of becoming hostile toward our Christian brothers and sisters who think differently than we do on this issue. As I have already mentioned, I have taken college classes on Genesis, and college science classes, and theology classes that discussed the various ways to interpret the creation account of Genesis, and I have read a good amount of other information on this issue, and the fact is that while the earth seems to be young, and while the Bible seems to support that hypothesis, we cannot know *for sure* in this life, and so again, like I just said, we should not be dogmatic about it one way or the other. The real issue should be <u>Creationism, as opposed to Darwinism</u>, not young earth vs. old earth. But I digress, for while this is an important issue, we have discussed it adequately here, and so now we will move on, as the main point of this section is to show some of the evidences used by YEC advocates to support the idea of a recent global flood, which in turn, in their minds, supports the idea of a young earth.

Now, pretty much everyone these days (or so it seems), with the except on of maybe some who are in third world countries, has heard the stories of dinosaurs and how they lived millions and millions of years ago, and also that they all died millions and millions of years ago. But is that really true? Is it necessarily the case, based on the evidence available to us today, that we should believe that dinosaurs lived and died millions and millions of years ago? After all, if they dic then that proves that the earth is far older than the YEC advocates claim. We are going to answer that question in just a moment, at least from the perspective of the YEC proponents, which I happen to be one of, but first I need to address an issue that has really been bugging me lately regarding YEC proponents.

A Pressing Issue That Needs To Be Discussed

I was watching a video last night at my home with my wife where a particular young earth creationist was discussing various issues of bioethics. Now this individual has a B.S. in Horticulture (with first class honors) and a PhD in plant physiology, so he too is a credentialed scientist, and he has been a YEC advocate for some time. In his presentation, as he began with an attack on evolution (which I am perfectly fine with), every time he used a picture analogy, connected to the word "evolution" was the phrase "millions of years." He also talked as if this was a necessary connection throughout his discourse.[21] Now like I said I am an avid supporter of YEC, but this type of thing really ticks me off, because it ultimately makes the young earth creationists look foolish and ignorant to the informed and learned individual of science. What do I mean, and why do I say this? Well, there are several reasons. One, millions or billions of years is not *necessarily* tied to the idea of evolution. Sure the evolutionists believe that the earth and the universe are billions of years old, but so do many, if not most of the creationists these days, and based on my studies it has been that way for quite some time. YEC started gaining scientific headway largely in the twentieth century thanks to the efforts of Dr. Henry Morris,[22] but the prevailing opinion of creationists still

---

[21] I have chosen not to cite this video for the sake of the reputation of the man giving the presentation in it.

[22] Dr. Henry Morris had a B.S. in Civil Engineering from Rice University,

seems to be that the earth and the universe are billions of years old. So, to claim that millions or billions of years is necessarily tied to evolution is to accuse our old earth creationist brothers and sisters of being evolutionists, which none of them, be they true creationists, would either accept or appreciate. Now don't get me wrong. I understand the zeal of the YEC advocates against the millions of years, for were it not for that zeal then why be a YEC advocate at all, right? But that is not the issue. The issue is that the millions of years can be scientifically deduced by means other than evolution, such as the supposed age of stars and how far away they are from us relative to the fact that their light is already present to our sight here on earth; the principle of geologic uniformity used in radiometric dating and the age of rocks and fossils that are deduced from such a principle; many principles evoked from the idea of the big bang, and so on.[23] Granted there are sound ways to "defeat" all of these old earth arguments, one of which we have already seen in this book, but these are nevertheless the means by which the old earth creationists discern that the earth and the universe are billions of years old, and even that Adam

---

Masters in Hydraulics and a PhD in Hydraulic Engineering from the University of Minnesota. He was also the professor and chair of civil engineering at the University of Louisiana at Lafayette, and he taught at Southern Illinois University and the school that is now known as Virginia Tech.

[23] Some of these issues are addressed in the book mentioned earlier by Dr. David Dewitt, *Unraveling The Origins Controversy* (Lynchburg: Creation Curriculum L.L.C., 2007), 129-134.

might have lived many millions of years ago. This does not make them evolutionists though, nor does it make them evil or un-Christian. There are those who are Christians and who also believe in evolution, for I have a good friend who is such a person as that, and that is a different issue altogether, but even they are to be treated with an appropriate level of Christian courtesy and brotherly love, for if you are reading this and you are a Christian I do not need to tell you how our Lord has commanded us to treat all people, especially those who are our family in Christ.

So, one of the reasons for bringing this issue up is because, when we link millions or billions of years necessarily to evolution, it shows our ignorance, since that is, quite simply, not the case. The second reason that I bring this issue up is because in this man's presentation in this video the idea of millions or billions of years was completely irrelevant to his topic of discussion. Many YEC advocates when they speak (based on my experience) are so dead set against the millions of years that they spend just as much, if not more time discussing and arguing against that than they do discussing whatever issue they are actually there to speak about. If we want to look credible and intelligent, and if we want to be taken seriously by those who might seek to oppose us, then we must remain focused on what is important. Personally I no longer think that the age of the earth is an issue that should be given much consideration *in and of itself*. Of course there are certainly serious implications involved with the idea of an earth and a universe that is billions of years old and a species, such as man, that is only millions of years old, or younger, for this makes man seem incredibly insignificant in the grand scheme of things, and as a matter of fact the only thing that is mentioned more than humans in the Bible is God Himself. For instance, there are a total of 79 Hebrew and Greek terms in the Bible that refer to man, woman, or humans in general. The terms for "man" and "woman" alone are translated such over 2400 times in the ESV translation, and the terms for "people" are used a total of well 3027 times throughout the ESV translation of the Bible. That is 5427 times that the terms for only three English words regarding humans are used throughout the Bible, and that does not include terms for "children," people's names, and other terms that would also be related to humanity. To give you an idea of how many that is, there are just over 20 Greek and Hebrew words used in the ESV translation of the Bible translated as "sin" and they are used a total of only 753 times throughout the Bib e, and sin is the biggest and most prominent problem in the entire Bible, for it is the root problem of humanity. The Greek and Hebrew terms in the Bible related to "God" or "god" and pronouns referring to this word are only used 4621 times throughout the entire Bible. Now of course this does not include all of the various terms for God such as "Jesus," "Holy Spirit," "Messiah," and so on, which, when combined with the use of the terms for "God" or "god" brings the total use of such terms to a few hundred more than the three terms used above for humans. But remember that those three terms do not include names of people, terms referring specifically to children, and so on. My point is this, that when we look at how prominent humans are in the total span of redemptive history and how prevalent we are from beginning to end in the Word of God, to claim that we have only been present here on earth and in the universe for only a *small fraction* of the time that it has existed seems absurd, especially when all the way back in the very first chapter of the Bible man and woman are both mentioned as having been created already. Now I know about the progressive creation theories and the day age theories and all of that, and if people want to believe that stuff then that is their prerogative, but I do not now nor have I ever seen any legitimate evidence that even lends us to needing to make such conjectures, whether that evidence be scientific or biblical. So while the issue of the age of the earth and of the universe may be an issue that needs to be discussed for various reasons, the issue should not simply be the age of the earth and the universe, but rather we should be far more concerned with the peripheral (meaning surrounding, not minor) issues involved with such discussions, such as the implications of an extremely old earth and young humans, biblical interpretation methods for Genesis, and so on. The age of the earth and the universe in and of itself simply has no direct bearing on our lives, and so it is not a fundamental, or core issue that much time should ultimately be spent on. The implications of such things, like we just saw, are very important, but to argue over the age of the earth and the universe for its own sake is a waste of valuable time, and time is a precious commodity that one can never regain once it is lost.

The bottom line here is this: I have seen far too many young earth creationists ruin their credibility by making foolish statements and claims; like that millions of years is necessarily tied to Atheism or evolution. I understand that the YEC advocates often think that they are fighting for biblical inerrancy, and I strongly sympathize with such a sentiment and to some extent even agree with it. But the fact of the matter is, whether the YEC proponents want to admit it or not, that there is more than one way to interpret the creation account in Genesis, as well as many, if not all of the other creation passages in the Bible, and ultimately the age of the earth and the age of the universe are not core Christian issues. Even the issue of biblical inerrancy is not really the issue here. Dr. Norman Geisler says it best when he says, "...Scripture is true, just as the author meant it."[24] Although we, myself included, would like there to be an objective standard for knowing without a doubt what each and every biblical author meant in each and every verse of Scripture, the fact is that there is no such standard, and so

---

[24] Norman L. Geisler, *Essential Doctrine Made Easy: Key Christian Beliefs* (Torrance: Rose Publishing, Inc., 2007), 11.

on non-essential issues such as this it is vitally important that we remain calm and sensible. I know Dr. Geisler personally, and I know for a fact that he is an avid supporter of strict biblical inerrancy. He was one of the framers of the Chicago statement on biblical inerrancy in the 1980's, and he also wrote a book titled *Defending Inerrancy: Affirming the Accuracy of Scripture for a New Generation* (2011) that was co-authored by another friend of mine William C. Roach. However, I also know for a fact that Dr. Geisler is a supporter of both the old earth and the young earth position, although he tends to defend the old earth position more often, and he is clearly consistent in his views regarding what the Scriptures allow for regarding one's particular hermeneutical approach. William Roach, the other individual that I mentioned above that co-authored the book on biblical inerrancy in 2011 with Dr. Geisler, told me that he is a YEC advocate, and Dr. R.C. Sproul, who is for all intents and purposes an icon in the Christian theological industry (as is Dr. Geisler) and one of the other original framers of the Chicago statement on biblical inerrancy, while he used to be an old earth advocate, has more recently changed his position and is now a young earth proponent, and so we cannot simply argue that those who believe in an old earth deny the inerrancy of the Bible. Now if we were talking about theistic evolutionists that would be a different story, but even then there is some room for grace on the issue, although evolution as it is today presented cannot rightfully be interlaced with the biblical account of creation, even if we posit that God was the Guider of it. So let us who are in the debate over how old the earth is not get overheated and vehement over issues that are not critical to our way of life as Christians.

I am not one to press unity over core doctrinal issues, but this is not a core doctrinal issue, and the issue at present is over Creationism vs. Evolutionism, two competing worldviews that can both be used as different starting points for doing science. The issue of the need for Christian unity on non-essential matters will be the topic of discussion in the Appendix, so now that we have gotten the issues discussed above cleared up let us return to the issue of dinosaurs and their supposed dying out millions of years ago.

Have Dinosaurs Really Been Dead For Millions of Years?

So what about the dinosaurs? It is a proven fact that they died out millions of years ago right? Well, not so fast! That is not true at all. If you remember back to our earlier discussion on historical science and how historical science is science that cannot be proven, you should be able to easily deduce from that the fact that since all that we have left of dinosaurs are bones and fossils for the most part (we will come back to that last bit in just a minute), the only thing that it seems we can be sure of at this point is that all of the dinosaurs are dead now, but we cannot actually know for sure when they died. But why question something that so many people believe? We have already discussed that issue, and nothing has changed since that discussion. Just because most people, or even all people, believe something that does not make it true. That is a fact, plain and simple. So what evidence is there to suggest that dinosaurs lived more recently than millions of years ago? Several things can be mentioned on that note on behalf of the YEC proponents.

First, there is a film that came out in 2010 called *Dragons or Dinosaurs: Creation or Evolution*, put out by Cloud Ten Pictures. This film is invigorating and incredibly interesting, and if it does not make you seriously reconsider your notions of how long ago dinosaurs died out (assuming you, prior to watching this film, held standard mainstream beliefs regarding this issue) then quite frankly you either were not paying very close attention when you watched the film or you are a closed minded person who lacks integrity. Now do not get me wrong, I am not saying that if you saw this film and it did not persuade you to become a YEC supporter then you lack integrity. What I am saying is that there is enough information in this film that is legitimate evidence and also contrary to popular opinion that it should make you seriously question the popular opinion about how long ago dinosaurs died out.

This film gives examples of various dragon legends throughout the centuries and compares them to what we know about dinosaurs; it shows many different pieces of artwork and cave drawings from around the world with drawings and pictures of what can only legitimately be described as certain types of dinosaurs that we know of, such as the Brontosaurus; it discusses stories that go back only a few hundred years of giant fierce birds (that looked something like a Pterodactyl) that were eating people and animals somewhere in the world (I don't remember which country it was), and how the people of the city had to band together and kill the creatures before they took over the town because it got so bad that they could not even go outside at night for fear of being eaten. This is not a fairy tale or some made up story or myth. This actually happened only a few hundred years ago! This video also tells of stories in certain remote villages of people seeing what could only be described as a small dinosaur, and its description is unlike any animals that are alive today. These stories are also fairly recent stories. The film also makes the point that the term "dinosaur" did not exist until the 1800's, and so it is not surprising that terms like "dragon" or other terms and phrases, including various descriptions of extremely large animals, like that found in the book of Job in the Bible,[25] were used in the past and that no one talked about "dinosaurs" before the 1800's,

---

[25] Most people argue that this description in Job is of an elephant, but Job is very clear in saying that this creature had a tail like a cedar tree. Have you seen an elephant's tail? It is very small, and nothing except dinosaurs in the animal kingdom have ever had tails that are big enough to be described as looking like a cedar tree.

because the word did not exist, but that does not mean that they were not around. With all of this evidence, along with the fact that stories of "dragons" and pictures of dinosaur like creatures dating hundreds to thousands of years ago is such a universal and common occurrence, the main point of the film is to make it clear that there is very good evidence to support the idea that dinosaurs lived very recently, among people. I highly recommend this film to anyone who has not seen it. There is also a corresponding book by the same title that was authored by Darek Isaacs and that came out around the same time as the film.[26]

The second thing that we are going to discuss briefly here regarding dinosaurs is a recent discovery of a particular *Tyrannosaurus Rex* thigh bone that still had actual soft tissue and blood cells in it. Dr. Morris and Mr. Sherwin tell of the incident in the book mentioned earlier in this chapter, *The Fossil Record*:

> "A recent discovery has opened up entire new areas of study. A large tyrannosaur thigh bone, deemed to be seventy million years old, had to be sliced in two for transportation. Surprisingly, inside the bone Dr. Mary Schweitzer found soft tissue that was flexible and pliable. Its hollow blood vessels contained actual blood cells. This

---

[26] Derek Isaacs, *Dragons or Dinosaurs?* (Alachua: Bridge-Logos, 2010).

shocked researchers. Even under ideal circumstances, organic tissue like this is known to break down in a rather short period of time, especially in the presence of water, and these conditions were far from ideal. Even fragile proteins and enzymes were present, indicating that this specimen must have been fairly recently deposited, far more recently than its assigned age. Soft tissue, DNA, and blood cells – as well as 'fresh-looking bone' – had previously been discovered in a number of old fossils, calling into question the standard view of fossil age and the fossilization processes.

The fossil containing soft tissue was entombed in porous sandstone, with the certainty of penetration by groundwater. Since biological material is quickly broken down in the presence of water, it seems inconceivable that the organic material could have avoided decomposition for so long. This raises the possibility that the formation in which it was found is misdated. While not 'proving' a young age for the fossil, the discovery is obviously much more compatible with recent rapid burial and fossilization than with an age of multiplied millions of years. Indeed, it is hard to imagine how soft tissue could have been preserved even the 5,000 years or so since the Flood of Noah's day, when creationists propose the dinosaur was probably buried. This seemingly 'young' fossil, so rapidly deposited that even its soft tissue escaped alteration, fits the biblical scenario and timeframe much better than an old-earth, evolutionary history."[27]

Now before we take a look at this quote I want to first point out again the last sentence of it. If you go back and reread it again you should notice that Morris and Sherwin have intimated yet again that an old earth is necessarily tied to evolution.[28] Now I am not sure whether or not this was on purpose on the part of these two authors, but if it was, as I said before, it is uncalled for. I respect Dr. Morris a great deal and I have spoken to him personally for at least a half an hour on one occasion, and he is no doubt a man of integrity, and so I would assume that he just doesn't realize that this insinuation is out of line. As for Dr. Sherwin, I have also met him but I only spoke to him for a moment and so I do not know much about him, but to give

---

[27] Morris and Sherwin, *The Fossil Record*, 80-83.

[28] It is possible, I suppose, that Morris and Sherwin simply meant to say "old earth" *and* "evolutionary" with this statement rather than necessarily tying them together, but due to the tendency discussed above of YEC advocates to conjoin old earth ideas with evolution, it seems more likely that this tendency was exhibited in this statement by Morris and Sherwin.

him the benefit of the doubt I will assume that he is also a man of integrity who simply does not notice the flaw in such an allusion.

To be sure, as Morris and Sherwin make clear here, this discovery does not prove anything about the age of the dinosaur fossil here described, nor does it give any necessary indication of the age of the earth or universe in general, but it is very indicative of insinuating that the dating of at least this particular fossil of seventy million years is a bit, or rather very ridiculous, for even animal and human bones these days fossilize relatively quickly under normal circumstances, and although this bone was no doubt far bigger, the pictures in Morris and Sherwin's book on page 81 show very clearly that there was still an incredible amount of vibrant color and "life" in the various tissue samples that were in this particular bone, to the point where they almost look like they were taken from an animal that was still living. I don't claim to be a medical expert, but I have taken anatomy classes and physiology classes in college, and I have seen bones broken in half that were not all that old, such as just a few years old or so, and they most certainly do not look like that. Now of course, like the idea that we just alluded to above, a Tyrannosaurus Rex would have been much larger than anything still around today, but still, if bones today can easily become fully fossilized in a short period of time, especially when water is present, why should we believe that it is realistic that a dinosaur bone could honestly have remained partially un-fossilized for anywhere even remotely close to seventy million years? The only way that this becomes possible in anyone's mind is if they accept the preconceived notion that "anything is possible" in the most literal of senses, and quite simply, as a man of intellectual integrity I refuse to accept such an absurd notion as that, as everyone should know that there are many, many things that are just not possible, like humans flying on their own with no mechanical help, or square circles. Even my wife, who's PhD is in Microbiology/Immunology, said that the half-life of blood cells is only about one month, and so the likelihood of blood cells remaining for even a moderate fraction of the time indicated by the dating of this Tyrannosaur bone (seventy million years) is incredibly unlikely, if not downright impossible.

While the idea of dinosaurs living recently is not necessarily indicative of a young earth or a recent creation, it nevertheless undercuts a major establishment in the idea of an old earth, namely the idea that these massive creatures must have died out many millions of years ago, for if that is true then a young earth is out of the question, but YEC scientists such as Morris and Sherwin, as well as the individuals responsible for the *Dragons or Dinosaurs* film, have made it clear that the death of all dinosaurs millions of years ago is not a proposition that we need to, or are required to accept.

Can YEC Proponents Do Good Science?

So, we have looked at some of the types of arguments that the YEC advocates use to support their young earth views. To be sure they are not all scientific arguments, but does that mean that they cannot do good science? I would argue that they can do just as good of science as those who oppose the young earth position. Sure they start with a presupposition that is religious and not scientific, but so do the evolutionists, as we have already seen. Of course, the issue of whether the earth is young or old is only one aspect of science, but YEC advocates do not *merely* focus on that issue, even if everything, or almost everything that they do relative to science is for the expressed aim of providing further evidence that the earth is young. After all, many evolutionists do everything that they do relative to science for the expressed purpose of trying to prove that evolution is true, do they not? So why should the YEC scientists be looked down upon for doing so when many of the mainstream scientists are doing the exact same thing, just with a different aim in mind? The fact is that they shouldn't!

There are YEC scientists that are astronomers, biologists, psychologists, philosophers, botanists, medical doctors, as well as many other types of scientists, and there is no good reason why we should assume or assert that they cannot do just as good of science as anyone else.

Whether or not they agree or disagree with a particular position on the age of the earth, the age of fossils, the age of rocks, or whatever, is completely irrelevant to whether or not they can do good science, as all of these issues are matters of how one interprets the available data, and there are multiple ways to go about such interpretations, several of which are at least seemingly valid. The fact is that they can do and are doing good science. It is absolutely a shame that organizations like ICR (Institute for Creation Research) that are headed by intelligent, knowledgeable, and capable people like Dr. John Morris are refused accreditation for their institutions of higher learning simply because they do not conform to the status quo. Since when was America the type of country that determined, by law, who is right and who is wrong on matters of science, *especially matters of science that deal with historical science that cannot be proven in the first place*?[29] I don't know about you, but I am deeply troubled by such censorship in a country that claims to be the "Land of the Free." I am not claiming that anyone should be able to teach whatever they want, but I am claiming that no one should have the right to dictate what should and should not be allowed to count as good science simply based on whether or not they agree or disagree with it without any harden fast proof or real authentic evidence

---

[29] Obviously America has been that way for some time now, but it should not be that way and I would imagine it was not the intention of our founding fathers either.

on their side. The fact that this is happening all across our country disturbs me greatly, and it should disturb you as well. We will talk about this issue more in chapter 11 of this book, but for now I simply want to make the point again that YEC proponents can do, in general, just as good of science as non-YEC proponents can.

Conclusion

In conclusion, we have looked at some of the specific advocates of YEC and their credentials, and we have seen that they are just as well educated in general as those who oppose YEC. We have looked at several of the major arguments that the YEC proponents use to support their views, and we have seen that they can also do science just as well as those who are not young earth creationists. We have also seen that YEC proponents need to be sure and make correct connections between various ideas, and that they need to stop insisting that an old earth is necessarily tied to evolution, because it is not. It is important that we note here that the main issue is not who is right and who is wrong in the science industry, although that is an issue that needs to be discussed also. The main issue here is that we all need to realize that neither macro-evolution nor Creationism, and neither old earth nor young earth can be proven, and they can each legitimately contribute to the field of scientific *theory* and investigation, regardless of which one is right. Now that we have taken a closer look at both Intelligent Design and

Young Earth Creationism we need to take a look at some of the major differences between the two, which is what we are going to do in the next chapter.

10

What Are Some of the Differences Between Intelligent Design and Young Earth Creationism?

"Differences between the ID movement and the earlier "scientific creationism" movement include several things. First, ID as such is not committed to teaching a specific view of the earth. The question is simply left open. Second, ID makes no affirmation about the nature or scope of Noah's flood. Third, ID advocates make no identification of the cause of Intelligent Design with God or any supernatural being. Fourth, they oppose laws mandating the teaching of creation or Intelligent Design. Rather, they concentrate on showing that some intelligent cause (whether inside or outside the universe) is a more likely cause for first life and new life forms."[1]

- *Dr. Norman Geisler in his book Creation & the Courts*

First off, due to the fact that we just discussed ID and YEC in our previous two chapters, this chapter will be shorter than most of the previous chapters in this book, as many of the differences between ID and YEC can be found

---

[1] Norman Geisler, *Creation & the Courts: Eighty Years of Conflict in the Classroom and the Courtroom* (Wheaton: Crossway Books, 2007), 26.

simply by going back and comparing the previous two chapters, and so for the sake of not being repetitive we will not be going back over the information from the previous two chapters in this chapter, with a few minor exceptions.

Now, as we noted in the last chapter (one of the "minor exceptions" mentioned above), "scientific creationism" was merely a synonym for YEC some years back when the term was more widely used, and so we can see here in the above opening quote to this chapter that there are several major differences between ID and YEC. But before we go any further it needs to be stated that the above quote, as well as the discussion that will follow below, is not intended to exude the idea that ID proponents cannot or do not hold to some of the same views as the YEC proponents do, for as we have already seen, some ID advocates are also YEC exponents, such as philosopher of science Paul Nelson. However, we need to keep in mind that the purpose of this chapter is to show, while individuals may very well be both ID and YEC advocates, that ID and YEC are, nevertheless, not the same thing, and so they should be viewed based on their own respective concepts and merits when discussing each of them. What particular individuals believe is an entirely different subject matter altogether. So, in this chapter we are going to discuss some of the specific differences between ID and YEC and their proponents, and we are also going to briefly discuss some of the issues that are involved with some of these differences. Let's get to it.

The Issue of the Age of the Earth

One of the most obvious differences between ID and YEC, as the opening quote in this chapter by Dr. Geisler pointed out, is that YEC advocates, by definition, take a precise position on the age of the earth, and ID does not, as it is merely a particular type of science, namely the study of patterns in nature. We can see here right from the start that a definitive position, or even a tentative position, on the age of the earth cannot be reconciled with what ID is according to its definition, just like when we saw that evolution, based on its definition, cannot rightly be classified as science (or in other words evolution cannot be reconciled with the definition of science), because the two ideas simply do not mix. To be sure, people that advocate ID can and sometimes do have a particular position that they take regarding the age of the earth, but that position is completely separate from ID itself, just like all scientists in all scientific fields can take various positions on different issues and yet their views on those various issues are separate from the particular science that they are involved in. For instance, a geologist, let's call her Nancy, can decide that she believes that it is okay to commit an abortion, but, ethical discussions aside, that has no direct bearing on her ability to do geology, let alone on geology itself. And so in the same way ID proponents can believe in a young, or an old earth and yet that has no direct bearing on their ability to do ID science, let alone on ID itself, because ID is by definition science, not a worldview, and so ultimately it stands a one, apart from all of the beliefs of those who do ID science, and it also stands apart from the beliefs of all of those who agree with the doing of such science (but do not actually do it themselves), let alone the beliefs of those who do not agree with it. In other words, ID is ID, and the beliefs of those who either do ID science or agree with ID science are separate from ID itself, and we should all keep that very important distinction in mind.

Why do I go through the trouble of explaining this distinction to you in this particular section of this chapter, you might ask? Because I want to make it very clear to you that what I said at the start of this section, viz. that ID does not take a particular position on the age of the earth, is true regardless of whether its proponents do or not. One of the problems with our culture these days is that people have, in our postmodern society, decided to remove, or at least attempt to remove, categories from our thinking, because categories are supposedly "oppressive" and so there is this idea that we have to subvert even the very distinctions and definitions that make things what they are (categorically speaking, not essentially speaking). This is a big part of why we are having so much trouble in our culture understanding things. No one seems to be able to understand anything except for the simple and the mundane these days, because no one, for the most part, wants to be told any form of "objective truth," but instead everyone wants to decide on their own terms what is what. Now of course this is not the place for an exposition on postmodernism, subjectivism, or relativism, although I would no doubt enjoy that greatly. My point here is simply that if we are to remain coherent in our thinking, and if we are to have integrity in our dealings with various systems of thought, ideas, and so on, including the various sciences, then we must necessarily retain the definitions that make them what they are (again categorically speaking), as well as the distinctions that allow us to distinguish between the more subtle nuances of various terms and concepts. In short, ID is not identical to what its proponents believe, but rather it is wholly separate, and that distinction is vital.

So, ID does not take a position on the age of the earth, even though many of its proponents do. Now what about the YEC advocates? Obviously, as we have already pointed out, YEC advocates necessarily take the position that the earth is young, relative to the millions and billions of years that those who oppose their view believe in. That is pretty cut and dry, for they are not called *young earth creationists* for nothing.

The reality that ID does not take a position on Noah's flood can be subsumed under the above discussion, for again even though many ID advocates may take a position on the flood of Noah's day, that has no essential impact on what ID is. Also, Noah's flood is certainly not a "pattern of nature", as it was a one-time global event and so there is no reason for it to be studied under the science of ID anyway.

The Cause of Design/Creation

Another difference that is alluded to in the above quote by Dr. Geisler is that ID makes no claim about who or what the "Intelligent Designer" is. Sure many ID proponents believe that this Designer is the Judeo-Christian God of the Bible, but some of them also believe that it is Allah (who is NOT the same as the Judeo-Christian God of the Bible); some could believe that the Designer is Brahma, the creator god of the Hindus, and so on. And of course an ID proponent could even be an atheist and simply believe that life and this world was designed by aliens, which of course, assuming they are also a naturalist, in their minds, would have arisen from purely natural causes. Of course the atheist then runs into the problem of where everything initially came from, namely who designed and brought into existence the nature itself, for nothing can create itself, because then it would have to exist before it exists, which is absurd and a contradiction, and so there must be something outside of nature that started it all (i.e. brought everything into existence). Nature also cannot be eternal, but we discussed that in an earlier chapter. Nevertheless, my point here is that ID itself, as a science, makes no claim as to who or what the

Intelligent Designer is, even if its proponents do. The previous statement is where I differ from Dr. Geisler on this issue, for I do not think it is fair to argue, like Geisler has in the above quote, that just because ID advocates do not make any public claim as to who or what this Intelligent Designer is, that they do not make any claim at all about who or what it is.[2] After all, I know very well that Dr. Geisler himself, a passionate defender of ID, would most certainly claim, if you asked him (especially while not in a public setting) who this Intelligent Designer is, that it is in fact the Judeo-Christian God of the Bible, as would I, and so that is why I am claiming that a better way to say it is simply that the science of ID itself makes no claim to who or what the Intelligent Designer is, regardless of whether its proponents do or not.[3]

Now, as for the YEC advocates, to my knowledge, although I could be wrong, all YEC advocates are either Muslims or Christians, and so they all take a strong stand on whom the Creator is, or so it would seem. This seems like another obvious difference between ID and YEC, but in actuality, although YEC advocates generally claim that the creator is either the God of the Bible or Allah, YEC itself does not require that a specific creator be named any more than ID requires that a specific designer be named,

---

[2] At least that seems to be what Geisler is implying by his statement that ID advocates make no such claim.

[3] Let me be clear here that I mean no disrespect to Dr. Geisler on this or any other issue. I respect him greatly. I just disagree with him on this point.

and so this is actually a similarity and not a difference between ID and YEC. Also, contrary to the claim of Dr. Geisler,[4] we have seen that both ID and YEC proponents, although maybe not publicly, do in fact generally make some sort of claim as to who the designer, or the creator, is, even if it be a private claim. These similarities however are trivial at best and they most certainly do not in any way indicate that ID and YEC are anywhere close to the same thing.

Laws Mandating Teaching

This particular difference is a little less clear than the first one we mentioned above, and it is a difference between ID and YEC *proponents*, rather than ID and YEC themselves. Again I think that Dr. Geisler here in the above quote has overstated this point, even if unintentionally, which is most likely the case. While many ID proponents in the public square are hesitant to demand that ID be taught in our schools, nevertheless it is not right to say that no ID proponent is arguing that we should mandate that ID be taught in the schools, for after all that is one of the reasons that I am writing this book to you, in hopes that you would see the need for alternatives to Darwinian theory, such as ID, to be taught in our schools. I would also imagine that this is the same reason, in part at least, that Dr. Geisler wrote his book *Creation & the Courts* that the quote at the beginning of this chapter was taken from.

---

[4] Again I mean no disrespect to Dr. Geisler.

There has recently been several votes in various states across the U.S. as to whether or not we should allow ID to be taught in the public schools, and I know for a fact that at least some of the votes were on the "yes" side even though the vote was predominantly "no" in each case, and so those people are publicly claiming that we should make laws to have ID taught in the schools. Of course these people are politicians and not scientists, but that is beside the point. It is no doubt because of the Dover case ruling of 2005, mentioned in an earlier chapter of this book, where U.S. District Court Judge John Jones III ruled that "Intelligent Design and creation its progenitor are not science and should not be taught in...science classes, and...Intelligent Design and other forms of creation are essentially religious and are, therefore, a violation of the First Amendment establishment clause,"[5] that most ID and creation proponents alike are weary of speaking out and saying that ID and Creationism need to be taught in the classroom. However, I have successfully shown in this book already that ID is in fact science, unlike the Dover case claimed, and I have also successfully shown that evolution is religion and not science, and this particular chapter is here to show that ID is not something that necessarily stems from Creationism, for in fact one can study the patterns of nature as an atheist, a Christian, a Muslim, a Buddhist, a Hndu, and so on. One does not have to believe in anything supernatural to study patterns in

_____

[5] Ibid, 29-30.

nature, which is all that ID is, namely the study of patterns in nature. So, I see no reason why we shouldn't *demand* that ID, at least the basics of it, viz. the study of patterns in nature and how they are often times very uncommon compared to what we find in instances of observed natural processes, such as when erosion takes place, be taught in our school science classes, for there is absolutely nothing at all in that statement that indicates any type of religion or anything other than the systematic study of nature (i.e. science). And I think that many of the current ID advocates would tend to agree with me on that, whether they would choose to admit it publicly or not.

YEC advocates, on the other hand, do tend to be more vocal about wanting Creationism taught in the schools, or so it seems, for after all it was required to be taught in the schools for many generations until the twentieth century. And so I do see a bit of a difference in the fact that the YEC proponents seem to tend to be more active publicly in asserting that YEC should be taught in the schools. But, as we saw, YEC, in the form that we have discussed it, is necessarily tied to religion, and more specifically to the Bible (or possibly the Qur'an for the Muslims), and so it may well be something that should not be taught in the school science classes.[6] However, the

---

[6] That is, YEC as a Christian or a Muslim Movement is necessarily tied to a religion and so it should not be taught in science class. I suppose that it is possible for someone to be non-religious and yet still believe in a young earth, for I see no contradiction there.

contributions to science that the YEC scientists have made, such as the RATE (Radioisotopes and the Age of the Earth) project, where a group of YEC scientists discovered serious flaws in radioisotope dating due to the actuality of non-uniform rates of decay of various elements because of diverse environmental circumstances,[7] as well as the other contributions mentioned n earlier chapters of this book, *should* be taught in our science classes, as they are legitimate scientific findings and our citizens, be they children or adults, have a right to know about these things, and that Darwinism has many serious flaws, which has been pointed out in many different books, lectures, and films over the last several decades. This means that while the worldview of YEC seems to have no place in the science classroom, there are many scientific ideas and issues that have resulted from YEC scientists' work that nevertheless fit quite nicely in the science classroom.

So, we have seen that ID proponents tend to be squeamish about publicly declaring that we should be teaching at least the basic tenets of ID in the public science classrooms across the country. We have also seen that I am not one of those people and that I firmly assert that we should in fact be teaching aspects of ID, as I stated above, in science classrooms, both public and private, for it is actual science, not religion. And we have seen that YEC advocates tend to be at least a little more vocal about the

---

[7] John Morris, *The Young Earth* (Green Forest: Master Books, 2007), 49, 53, 55-70.

idea of teaching YEC in the science classroom, and yet YEC itself is a worldview and so it most likely should not be taught in the science classrooms. Now, having said that, I also do not think that Darwinism should be taught in the science classrooms, since it too is a worldview rather than science, as we saw earlier in this book. However, since there is probably no chance that the U.S. is going to take Darwinism out of the science classrooms any time soon, I think it is only fair that YEC be taught alongside it as well, but even if that does not happen we at least need to be making our children and young adults, by way of the science classroom, aware of the various contributions that YEC scientists have made to the various fields of science that they have done their research in. Although the difference between ID and YEC that their proponents are not equally active in speaking on behalf of their respective views publicly, relative to getting them into the science classrooms, is a minor difference, it is nevertheless a difference. It is true that ID proponents in general seem to be more comfortable just being allowed to do ID science, although there are some of them that are more vocal than others, such as the politicians, but it is also clear that both ID and YEC advocates want to be heard, and that they both are tired of the Darwinian nonsense that has pervaded our culture for well over a hundred years now.

The Main Emphasis of ID and YEC

There is one final difference that I would like to point out here in this chapter between ID and YEC, and that is what each one puts its main emphasis on. This should again be a fairly obvious distinction, but since so many people want to argue that ID and YEC are the same thing just with different names, this final peculiarity between the two needs mention. First we will briefly discuss what the main emphasis of ID is on, and then we will in turn briefly discuss the main emphasis of YEC.

What is the main emphasis of ID? Well, ultimately the main emphasis of ID and its advocates is that there are patterns in nature that do not seem to conform to the general conditions that we find under purely natural circumstances. As you can see, the only reason that this would be a problem for anyone is if they have an a priori commitment to Naturalism. Let me just say that it is anyone's prerogative to have such a commitment, but the only place that such a commitment should be expressed outwardly, let alone forcefully (relative to the demands of the curriculum, not in an abusive sense), is in a philosophy class about Naturalism. Any other venue besides where the expressed purpose of the class is to be the study and understanding of Naturalism is not the place for an a priori commitment to Naturalism to be expressed (relative to classroom settings), other than to simply tell one's students what your particular position is on that issue. The science classroom is most certainly not the place for teachers to brainwash their students with a government approved worldview, wh ch is essentially what our public science classrooms are for these days. I will talk more about this in our next chapter on the importance of a free thinking society. For now my point is merely that the main emphasis mentioned above of ID, namely that there are patterns in nature that do not seem to conform to the general conditions that we find under purely natural circumstances, should afford absolutely no problem for the public, or private, science classroom. It is not necessarily religious in any way, nor is it in and of itself anything other than a general statement about reality.

So what is the ma n emphasis of YEC? Simply put, the biggest and most prominent emphasis that YEC advocates put on any particular subject is the matter of the age of the earth, namely that the earth is young (normally six to ten thousand years old), and also that it was created and not the result of random chance. The first part of this emphasis should pose no direct problem for the public or private classrooms other than the fact that it challenges the status quo, which, to be honest, is often times a good thing because it makes us reconsider our preconceived notions anc actually think about the issues at hand. The second part of the emphasis, however, is in fact an implication that cannot be tested or studied by science, at least not the hard sciences. Sure we can come up with different syllogisms and philosophical arguments that support the idea of everything being created, and we can gather all kinds of evidence throughout nature insinuating that there is a Creator and that he/she/it created the universe and everything in it, but the fact of the matter is that we cannot prove that an immaterial entity (which is what the YEC advocates appeal to for their Creator) exists through science, and so the creation aspect of YEC seems to be an area that is best left to the religion or philosophy classroom and not to the science classroom. That leads me to something that I just don't understand. Why are the creationists so dead set on getting their theories about creation taught in the science classrooms? Are there not other subjects being taught in school? And why can't we create a new subject for students called "Origins Theory" or even "The History of Origins Theory" where various theories of the origin of life are taught from a neutral perspective, where the students are allowed to decide for themselves which origin theory they want to believe. Granted they should choose which to believe based on merit and not their own personal biases, or the biases of the teacher or anyone else either for that matter. Nevertheless, the main emphasis of YEC is two-fold, namely that the earth was created by a supernatural entity and that the earth is quite young relative to modern day scientific dating trends.

So, we see here also that there is yet another major difference between the driving emphases of ID and YEC. To recapitulate, ID emphasizes that there are patterns in nature that do not seem to conform to the general conditions that we find under purely natural circumstances, and YEC (Christian or Muslim) emphasizes that the earth was created by a supernatural entity and that the earth is quite young relative to modern day scientific dating trends. These emphases are absolutely nothing alike, and to be even more specific on this matter the ID emphasis is something that can be shown to be objectively true, and the YEC emphases, neither of them, can be shown to be objectively true, because one of them deals with supernaturalism (i.e. the invisible, un-scientifically testable realm) and the other deals with historical science, which we have also seen cannot be proven. And so we see that ID and YEC have completely different emphases.

Conclusion

In conclusion, we have seen several major differences between ID and YEC. We have seen that ID itself takes no position on the age of the earth, even though its proponents might (because it is strictly science), but also that YEC by definition does. We have also seen that ID makes no claim to who or what the Intelligent Designer is, again even though its proponents might, and that YEC also does not demand a name for the Creator, which is in fact a similarity between the two, albeit a minute and insignificant one. We have seen that YEC proponents tend to be more publicly vocal about demanding that YEC be taught in the science classrooms than the ID proponents tend to be about demanding that

ID be taught in the science classrooms, but we also need to note that that is not necessarily the case, and that ID proponents need to take a stand for such an issue because ID is in fact science and not religion, and so it does have a rightful place in the science classrooms. And finally we saw that the main emphases for ID and YEC are completely different. Therefore, along with the other differences that can be seen by going back through the previous two chapters of this book and comparing ID and YEC, it is extremely obvious that ID is not something that stems necessarily from Creationism, and that ID is a science all of its own and it should be treated as such, and that it is very, very different from YEC, which has also made some contributions to science that have their rightful place in the science classroom, albeit possibly detached from the Creationism aspect of YEC. It is important to remember that there are other venues besides the science classroom to get things that are not science into the schools, and in front of our children. We must not try to force religion into the science classroom, for that is what religion class is for (or social studies, etc.).

11

The Importance of a Free Thinking Society

"We should realize that in our country we enjoy freedom of religion, not freedom from religion."[1]

- *Dr. Norman Geisler (emphasis original)*

There are many things that we enjoy as Americans that many, many other nations do not. For instance, at least to some extent, we have the right to an education. Many countries are so poor that the majority of the children do not ever get to go to school. This is something that most of us obviously take for granted. Another example is that we, as Americans, are essentially allowed to have as many children, regardless of gender, as we want. I met an elderly man when I lived at Ft. Benning, GA who was a WW1, WW2, and Korean War veteran (infantry), whose father had had four different wives and a total of over thirty children. He had so many kids that he named several of them the same thing, just with different middle names. We didn't believe him, so he pulled out his

---

[1] Norman Geisler, *Creation & the Courts: Eighty Years of Conflict in the Classroom and the Courtroom* (Wheaton: Crossway Books, 2007), 15.

father's obituary from the newspaper from when he had died and showed it to us. It was a whole article about his dad and all of his wives and kids. Also, the pastor of our church has 12 children, many of them girls, and another family in our church has 8 children, several of them girls. Now although these examples are a bit extreme, especially the one from Ft. Benning, and granted this kind of thing doesn't happen much anymore, this is something that China has denied their citizens the right to do for some time now. As I am writing this there is a man who has gone into hiding in China because his wife was forced to abort their seven-month old daughter[2] because they already had one daughter in their family.[3] The husband is in hiding because he decided to speak to the foreign media about the incident.[4] This is not just a violation of a human's right to give birth to a child made in the image of God.[5] This also

---

[2] The government kidnapped his wife and gave her a shot to kill the baby, and soon after that she gave birth to a dead baby.

[3] It is generally illegal to have more than one daughter in China. This has led to a wide variety of problems in China, including the selling of "black market" female babies and young children to various sex trafficking organizations around the world.

[4] Malcom Moore, "Husband of Chinese woman forced to have abortion 'disappears,'" The Telegraph, http://www.telegraph.co.uk/news/worldnews/asia/china/9356169/Husband-of-Chinese-woman-forced-to-have-abortion-disappears.html (accessed June 29, 2012).

[5] I would like to add here that anyone who wants a quick synopsis of what the image of God is all about without getting incredibly deep into theology should check out Christian rapper Pro's song titled "In His Image," featuring Christian rapper Andy Mineo, formerly known as c-lite, as there is a lot of great general theology in this song regarding the image of God, and it also sounds great.

shows that these people do not have the right to freedom of speech, which is something else that we, in general, benefit from here in the United States. So we have many rights in America that other countries do not offer their citizens, but what about our right to think whatever we want to think as American citizens? No, this right is not listed in the constitution, and in and of itself it seems quite intuitive that we do in fact have this right, but is that really the case, and if so then what exactly should that right consist of? In this chapter we are going to take a brief look at a couple of different scenarios in which this fundamental human right is either diminished or abolished under certain conditions, and we will evaluate such situations to determine whether they seem appropriate or not based on the basic understanding that all humans have certain inherent rights as human beings created by God in His image as stated in Genesis 1:26-28. We will then proceed to discuss how these situations apply to our current cultural condition in America, followed then by a quick look at what exactly I mean by a "Free Thinking Society," and why it is vitally important that we be such a society if we are to remain, or rather return to being the nation that we were founded as, namely the "Land of the Free." We will then end with a summary of our discussion in this chapter and some closing remarks, as usual.

What Does a Lack of Free Thought Look Like In a Society?

A classic example of what it looks like for a nation's citizens to lack the right to think (this includes the right to believe also)[6] for themselves is in the case of nations in which Islam has mandated Sharia law for its citizens. When this is the case, the law is essentially that everyone in the country must adhere to the moral and religious preferences and codes of Islam. This can be played out in several different ways.

One way that this scenario can exemplify the citizens of such a nation not having the right to think for themselves is by the fact that the citizens of these countries (and there are countries in the world like this today) are being required to adopt Islam as their official religion. This is because "Islam rejects the secular Western idea of the separation of religion and morality from the duties of the state."[7] These people must also not only adopt Islam as their religion, but they must practice the various traditions of Islam, and they must adhere to the various stipulations of Islam. For example, women are

---

[6] I realize that thoughts and beliefs are different, but thoughts are fundamental to beliefs, as we cannot form beliefs without first thinking about whatever it is that we are considering whether or not to believe, with the exception of certain specific beliefs, such as moral beliefs, that are self-evident Also, we do not act based on our thoughts, but rather most fundamentally we act based on our beliefs (when we act rationally that is), and so for our purposes here we will be including belief as being entailed in the issue of "free thinking."

[7] Irving Hexham, *Understanding World Religions: An Interdisciplinary Approach* (Grand Rapids: Zondervan, 2011), 426.

required to be incredibly submissive to their husbands, to the extent that, according to Mary Jo Sharp, women are required to subject themselves to being severely physically abused by their husbands if they upset them, even if just for not satisfying their husband sexually.[8] I realize that our nation, and more especially our president Barrack Hussein Obama, in recent years has gone to great lengths to establish the idea that Islam is a peaceful religion, but in fact this is merely a facade with regard to what Islam is really like. In reality Islam is an incredibly violent, totalitarian religion that seeks to convert the whole world, by force if necessary.[9] There are of course various sects of Islam, and some of them are more lenient than others, but the primary purpose of Islam is to see to it that the whole world comes to worship their God, Allah, the same way they do. According to Muslim scholar Afif A. Tabbarah, "Islam is a continuous strife to establish the Word of God [as seen primarily in the Qur'an] on earth, to establish the proper system which brings content and bliss to mankind."[10] When following this line of thinking it becomes clear that when Islam claims to be a peaceful religion, in fact what that means is that if the whole world would worship Allah

---

[8] Mary Jo Sharp, "Did Muhammad Believe in Women's Rights?" in *Christian Research Journal* 34, no.5 (2011): 21-27.

[9] For an excellent, thorough, and objective analysis of Islam, its leaders, and its teachings see Norman Geisler and Abdul Saleeb, *Answering Islam: The Crescent in Light of the Cross, Updated and Revised Edition* (Grand Rapids: Baker Books, 2002).

[10] Afif A. Tabbarah, *The Spirit of Islam* (Beirut: Dar-El-Ilm Lilmalayin, 1978), quoted by Irving Hexham, *Understanding World Religions*, 427.

and embrace Islam wholeheartedly, then there would be peace on earth, and since Muslims are called to convert the "unbelievers" to Islam, even by force if necessary, then they are "striving for peace," for like we just said, if everyone is Muslim then there will be worldwide peace according to Islam. That is, however, not what Obama and others are touting regarding the "peaceful" aspects of Islam.

Sura 2: 190-195 (regardless of what language you read it in)[11] tells us about how the Muslims are to go about seeking to convert people, and more specifically this passage is about "Jihad," which is often misinterpreted as meaning "holy war," but which is more accurately understood by Muslims to mean a "spiritual struggle."[12] This spiritual struggle is the fundamental call of all Muslims, whether they adhere to it or not, for it is part of their holy book and the commands therein and therefore part of their sacred responsibilities as Muslims. This passage from the Qur'an reads:

---

[11] I say this only because Muslims claim that only the Arabic versions of the Qur'an truly teach what the Muslims believe, and that if you cannot read Arabic then you cannot really understand Islam. This is, however, a ridiculous claim that there is absolutely no way to legitimately support, as Arabic is a language that can clearly and effectively be translated into other languages, and so there is no reason that we should assume that non-Arabic translations of the Qur'an cannot also intimate what the Arabic text says. Even though the Muslims claim that Arabic is the language of god (Allah), this is a completely arbitrary claim that there is absolutely no way to prove, plain and simple.

[12] Ibid, 428.

190 Fight in the way of Allah against those who fight against you, but begin not hostilities. Lo! Allah loveth not the aggressors.

191 And slay them wherever ye find them, and drive them out of the places whence they drove you out, for persecution is worse than slaughter. And fight not with them at the Inviolable Place of Worship until they first attack you there, but if they attack you (there) then slay them. Such is the reward of disbelievers.

192 But if they desist, then lo! Allah is Forgiving, Merciful.

193 And fight them until persecution is no more, and religion is for Allah. But if they desist, then let there be no hostility except against wrong-doers.

194 The forbidden month for the forbidden month, and forbidden things in retaliation. And one who attacketh you, attack him in like manner as he attacked you. Observe your duty to Allah, and know that Allah is with those who ward off (evil).

195 Spend your wealth for the cause of
Allah, and be not cast by your own hands to
ruin; and do good Lo! Allah loveth the
beneficent.

Some people have argued that this passage clearly shows
that Muslims are called on to merely be defensive fighters
for the cause of Allah, only responding to attacks that the
nonbelievers foist upon them. But in actuality this is a
misleading assertion, for n actuality true, committed
Muslims realize that the form of "attack" that Muhammad
was referring to when he wrote this passage (albeit in their
minds as Allah told him to) was simply the act of refusing
to convert to Islam, or in other words devout Muslims who
are truly committed to the "cause of Allah" as set forth in
the Qur'an see that anytime someone refuses to convert
to Islam they are in essence attacking Islam and the cause
of Allah, and so they are worthy of being "slain wherever
they are found." Also, the section in verse 194 that says to
"attack him in like manner as he attacked you" is not
meant to be taken in a literal sense, in that if someone
merely refuses to believe and convert to Islam then the
Muslim is in like manner to merely refuse to believe the
other person's religion and convert to it, but rather the
manner in which the Muslim is attacked by the unbeliever
is of a capital criminal nature, the most heinous offense
possible to a Muslim, namely to refuse to convert to Islam.
In other words the "unbeliever" attacks the Muslim, by
refusing to convert, in the most serious nature possible,

and so in turn the Muslim is to respond in the most serious nature possible, viz. by slaying him/her wherever they are.

So we see here that the *true* Muslims are those who slay (kill) the unbelievers and who physically fight for the "cause of Allah." Muslim Sayyid Abul A'la Mawdudi confirms this in his book *Let Us Be Muslims*, published by the Islamic Foundation, when he tells other Muslims,

> "You have no alternative but to exert your utmost strength to make it [the kingdom of God as the Muslims see it] prevail on earth: you must either establish it or give your lives in this struggle....if you passively accept to live under another Din [a law other than Muslim law], you are not a believer in the true sense of the term."[13]

The point that I am making here is not primarily religious, but rather the point is that in countries under Muslim rule of the truest kind, people are required to either convert or die. This is not just a lack of freedom of religion, but it is a lack of the right to think what one wants without the fear of serious consequences if they disagree with those in charge. Obviously no one can truly deny

---

[13] Sayyid Abul A'la Mawdudi, *Let Us Be Muslims* (Leicester: Islamic Fountdation, 1991), 287-288, quoted by Irving Hexham, *Understanding World Religions*, 427.

someone the right to think what they want, but people can most certainly be bullied to conform their thinking to that of others to the point where they may feel as though they have no choice in the matter. In the case of *true* Islam, both unbelievers and believers alike are ultimately required to think as Muhammad thought, or else die. Of course this is to some extent how most religions work, namely that you either agree with a certain set of statutes or you cannot be a part of that religion, but this is something far more serious. Most religions, besides Islam, do not threaten people with death if they refuse to convert to that religion. Sure the Crusades were similar situations, but, as we saw earlier, anyone who knows anything about Christianity and what the Bible teaches knows that the Bible never teaches Christians to kill anyone for any reason, but rather most often times we are instead called to simply subject ourselves to injustice, without compromising our faith and beliefs of course.[14] The Crusades were rather the result of what happens when a religious organization is taken over by corrupt individuals who thrive off of manipulating other people for their own gain. So again the point here is that Islamic countries under true Muslim rule are a prime example of a society that does not have the right to "think freely," and more specifically Islam is a prime example of a religion

---

[14] This is not to say that there is no place in the Christian religion for justifiable war, revolution, or military service, because there is, but those are other issues entirely.

that denies people the right to think whatever they want, unless of course everyone on earth wanted to think and believe that what the Muslims teach is true, which is obviously not the case.

The Catholic Church and the Pope

Now before I address this issue allow me to say that I mean no offense to anyone who reads this that happens to be Catholic. There are many doctrines that the Catholic church holds to that myself and other evangelicals agree with wholeheartedly. This particular issue has more to do with church administration and leadership than it does with church doctrine, although there are certainly some doctrinal issues at work here.

The Catholic church is another great example of a society where people do not have the right to believe whatever they want *without the fear of serious consequences.* Allow me to explain.

The pope, for all intents and purposes, has become somewhat of a god on this planet since the beginning of the inception of the Catholic church many centuries ago.[15]

---

[15] The things that I am going to say here are either common knowledge to anyone who knows how the Catholic church is run, and it is all readily available information for anyone who cares to research it. These things are a matter of record, and so, as common and available knowledge, I will not, for the most part, be citing any sources here. This is merely information that I have acquired through my various theology and religion college and seminary courses. I also will not be capitalizing the word "church" after the word "Catholic," as I

Of course he would most assuredly not admit to this, for to do so would be tantamount to blasphemy and idolatry of the highest of sorts. Nevertheless, the fact that he enjoys the complete and total religious rule over roughly one billion people worldwide, that he lives in a sovereign state over which he rules, and that if anyone in the church questions him, regardless of their stature in the church, they risk possible immediate and complete excommunication, which in the Catholic church includes being permanently (although not always permanently if proper repentance is allowed and made) cut off from all sacraments (forms of grace), henceforth condemning them to eternal damnation in Hell. It is this last fact, namely the eternal condemnation of those who oppose the pope, that we are now briefly going to discuss.

The pope is essentially "in charge" of the entire Catholic church and every member of it, as stated above. This may not seem like a big deal, but think about the fact that the Catholic church claims to represent the Christian

---

am not referring to the universal Catholic Church that consists of all believers everywhere but rather the Catholic church that sits under the papal system which finds its home at Vatican City in Rome, Italy. I realize that "Catholic Church" is the proper way to type the name of the organization, but I do not feel that it is right to give credence to a false church by giving it a capital letter in this sense, and I do not want to confuse the papal Catholic church with the universal Catholic Church, and so I will refrain from such capitalization. Again I mean no offense by this, but as a conservative evangelical I must stick to my own religious convictions on such matters, and I do not believe, with good and sound reason, that the Catholic church is part of the universal Church, although some of its members may be.

Church and community. Now, without going into detailed church history as to how the pope came to be viewed as infallible "ex cathedra,"[16]

let us briefly discuss what it means for someone within the Catholic church to challenge the authority of the pope, or any of the teachings of the Catholic church, or their traditions for that matter.

This challenge might play out in the Catholic community, for instance, by a particular bishop in the Catholic church deciding that he no longer believes that Mary is divine.[17] The Papacy, as well as the Catholic church in general, clearly affirms that Mary is in fact divine, and so

---

[16] I actually read a theological journal article in undergraduate school that pointed out that in fact, although it is claimed that the pope's words are only infallible "ex cathedra," it is actually the case that no one is ever allowed to even question the pope about anything that he says with the intention of insinuating that he might be wrong. This is, quite simply, unacceptable in the Catholic church regardless of who you are. You simply do not question the words of the pope, regardless of where he has spoken them from, for if he were allowed to be questioned on anything that he said then it might be presumed that he could somehow be wrong, and then the entire Catholic enterprise would collapse, for it all hangs on the infallibility of the pope ultimately. See Louis Weil, "The Papacy: An Obstacle or a Sign for Christian Unity?" in *International Journal for the Study of the Christian Church* 4, no. 1 (2004) 6-20.

[17] This is, whether people realize it or not, something that the Catholic church believes. They do not just pray to her, but rather they truly believe that she is, in some sense, divine. See the chapter "Was Mary the Mother of God" in Erwin Lutzer, *The Doctrines That Divide: A Fresh Look at the Historical Doctrines That Separate Christians* (Grand Rapids: Kregel, 1998), 51-65.

this bishop would have to answer for his lack of belief in this very key doctrine of the Catholic church. Ultimately, unless he decides to begin believing again that Mary is divine he will lose his bishopric and will be excommunicated from the Catholic church if he decides to stand fast by his new conviction. Now of course today the Catholic church seems to be a little less forthcoming with excommunicating people as many people at that point would simply decide to leave the church on their own, and possibly change their religion (perhaps to Christianity)[18]. But assuming that this bishop wishes to remain a bishop and, instead of just keeping this belief to himself, also begins teaching this newfound belief to his congregation, this would most certainly be unacceptable to the pope and the Catholic church and they would be "forced" to excommunicate him for what they would see as a heretical belief.

Now it would not have to be a bishop or a cardinal or any leader in the church necessarily for excommunication to take place. It could be anyone at any

---

[18] Catholicism is not a denomination of Christianity due to certain major doctrinal differences from the Christian faith, most especially the issue of the Catholics believing that Mary is divine and the fact that they pray to her, and also because they believe in a works based faith and salvation. This is why I refer to Christianity and Catholicism as separate religions. Ultimately Catholicism would most accurately be defined as a cult derived from Christianity, such as Mormonism and the Jehovah's Witness religion, even though it has its roots in the Christian church and shares much of the same history as the Christian church.

Catholic congregation in the world under papal rule. Any one of the roughly one billion Catholics in the world could be excommunicated at any given time, ultimately for any reason that involved them disagreeing with the pope, church doctrine, and so on. Now to be sure, in non-Catholic churches, including evangelical churches, if the church is run in a biblical manner, anyone who does not hold to the essential doctrines of the faith would be encouraged to do so, and certainly under the rules of church discipline as presented in the Bible there are reasons for "excommunicating" people from the church. Even Paul in 1 Corinthians, chapter 5, commanded the church at Corinth to kick someone out of the church for "living with" (a euphemism for sleeping with) his step mother, and in the same chapter he commanded the church not to even eat with sexually immoral people. But the major difference between the Catholic church and the evangelical church is that we do not claim that the person who is excommunicated is cut off from salvation. We simply remove them from the church so as not to corrupt other members with their excessive moral and spiritual disobedience and admonish them to repent and return to the church and to God. If they are truly Christians then they will retain their salvation even if removed from the church (John 10:27-30), although they will be on God's "bad side" and will certainly miss out on more and more great blessings the longer they remain in their un-confessed sin. . The Catholic church, on the other hand, due to the fact that they believe that the continual partaking of the various sacraments is required for sustained eternal salvation, when they excommunicate someone for, say, disagreeing with church doctrine or the pope, is in essence condemning that person to Hell (at least as far as they believe). I personally do not understand how this is much different, other than the method used (physical murder versus "damnation"), from what we discussed above regarding the Muslims. Both the Catholic church and the true Muslims take formal and active steps in purposefully condemning people to Hell (although the Muslims also physically kill people) strictly for disagreeing with them. This is not the same as the evangelical Christian telling someone that if they do not believe what the Bible says then they are damned to Hell, because for the Catholic church they believe and assert that they, the church and the pope themselves, have the power to damn people to Hell (albeit by the authority of God as they see it), and the Muslims are taking it upon themselves (albeit by the authority of Allah and the Prophet as they see it) to take the lives of the "unbelievers," thereby condemning them to eternal punishment. But the evangelical Christian believes that it is only God Himself who has the authority to condemn someone to Hell, and we most certainly do not believe that we are supposed to kill people who do not believe what the Bible says and who refuse to convert to Christianity. In this way we can see that the Catholic community, on doctrinal and moral issues that the

Catholic church or the pope has spoken on, does not have the "right" to think whatever they wish without fearing not only being excommunicated from their community of friends and family, but also eternal damnation by way of the decree of *man*, namely the pope and the Catholic church. In the evangelical community one is not kicked out of the church merely for what one thinks, but rather church discipline is based on actions, whether that be teaching other people in the church heresy or by acting in an immoral manner and refusing to repent of those actions. But the Catholics, as well as the Muslims, deny people the right to ever think what they want (assuming they find out what those who disagree with them think) without living in fear, or living at all (whether eternally or physically).

Now, before we continue on to the remainder of this chapter let me say that the above statements were not intended to "bash" either Muslims themselves or the Catholic church, but rather they were merely to show some examples of societies in which people do not have the right to think whatever they want (again assuming other people know what they are thinking by some means). I do however need to clarify that I firmly stand by all the above statements that I have made in this chapter so far, as they are the result of both my personal and academic studying and they are all true statements. The Catholic church and Islam were simply the two best examples I could think of for the topic that we are discussing in this chapter. I did not choose to go out of my way to purposefully "pick on" these religions, but rather they were just the two that I chose to use do to their relevance to the topic at hand. I am sure that there are other societies in the word that also do not allow people to think whatever they want, and they would also be examples of my point in this chapter, but as I have not studied those other societies, I cannot rightfully engage in discussing them, as that would lack integrity.

Ultimately, these two societies, namely the Catholic church and Islam, do not respect the inherent right that all humans have to think and believe whatever they want. Now, let me clarify my previous statement here. As a Christian I firmly believe that every person on this planet has a responsibility to agree with everything that the Bible actually says (false interpretations aside) to the extent that they understand it, whether they want to or not, and so in that sense I do not believe that humans have a right to think and believe whatever they want (we will discuss this more below). However, several things make my view on this different from the societies discussed above. First, that is my own personal conviction, and even many evangelical Christians do not agree with my above assertion that we are all required to believe every single thing that the Bible teaches (again all false interpretations aside), especially to be true Christians, and I do not condone censoring people or killing them just for disagreeing with me. I am also aware that everyone does not understand everything in the Bible, nor does anyone understand absolutely all of it, as there is certainly much mystery within the pages of Scripture, and no one can truly ascent to something that they do not understand other than to the extent that they do in fact understand it.[19] For instance, I do not fully understand the resurrection of Christ, but there is enough evidence for its reality that I understand that it is most likely true, and so to that extent I understand and accept it as true. I am sure that some people might disagree with me on this, but I do not believe that anyone can truly accept anything that they do not honestly understand, meaning that, any truth proposition can only actually be accepted as truth to the extent that the one who is accepting it understands it, for it is impossible to intellectually and rationally ascent to something that is not rational to (not understood by) the mind. And so I think that we are all, as humans, required to accept everything in the Bible as truth to the extent that we understand it, because it is the true and living Word of God, and because God created us to serve, worship, and glorify Him, which includes accepting what He says as

---

[19] This is why I said above that people should believe the Bible to the extent that they understand it. I am simply saying that it is impossible to ascent intellectually to and therefore truly accept something that we do not understand. So my point is that we cannot accept what we do not understand, because that which we don't understand is unintelligible to us, and that which is unintelligible is unknowable and ultimately unacceptable to the mind to the extent that it is unintelligible, no matter how much we want to believe something. Even faith can only be had regarding that which one understands to the extent that one understands it.

truth, as He is the author and embodiment of truth. But I am not planning or willing to kill or excommunicate anyone who disagrees with me (or with what the Bible says), especially simply for thinking differently than I do, nor do I expect anyone to actually be able to accept 100% of what is in the Bible to be absolutely true, for as we just saw it is impossible for anyone to do so, because it is impossible to truly understand everything that the Bible teaches, due to the fact that there are certain mysteries in it that cannot be understood by our human minds. After all, God said that His ways and thoughts are different than our ways and thoughts (Isa. 55:8). The Muslims, while they may try to help you understand the Qur'an and its teachings initially, the most avid and the truest Muslims ultimately will expect you to accept them and follow them anyway. The Catholics expect you to strive to understand the Bible and the teachings of the church as much as possible, but they too ultimately expect you to accept their teachings and believe them whether you understand and agree with them or not, for the pope and the church in their minds have the final say, especially in all matters of faith and religion.

The second thing that distinguishes my view on this issue from that of the Catholic church and Islam is that the authority that I am claiming (namely biblical authority) requires universal subjection is *God*, not man, and the Bible can and has in fact been proven beyond a *reasonable doubt* to be the very Word of God, Creator of the universe and everything in it.[20] The Muslims cannot live up to the challenge of proving that either the Hadith or the Qur'an is in any way, shape, or form the actual words of God.[21] Also, the Catholic church cannot in any way prove that they, including the pope, have any authority other than what the Bible itself says, which is the same authority that any Christian can claim regarding their teachings that are Scriptural.[22]

---

[20] There is an incredible array of books, videos, and lectures available from a very wide variety of sources to confirm this statement. All you have to do is look for them and you will find that I am telling you the truth on this matter.

[21] Again see the book *Answering Islam: The Crescent in Light of the Cross* by Norman Geisler and Abdul Saleeb (to prove my point about Muslims not allowing people to think what they want, this name, Abdul Saleeb, is a pseudonym, a fake name used by a former devout Muslim who helped Dr. Geisler write this book. He used a fake name because he fears that if the Muslims find out who he is and that he has turned against them and their religion, then they will find him and kill him and his family, which, based on how Muslim society operates, is a very legitimate concern) for a comprehensive and extremely scholarly critique of Muhammad, Islam, and the Qur'an.

[22] There is nothing in the Bible that says that Peter was the first pope, or that Jesus built the church on Peter. This is in contrast to the claims of the Papacy that the pope and the Catholic church get their authority based on Matthew 15:18. Mathew 16:18, where Jesus tells Peter that "Upon this rock I will build my church," when viewed in the Greek, actually shows very clearly that Jesus does not use the same word for "rock," *petros* (which refers to a pebble or small stone), which he uses in the first part of the verse to refer to Peter, in the second part of the verse, but rather the word *petra*, which more accurately refers to a very large stone, or a cornerstone. Jesus, in this passage, when He said "this rock," was referring to Peter's previous confession that Jesus is the Christ. Jesus was claiming that He would build the church on Himself, that He, Jesus, would be the cornerstone

Do These Examples Provide Appropriate Rights To Individuals Based On Genesis 1:26-28?

Genesis 1:26-28 says,

"Then God said, 'Let us make man in our image, after our likeness. And let them have dominion over the fish of the sea and over the birds of the heavens and over the livestock and over all the earth and over every creeping thing that creeps on the earth.' So God created man in his own image, in the image of God he created him; male and female he created them. And God blessed them. And God said to them, 'Be fruitful and multiply and fill the earth and subdue it, and have dominion over the fish of the sea and over the birds of the heavens and over every living thing that moves on the earth (ESV).'"

Now we can see several things here. First, we see that God created both male and female in His image.[23] This means

---

on which the church would be built. This is confirmed in passages like 1 Corinthians 3:11 where Paul indicates that Jesus Christ is the foundation of the church. The other arguments used by the Catholic church to affirm the legitimacy of the papal system can also easily be explained as being false, and so there is no good reason to except papal or Catholic ecclesiastical authority on any grounds.

[23] What exactly the image of God consists of is a hotly debated topic. For our purposes here we are strictly concerned with the fact that, as all humans are created in the image of God, we all share an equal level

that male and female are created equal, both in the image of God, for there is absolutely no indication anywhere in the text that insinuates that the man or the woman received less or more of this image of God than did the other, for to be sure even thinking about this passage in that way is to misunderstand the passage altogether.[24] This passage states that male and female[25] were created *in* the image of God, not *with* the image of God, and therefore it is a part of how we are made or formed to be human that is in view here. It is, shall I say, not that we have had some part of God's image *added* to us, but rather this image, namely the image of God, is *part of* us, that is, it is part of our very essence as human beings. And so it is not that some part of the image of God has been attached to us as humans, something that could possibly fall off of us, something that we could lose, or something that could be somehow diminished in some way, as if it were somehow some sort of semi-external thing to our existence as humans, but rather it is in fact part of the very foundation of our existence as humans; it is not part of who we are, but rather it is part of what we are. This fact is why all humans, from the moment at which they become a

---

of inherent dignity and intrinsic value and self-worth, regardless of race, social status, gender, or any other possible factor.

[24] The roles of the different sexes is another issue for another book, and it does not concern us here.

[25] "Male and female" here is ultimately a euphemism for all of humanity, as we are made up of two sexes, male and female. However this passage is also referring specifically to the first man and woman, Adam and Eve.

human (notice I did not use the term "person"), which is at conception, have a certain and undeniable dignity and self-worth in and of themselves, given to them by God, that should be recognized by all other humans, as we are all equally created in God's image, for remember that the phrase "male and female" in Genesis 1:26-28 ultimately entails every single person.

The other thing that can be seen in this passage is that the same commands were given to both the man and the women (i.e. all humans). "God said to *them*" indicates very clearly that He was speaking equally to both the male and the female. But what is it that He says to them? Ultimately He commands them to have dominion over the earth and to subdue it, or, put another way, He put humans, all humans, in charge of the world.[26] This is important to our discussion in this chapter because it shows that not only are all humans equally created in the image of God, but from the very beginning of our existence as humans we have all essentially been given the same responsibility, dominion, and prominence over the earth.

These two points above regarding Genesis 1:26-28 are a clear indication that we all as humans essentially

---

[26] I am aware that there are some people, such as one of my seminary professors, that disagree with me here that this passage was a command by God, but that is another argument for another book, and the linguistic and textual evidence does in fact support my position that this is a command, even on a basic reading of the text.

have the same fundamental rights. Now of course the right to have dominion over the earth and subdue it is just that, to have dominion over the earth and subdue it, and it says nothing of the right to "free thinking." However, the above points show us that, and read *carefully* here because this is my main point in this chapter – we are all created equal; none of us is any better than the other inherently; and so no human has the right to demand specifics from any other human regarding the inner most things of our being, which includes our thoughts. That authority is strictly reserved for the One who is above every human in worth, character, and dominion; the One who created us in His image, namely the Lord God Himself. In other words, God has the right to demand that we think, talk, act, believe......a certain way, because He has *inherent authority* over us, but no human has such authority, as we are all, as we just saw above, created equal, with the same *bestowed authority* (Rom. 13:1), and none of us is inherently better or higher than any other of us, and so no human has the right to tell anyone else what to think, as thinking is an act of the soul, an inward act that cannot be controlled by another human, unlike physical acts where, although they may have their genesis in the mind (soul) they are nevertheless outward actions, and therefore they have the ability to affect others *directly*.[27] What we write,

---

[27] The government and various people in positions of authority sometimes have a right to prohibit certain actions from people, such as murder, theft, and so on, but no human has a right to prohibit or demand specific thoughts or beliefs from any other humans for the

say, or do has the power to change other people's lives, but even then there are limits to man's inherent authority to "protect" himself and his fellow man. It is one thing to put someone in jail for committing murder, it is quite another to murder someone simply for disagreeing with you, no matter how strong the disagreement may be or what it is about. Now we do not have the time or the space here to get into a discussion of ethics any deeper than we already have. My point is simply that it is not the right of humanity to dictate what other humans think or believe, regardless of whether or not they express those beliefs to others. It is true that we should not necessarily allow strangers to teach moral principles that conflict with our own to our children,[23] or similar such things, but all humans have a right to think whatever they want *within the realm of humanity*; when God enters the picture that is a different story, like we said, because He is *inherently and infinitely more valuable and authoritative* than any and all humans, and so He, and He alone, has the right to tell us what to think and believe.

So, to wrap up this section, according to Genesis 1:26-28 and the principles set forth above that flow from this passage, cases in which people are not allowed, by other humans, to think and believe whatever they want in

---

reasons discussed above, and even the authority that the government has is given to them by God (Rom. 13:1)

[28] This is why worldview teaching should be expelled from our school systems as much as possible (unless of course it is just an overview, such as in philosophy class), as that is the responsibility of the parents.

and of themselves are a clear violation of inherent human rights, for no human has the *inherent authority* to require anything from any other human with regards to our innermost workings, which include our thoughts, since they in and of themselves are in the soul and are therefore personal and not public (even if expressed outwardly), and no man has the *inherent authority* necessary to give another human the authority to do so either, because God has not given any man such authority, and only He possesses the *inherent authority* required to bestow such authority on man (again, Rom. 13:1), which He has not given to any human. Now this does not mean of course that anyone should be allowed to *teach* anyone else anything that they want, as stated above, for to allow someone with authority over others to teach falsity as truth (as the evolutionists do) is the height of foolishness and stupidity. But, as far as thinking and believing goes, people have an inherent right, relative to other humans, to think and believe whatever they want, and this right should not be violated.

How All of This Applies To America

Now, how does all of this apply specifically to America as it currently stands? Well, in America, at least over the last eighty-seven years (since 1925 starting with the Scopes trial) there has been a serious battle going on in our nation's school systems regarding what should and should not be taught in our schools regarding science.

However, it has not been confined to the schools, but rather the national media, as well as pretty much every major museum (especially the Smithsonian), and even National Geographic and every major publication that deals with science, have all become deeply and passionately biased regarding what is and is not science (i.e. evolution reigns supreme), and therefore what should and should not be considered worthy of being taught as science in the public school systems.

A documentary came out in 2008 titled *Expelled: No Intelligence Allowed* (mentioned earlier) in which Ben Stein did a thorough investigation into our nations academic realm regarding the issue of teaching, or even mentioning, Intelligent Design in public jobs and teaching positions. If you have not seen the video I strongly encourage you to get a copy and watch it, as it will open your eyes to much of the reason that I am writing this book to you. Throughout the video Ben Stein shows us many different people who have been "removed" from their various public positions for either teaching Intelligent Design or even for simply mentioning that it might be a viable option worth looking into further. But it gets worse! These people, especially the college professors and school teachers, are not just fired from their positions merely for disagreeing with the status quo (remember the free thinking issue, this is where it comes in), but they are most often times blacklisted to the point where they cannot find a job anywhere in the country at any public schools or universities, at least a job in their field that pays well and carries prestige. Even at many supposedly Christian schools and universities (such as Baylor University) this is happening all across our country. Of course the schools and institutions that fire these people and then blacklist them deny that these people were "let go" because of anything to do with ID, but anyone who has a brain and can see the truth for what it is knows better than that. Jerry Bergman, the gentleman that I mentioned in our earlier chapter regarding YEC who has roughly nine college degrees and is working on another one, and who is also a member of MENSA, is one prime example of someone who has experienced this type of situation. In 1978 Bergman was denied tenure at Bowling Green because of his affiliation with the creation movement. When Bergman filed suit against the school claiming that they discriminated against him for religious reasons the court dismissed his case, as if they did not even want to listen to what he had to say, because, quite simply, the courts in this country are also primarily run by people who are *die hard evolutionists*. If you don't believe that statement then just read Dr. Norman Geisler's book *Creation & the Courts: Eighty Years of Conflict in the Classroom and the Courtroom* (2007) that I have mentioned numerous times already in this book. This kind of thing is happening all over the country, like I said above, and although lately there have been attempts to change such issues by various state governments, these attempts have all been to no avail.

I have already made my case in previous chapters regarding ID, YEC, and evolution, and we have already seen that ID *is* in fact science, and that evolution is in fact *not* science. So what does all of this have to do with a free thinking society? Well, put plainly, anyone who questions evolution openly in this country (i.e. thinks that it might not be true and mentions it to someone else who disagrees with them) in the public arena, and sometimes even in private, is forced out of their job and is then often times unable to get a job anywhere else, at least as far as public teachers and museum administrators are concerned. Jerry Bergman is by definition one of the smartest people in the world (that is why he is able to be a member of MENSA) and he is not even able to find a teaching position where he is allowed to teach graduate students in a public university, because you must get tenure before you can teach graduate classes and he cannot get tenured because of his creationist beliefs. This man, with all of his credentials, has taught at a COMMUNITY COLLEGE for over 17 years and he has also been an *instructor* of science, but never has he held a decent graduate teaching position (to my knowledge). He should be the head of a major scientific department at a major university! Now yes we did see earlier that Creationism, like Darwinism, is a worldview and not science, but why should Bergman's believing in (thinking it is true) Creationism, unless he is openly teaching his students that Creationism is a fact and that evolution is completely false, make any difference at all as to his level of competency as a professor? The fact of the matter is that it shouldn't, and it doesn't, at least not to myself and anyone else with a decent level of common sense regarding such matters.

The bottom line here is that our country has become a ***big bully*** to anyone who disagrees with them, especially on matters of "science." In the academic world, if you want to get and keep a good teaching job and be respected in your field (often times even in non-scientific fields) then you are essentially *required* to think and believe what the status quo is, which in the case of science is that evolution is a proven fact and that ID and YEC are stupid, foolish, and that anyone that thinks that they might even possibly be true is a total imbecile. How is this any different than what the pope and the Catholics do to their congregations when they disagree with them, or what the Muslims do to those who refuse to convert (minus the actual act of killing of course)? The fact is that it is the exact same thing (minus the particulars). In the realm of science, teachers and academicians are not allowed to think and believe whatever they want in this country, plain and simple. Sure they can technically think and believe what they choose, but if they must live in fear of being exiled, ostracized, and expelled from academia for their thoughts and beliefs, that is not freedom in the truest sense of the term, and, to be honest, it is not really freedom at all. This is essentially what I mean when I refer to a "free thinking society," namely a society where people can live their lives and think whatever they want without fearing repercussions from other humans merely for what they think. In the realm of science, it would be one thing if evolution was indeed a proven fact (which it never will or even can be as we have seen) and if ID and YEC had in fact been proven as definitely false, but that is simply not the case, nor can it be, for evolution and YEC deal with historical science, and so they cannot be proven or disproven completely, and ID is actually science, and so the very categories of *truth* and *falsity* are not even coherent categories to consider placing ID in, for science is the systematic study of nature by definition, which is something that someone does, not a truth proposition or a worldview. Hence, there s no legitimate reason for anyone to not be allowed to think or believe that evolution, or YEC, is possibly false, or that ID should be taught in the public science classrooms, without fearing the loss of a present or future job in public academia. Private academic institutions are allowed to require what their teachers believe and teach (within certain parameters), because they are privately funded.[29] The reason that public institutions are different is because they

---

[29] However, this is still far different from our above examples of the Catholic church and Islam, for in this instance we are merely talking about not being able to get a job at a private school if one does not adhere to the particular stipulations of the private institution. We are not talking about being condemned to death or damnation for one's beliefs.

are not allowed to uphold or demand any specific religious convictions for or from their faculty, and as we have seen evolution is in fact properly classified as a religion, so that is their first mistake relative to our discussion here. The second reason that public academia does not have the right to discriminate against people that work for them on the basis of their beliefs and thoughts is that public schools do not make their professors sign a "statement of faith" describing the particular thoughts and beliefs that the professors must agree with to teach there (nor are public schools allowed to require such a thing), and so it should be illegal to terminate someone's contract or job at a public school or deny them tenure based on their beliefs, thoughts, or convictions, even if they do mention them to their students in the classroom setting.[30] The same goes for the public museum industry, for public museums have no more right to discriminate on the basis of religion, thoughts, or beliefs than the public school systems do. And do not be fooled; the freedom to think what one wants, in the sense that I am using it here in this chapter, *necessarily includes the freedom to openly express those thoughts in private and in public without the fear of ridicule or discrimination for those thoughts.* There are of course some instances in which we cannot always preserve such a freedom since sometimes the circumstances are out of our hands, but our schools systems and our court systems do

---

[30] This is of course with the exception of sexist, racist, or other comments that are clearly out of line and that violate human dignity.

not include such instances or such circumstances, for they are in full and complete control over their respective systems, and so the freedom to think and believe whatever one wants without the fear of being ridiculed, ostracized, or fired from one's job should necessarily be upheld in such institutions as those.

The simple fact that this kind of thing is going on all across our country, namely people being fired for what they believe and think simply because they disagree with the status quo (a status quo that has not and cannot be proven as true, and that there is essentially absolutely no real evidence to support), especially in the realm of science, is a clear indication that we are quickly losing our title as the "Land of the Free." In this day and age we are basically taught to either fear and obey our government, which runs the public school systems, and obey their every beck and call, or accept their wrath in whatever way it may come to us, with absolutely no hope of the courts helping us out when we come to them, as they too are on the side of American government, which is largely run and operated by the driving worldview of evolution. If we are to ever return to the status of being a free nation in the strict sense, then our government has got to start standing up for the inherent rights of all human beings as discussed above. Otherwise there is no hope for us as a nation in the future. It is one thing to deny teachers and professors the right to teach that a widely accepted theory is absolutely false without providing adequate evidence that it is indeed such. It is quite another to deny teachers and professors the right to teach legitimate science (such as ID and certain scientific contributions of YEC) in the classroom simply because our government has espoused a contrary worldview and wishes to cram it down our throat.

Conclusion

I apologize for the long footnotes in this chapter. I realize that sometimes that makes the chapter harder to follow, but there are some grave misconceptions regarding Islam and the Catholic church, and as a student of religion I felt it pertinent to include an explanation regarding some of them in this chapter for various reasons. One of those reasons is because I wanted you, the reader, to get a different feel from this chapter than from the other chapters. I wanted this particular chapter to be primarily religious in nature, even though that is not the main topic for this chapter, because I wanted to make the point that these two examples, namely Islam and the Catholic church, are merely other examples of religious systems that are doing the same thing to societies that the Darwinists/evolutionists are doing to America (denying citizens the right to think for themselves), as evolution, as we saw already, is also a religion, just like Islam and Catholicism. And so, as they say, there is a "method to my madness." Also, the example of Islam and Catholicism is relative to our discussion because just like they kick people out of their systems if people do not adhere to their wishes and accept their beliefs, so the modern mainstream academic anc scientific community is doing the same to anyone who refuses to accept their evolutionary dogmas and theories.

In conclusion, we have seen two prime examples, namely Islam and the Catholic church, of societies that deny their citizens the right to think freely, as they please. We have also seen that this kind of criminal claptrap is completely contrary to the proper respecting of our inherent rights as human beings created in the image of God. And we have seen that this very same kind of thing is happening in our school systems, our museums, and our courts all across our country right here in America to anyone who disagrees with the status quo, namely that evolution is a "proven fact," which we have already seen multiple times over is an absurd and nonsensical assertion in the first place. We must fight for our right as American citizens and as human beings to think and believe what we want to without the fear of being ridiculed, reprimanded, and detested simply because we may disagree with the status quo.

In the next and final chapter we are going to take a brief look at everything that we have discussed in this book, why it all matters, and what we should do about it. So, let's get to it!

12

So What Should We Do About All of This?

"Evolution is promoted by its practitioners as more than mere science. Evolution is promulgated as an ideology, a secular religion – a full-fledged alternative to Christianity, with meaning and morality... Evolution is a religion. This was true of evolution in the beginning, and it is true of evolution still today... Evolution therefore came into being as a kind of secular ideology, an explicit substitute for Christianity."[1]

- *Dr. Michael Ruse (Philosopher of Biology)*

The above quote by Michael Ruse, a very prominent and well respected evolutionist who currently teaches at Florida State University, exemplifies precisely why I wrote this book, and what we have discussed in it. Michael Ruse is also, unlike many evolutionists, honest about the fact that evolution is not science (or not *just* science to Ruse), but rather a religion, as can be seen by the above quotation. On this we agree wholeheartedly with Dr. Ruse, and I commend him for his honesty in that regard. Ruse has also made the point, which extends from the fact that he knows that evolution is a religion, that the fight

---

[1] Michael Ruse, National Post May 13, 2000

between evolution and creation is not one between science and religion, but rather one between two rival religions. This is essentially one of the main points of this book, and so again I extol Ruse for such a proclamation. Now, like we saw in the earlier chapters, I do not necessarily think that Creationism should be taught in the schools either, but like I said, if we are going to teach Darwinism to students in public schools all over the country, then why not teach Creationism as well? Well, put plainly, the two worldviews clash so heavily that it would most likely confuse the students and maybe even cause them to reject science altogether due to their frustrations, which of course is not what we want, or at least it is not what we should want. Science is a great and amazing thing, and it has brought us many wonderful medical, societal, and technological advances. So what exactly should we do about all of the information that we have discussed in this book? First, in this brief and final chapter, we are going to recapitulate everything that we have learned and discussed throughout this book. Then we are going to take a quick look at how it all fits together regarding the title of this book, namely *Science vs. Religion: Is It Really That Simple?*, followed by a brief discussion as to what we can and should do about all of this.

Let's Recap

We began this book with a brief overview of logic and why it is important, especially regarding our discussions in this book. We took a look at the typical argument that "If we teach ID in the public school science classrooms then that will lead to teaching YEC in the public school science classrooms, and so we must not teach ID in the public science classrooms," and we saw that this argument is logically flawed in two ways, namely in that teaching YEC does not necessarily follow from teaching ID, and also that it is not necessarily a bad thing if YEC is taught in the public schools, for after all Darwinism is also a worldview and it is taught in the public school. This argument was obviously intended to discuss the teaching of ID and YEC in public school *science* classrooms rather than religion class or some other type of class.

Then we took a bit of an in depth look at why the prominence of evolution matters so much. We discussed its direct relation to racism, the removal of God from our nation, rape, bullying, and anarchy, which are all very real issues that America is facing today, although to varying degrees depending on which issue one is referring to.[2] We also talked about the fact that if something is not done about it soon (i.e. if we do not remove the teaching of evolution from our country soon) then we as a nation are doomed to ruin one way or another. Evolution is of course

---

[2] It should be noted here in passing that evolution is not the only reason for these types of issues, but it is nevertheless a robust progenitor of such illicit activity and evil.

not the only thing in our nation that is damaging our society, but it most certainly started becoming popular around the time that American society really started going down the tubes, and that is a correlation that we would do well to avoid ignoring.

After that we took a look at what exactly truth is. We looked at whether or not truth is relative, followed by a look at several definitions of truth, and we discovered the definition of truth that is most adequate and simplified, namely "that which is really so." This definition fits squarely with a correspondence view of truth, which ultimately means that truth corresponds directly with reality, hence truth is "that which really is so," or put another way, truth is "that which really is the case." Then we briefly discussed why knowing and believing truth is important.

Next, we took a look at whether or not mainstream science is actually looking for the truth, or whether they do in fact have a different goal in mind. We discovered that contemporary mainstream science is not in fact looking for the truth, but rather they are seeking to further their own evolutionary agenda, which is essentially to promote and propagate the evolutionary position in all areas possible, to the greatest extent possible, *almost* at any cost. This is one of the biggest problems with our society that we discussed in this book, for if you will recall, most of our country is run by some form of "science" related organization, and whether governmentally or by popular media evolution is engrained into virtually every aspect of our society in th s day and age.

Then we took a look at what Naturalistic Materialistic Scientism is. We saw that Naturalism and Materialism are both philosophical systems (i.e. worldviews) that deny the existence of the supernatural (this includes God), and that Scientism is essentially the belief that only science can provide us with the truth, no matter what that truth may be about. We saw that Materialism and Scientism are self-defeating and therefore irrational, and that togetf er, along with Naturalism, they form the central belief system of most modern day naturalistic evolutionists. Naturalism is the leading worldview of evolutionists, even for those who do not hold to strict Materialism or Scientism, and it is 100% antithetical to Christianit, as well as any other form of theistic belief.

Then we moved on to look at whether evolution is science or whether it is a religious/philosophical belief system. We discovered that evolution is in fact most properly classified and defined as a religion and that it falls under the umbrella of philosophy, but that it cannot, by definition, rightly be classified as science, for the two simply do not mix, as science is merely "the systematic study of nature," indicating very clearly that science is something that one *does*. namely *study*. And since evolution (in this case macro-evolution) is necessarily something that someone *believes,* namely that all life arose and descended from a single common ancestor, and that that ancestor arose randomly from non-life, which we saw is absolutely impossible, evolution, as we just saw above, cannot rightfully be classified as science. This no doubt may have come as a surprise to you as the reader, but it is nevertheless a very *core truth* of this book that needs to be remembered from this point on, as the fate of our nation may very well depend on such a truth as that. In the end we determined that Evolutionism, or Darwinism, is the religious/philosophical belief system that is founded on a belief in evolution.

After seeing that evolution is *not* science, we took a closer look at whether or not evolution can be proven. We saw very clearly that neither evolution nor anything else that requires the study of historical science can be proven, but rather only certain levels of probability can be sustained regarding such issues, which is ultimately the case regarding all science, as science is fundamentally founded on the basis of inductive logic, which necessarily deals only with probability and does not leave open even the possibility of 100% proof or complete certainty, no matter what anyone tel s us. This has major implications for the fact that scientists around the world flaunt their experimental findings as if they were unmistakable facts that are beyond question. This includes the assertion that evolution is a proven fact. The bottom line is that evolution cannot be proven, no matter what the men and women in white lab coats tell us. We should, however, not take this information as an indication that we are to be purely skeptical of science. That is definitely not what I am saying here. Rather I am merely letting you know that if we are to have and exhibit intellectual integrity regarding such things then we must be truthful and only give a proper level of credence to any given issue, rather than expressing, for instance, certainty where certainty is not possible, such as in the case of science. This does not mean that we cannot know things as a result of science, but rather just that we cannot know that we know things as a result of science, at least as far as proving hypotheses *true* goes,[3] for knowledge that something is true is not a necessary requirement for one to know that thing, but rather the condition is simply that it must be true.[4] We also discussed the differences between historical science and empirical science, and we saw that they are in fact quite different, although again both merely deal with probability rather than certainty. The major difference is that historical science, cannot completely falsify (prove false), or completely verify (prove true) a hypothesis, because it deals with past, unrepeatable events, while empirical science can at least completely falsify

---

[3] Again, like I said in an earlier footnote, science can falsify (i.e. prove false) a hypothesis, but it cannot prove it to be true.
[4] Along with one being justified in believing the thing and actually believing that the thing is true

hypotheses regarding observable and repeatable data and events.

Next, we took a look at what exactly Intelligent Design is. We discovered that ID is in fact science, for it is merely the study of patterns in nature, which meshes perfectly with the definition of science that we established in this book,[5] viz. *the use of the scientific method to study anything and everything that exists in nature.* All other definitions regarding ID focus on external, secondary aspects of ID, such as the implication that there must be an Intelligent Designer, and so they are therefore improper and mistaken in *truly* defining ID. It should hence be noted again that ID should in fact be taught in the public school science classrooms, as it is rightfully classified as science. We also saw that the individuals who support ID (such as William Dembski) are just as well educated and intellectually qualified as those who oppose it and that consequently those who hold that ID is a legitimate form of science should not simply be dismissed as uneducated and imbecilic.

Then we took a look at what Young Earth Creationism is. We saw that it has its roots in religion, as the basic presuppositions that it is founded on come from the Bible (or the Qur'an) primarily. We also saw, however,

---

[5] Remember that we got this definition through the use of definitions taken from secular, state approved science textbooks that are used at state, public universities across the country.

that there have been many significant and noteworthy scientific contributions made by various YEC exponents over the years, and that like the proponents of ID, we saw that the advocates of YEC (such as Jerry Bergman)[6] are also highly educated and intellectually sophisticated, just as much so as the opponents of the YEC position are.[7]

After discussing ID and YEC, we took a look at some of the major differences between ID and YEC and their proponents. We discovered that although ID proponents may in fact also be supporters of the YEC position (or Old Earth Creationism, or any other worldview position for that matter), this in no way affects the reality that ID is science and not Creationism. We must remember to properly distinguish between someone's personal beliefs and the research and or science that they do, for as we saw good science can be done *within* a wide range of different worldviews.

Finally, we discussed the importance of a free thinking society. We discovered that Islam and the

---

[6] It must be noted again here that Jerry, while not opposed to YEC, does not necessarily consider himself to be a young earth creationist per se.

[7] We must briefly note again here that just because someone is smart that does not mean that they are right. That is not what I am saying, for clearly there are many, many highly educated and intelligent individuals who support the evolutionary position, as well as various other positions, who are wrong. My point is rather that one's intelligence should not be questioned simply because of what they believe, for that is all too common of a mistake that is made by many, many people these days.

Catholic church and two prime examples of societies that do not allow their citizens to think and believe whatever they want without the fear of being ridiculed, ostracized, murdered, and/or eternally damned. We also saw that a similar phenomenon is going on right here in America in which teachers, professors, and museum workers across the country are being fired from their jobs and blacklisted simply because they disagree with the status quo ideology that evolution is a proven fact, which, again, for the *millionth* (sarcasm) time in this book, as we saw, is not only not true, but also is not even possible.

Now that we have briefly summarized everything that we have gone over in this book, we are going to close with a few comments as to how it all relates to the theme expressed in the title of this book, "Science vs. Religion: Is It Really That Simple?," and then we will end with a few quick comments on what we should do about all of this.

How It All Fits Together

As we just saw above, we discussed in the opening section of this book the basic principles of logic, and more specifically the particular fallacy known as the *slippery slope fallacy*. We took a look at a specific fallacy of this type involving the idea that if we teach ID in the public schools then that will lead to teaching YEC in the schools. This particular type of argument can be seen in books such as *Creationism's Trojan Horse: The Wedge of Intelligent Design*, published by Oxford University Press in 2004.[8] We discussed the fact that there are two ways to defeat a slippery slope fallacy. The first way is to show that the second statement, or consequence (in our case the teaching of YEC in the public school science classrooms) does not *necessarily* follow from the first statement, or hypothetical (in our case if we teach ID in the public school science classrooms). The second way to defeat the slippery slope fallacy is to show that it would not *necessarily* be a bad thing if the consequence followed from the hypothetical.

We then defeated this particular fallacy in the first way listed above by showing that ID and YEC are very different from each other. ID is actually science, and YEC is a worldview. We also showed some further specific differences between ID and YEC and their proponents, which made it clear that YEC does not necessarily flow from ID, nor are they even close to the same thing, and so the teaching of YEC in the public schools would not *necessarily* follow from the teaching of ID in the public schools, for not only are ID and YEC themselves significantly different from one another but the individuals who support such views are also often times very different as well. ID *is* science. YEC is *not*. Yes, as we saw earlier there are many significant scientific contributions that YEC scientists have provided the scientific community with that

---

[8] Barbara Forrest and Paul R. Gross, *Creationism's Trojan Horse: The Wedge of Intelligent Design* (New York: Oxford University Press, Inc., 2004).

need to be acknowledged, including in the public science classrooms, but YEC itself is a worldview, and not just a worldview, but a strongly religiously based worldview. Yes, Darwinism, or Evolutionism, is also a strongly religious worldview and it is taught in the public schools by law, and so there may at this time be room for YEC in the public science classroom alongside the Darwinian worldview, but as far as science is concerned, there is no reason to believe that YEC will make its way back into the public science classrooms just because we allow ID, true science, to be taught in the public science classrooms, nor should it necessarily.

We defeated the above stated slippery slope fallacy in the second way listed above by establishing the fact that there are many very credible people who are YEC advocates, like Jerry Bergman. We also pointed out that since Darwinism is taught in the school systems, and since it is a worldview, like we just saw above, there should be no reason why YEC should not also be taught alongside it in the classrooms. Ultimately however, as far as worldviews being taught in science class goes, we should all be very careful about this, for science teachers are not, generally speaking, by profession counselors, pastors, or therapists, and so they should not be teaching and/or supporting any particular worldview, at least not in the science classroom, other than personally (having a worldview but keeping it to themselves). This is the kind of thing that should be left to the parents and the religious organizations that the students are a part of. Now having said that, the point here is twofold: 1) YEC is a religious worldview just like Darwinism is, and so if we teach one in our public schools, then according to the fact that the government and the public school systems are not *legally* allowed to sponsor a particular religion or religious view, we should be teaching both of these worldviews in science class if we are going to teach either of them, and we should teach them as scientific theories to the extent that they relate to science, and no further; 2) YEC scientists have a lot of very valuable information to contribute to the various fields of science, and these contributions should not be overlooked by anyone, especially in the scientific community, as they are just as scientific as anything else that is truly scientific. And so the point here is that even if YEC was to end up being taught in the public schools again, it is not necessarily a bad thing, especially based on the fact that it was taught for many, many centuries prior to the takeover of Darwinism, and just look at all of the amazing scientific discoveries and achievements that were made during all of that time! I must note here that I am not supporting a pragmatic approach to what we should teach in our school science classrooms. Rather I am merely pointing out that since our government is required by law to be non-partisan with regard to supporting a particular religious view, as long as we are going to teach one religious view as science, such as evolution, and as long as that is acceptable to those in charge, then it should be equally acceptable to teach YEC as science in the public science classroom. I am not saying that all worldviews are equally valid and so we should teach all worldviews in the science class, but any worldview that has evidence supporting it, such as Creationism, that also has much to offer the realm of science, should be taught in the science classrooms; that is of course only as long as we are going to teach worldviews rather than strictly science in the science classrooms, which personally I do not condone. But having said that, neither evolution nor YEC is science, as we have seen, and so technically neither of these views should be taught in science class any further than their particular scientific aspects, for to teach religion and worldviews in science class instead of philosophy or religion class is to confuse subjects, and that is not an intelligent way to run our schools, regardless of what we are teaching. Again, I think that having a class just on origins theory or the history of origins theory is a great idea and would be a great place to teach such things, albeit in a neutral manner.

So, this shows us that the statement, "If we teach ID in the public schools, then that will lead to teaching YEC in the public schools, and therefore we should not teach ID in the public schools," should be rejected on the basis that it fails logically on all possible counts, and so it is necessarily a false statement, and should therefore be unstintingly rejected as such. Remember that even if my second argument, namely that it would not necessarily be a bad thing to teach YEC in the public science classrooms, is not as valid as my first argument (even though I think it is), that does not affect my overall desecration of the above slippery slope fallacy regarding ID and YEC and the public science classrooms, because one only needs to use *one* of the two ways of defeating such a fallacy as we have seen, and my first argument is perfectly valid regarding the fact that teaching YEC does not necessarily follow from teaching ID.

We must also always keep in mind that even though there are a growing number of atheists and scientists who are arguing against the principles and laws of logic and their legitimacy, the *fact* is that it is impossible to even deny the laws of logic without actually using them, for when someone says something such as "the laws of logic are illegitimate," they are evoking all four laws of logic, whether directly or by implication, such as the law of identity in that they expect you to take their statement as meaning "the laws of logic are illegitimate" and not "I want a pepperoni pizza." They are also using the law of non-contradiction in that they expect you to understand their statement as meaning "the laws of logic are illegitimate" and not also "the laws of logic are *not* illegitimate." And again they are using the law of the excluded middle in that they expect you to understand that "the laws of logic are illegitimate" means "the laws of logic are illegitimate" and not some combination of this statement and its antithesis. Finally, they are also using the law of rational inference in that when they say "the laws of logic are illegitimate" they are essentially presenting the syllogism: 1) I am making a statement; 2) My statement is that the laws of logic are illegitimate; 3) Therefore, I am making the statement that the laws of logic are illegitimate; thereby providing a rational inference (Premise 3) from their statement and the fact that they made the statement. So, we see here that for someone, anyone, to deny the laws of logic, they must necessarily use all four laws of logic in their denial, thereby making their denial self-refuting and therefore irrational, and so we must by necessity reject *any* rejection of the laws of logic on these grounds, as they are absolutely fundamental and cannot rationally be denied.

As far as how the rest of the information in this book fits into our argument as a whole, the fact that evolution is so incredibly detrimental to society in particular, and to humanity in general is a primary indication of why it is vitally important that we all stand up and start fighting for the removal of such a dangerous and unsubstantiated ideology from not only our public school systems, but from our nation also, as the real argument is not simply "science vs. religion," but instead it is about competing religious systems, one of which (Evolutionism) is sure to destroy our nation in the near future if left unchecked and engrained in our culture.

We looked at what exactly truth is so that we would better understand the concept of truth when we talked in the following chapter about whether or not modern mainstream science is looking for the truth. This made it clear that by mainstream science seeking to advance their evolutionary agenda, they are in fact most certainly not seeking the truth, for as we saw they do not care about the truth, but rather they care about staying in control of society to the greatest extent possible, and this includes our public schools, our museums, and even our media. We saw that American society is so engulfed in evolutionary dogma that to denounce evolution on a national level would mean at least a temporary collapse of our society. Nevertheless, for an injury such as this to be healed, surgery is necessary, and surgery always causes temporary setbacks, but, if done properly, brings great rewards and much needed healing in due time.

We defined and discussed Naturalistic Materialistic Scientism so that we could better understand the minds and thinking patterns of the evolutionists. When we realize that the evolutionists have an a priori commitment to Materialism and/or Naturalism we can better understand why they are so vehemently against the idea of teaching anything in the public schools that might insinuate that anything supernatural exists, let alone something that might indicate that they could be wrong! This is, however, just a power move by the people in charge intended to keep their prominent positions in this country and to keep those who disagree with them silent, which is very clearly a violation of the inherent human rights that we all have that we discussed in our chapter on the importance a free thinking society regarding Genesis 1:26-28.

When we saw that Evolutionism, or Darwinism, is a religious/philosophical belief system, and that evolution is *properly* classified as a religion, we became aware of the reality that it is *not* science. This should lead us to conclude that there is a serious problem with our government not only allowing but mandating that evolution be taught in public science classrooms, especially when we realize that it is not normally being taught as a theory, but rather as a proven fact, for as we saw earlier the courts ruled some years back that ID and Creationism could not be taught in public schools because they are religion, and that evolution is science, but we have in fact seen in this very book that evolution is religion, and ID is science! That is the exact opposite of what the courts said! Something needs to be done about that, and soon. But even if evolution is being taught as a theory in the public schools, that does not change the fact that the media, not to mention National Geographic and all major scientific publications, and virtually every major museum in our country that has anything to do with the hard sciences, purports evolution to be a proven fact, thereby solidifying this idea in the minds of our citizens (especially the young and easily impressionable ones) that evolution is a proven fact, for the media and our nation would never lie to us, right? WRONG! We must always remember that our media, public school boards, court systems, our government and our nation are all made up of people; real, flesh and blood, sinful, fallen, imperfect people, who have a natural tendency to seek the good of the self. This is what the Bible teaches us that natural man is like. We must remain keenly aware of the reality that just because we hear something on the news or in school does not make it true, and we must all learn and strive to be critical (although on a healthy level) regarding everything that we hear and read, and we must all check such things out for ourselves to see if they are true or not, and if not, then we should reject them and seek the truth instead!

We also looked at whether or not evolution can be proven. As stated above, we saw that macro-evolution actually *cannot* be proven, and so it is *impossible* for it to ever be a proven fact, as it necessarily deals with historical, non-repeatable, un-verifiable science. This should cause us to raise serious questions to our nation's media, museums, public schools, and government as to why they have been and are continuing to lie to all of us by telling us all that evolution is a proven fact, when in reality that is impossible! We should, nay, we *must* expect more from our government, our media, and our school systems, for they are the ones that are running our country, teaching (and often times raising) tomorrow's leaders, and the ones who are supposed to be honest with us.[9]

Finally, we saw some examples of societies that do not allow their citizens to think whatever they want, and we saw that America, and especially the American public schools and museums, is one of those societies to some extent, for we are not allowed to believe and think whatever we want without fearing the consequences of harshness, the accusation of insolence toward the absolute truth (according to those in charge, namely that evolution is a proven fact), and even the loss and/or denial of jobs, both present and future.

All of this relates to science and religion one way or another. The bottom line here is that the age old so called debate between science and religion, which in recent centuries has been mutated into a debate between evolution and various other religions, is in fact a mislabeled and therefore a misleading debate. The reality is that evolution is not science, no matter what the courts say. You do not need a law degree or a PhD to see that. The other important thing here is to realize that religion has almost always been the foundation on which true science has been built, for all throughout the vast majority of history science has been done in direct connection with

---

[9] I say this because news reporters and networks always claim to be completely honest with us, and of course because lying is always wrong.

some form of religion, and some of the world's greatest scientists, including Newton, Kepler, and so on did their ground breaking scientific work with the presupposition that the universe and everything in it was created by an all-powerful supernatura being, and although this is an idea that flies directly in the face of modern mainstream "science," it is nevertheless the truth. The _**fact**_ of the matter is that it is *not* as simple as "Science vs. Religion," especially when discussing evolution, ID, YEC, and other related issues.

What Should We Do About All of This?

It needs to be said here at the end of this book that to argue that a scientific view is false simply because it is religiously based on some level is a genetic fallacy. It is irrational to argue that something is necessarily false simply because of who, what, or where it comes from or what it might be attached to, and so we must reject all arguments that assert that ID, YEC, and so on are false because they may be re igiously based (YEC) or because they have religious implications. It is the height of hypocrisy for an evolutionist to argue that YEC is false just because it is religiously based and then turn around and support a religion such as evolution as true! And we have already seen that to cal ID false or anything of the sort is to misunderstand the nature of ID, for ID does not and *cannot* fit into any such category, since ID is science and science is something that one does, not a truth proposition. Also, and this is very important, remember in the last chapter when we talked about the idea that no one can make an intellectual ascent (i.e. accept as truth) to anything other than to the extent that they understand it? Well, the evolutionists all across our country, which includes much of our government, our public schools, and our museums and media, are all trying to make us believe that evolution is a proven fact, but there are several major issues with that. First, as we have seen, again, evolution cannot be a proven fact, because it deals with historical science. Second, and this is also very important, there are an innumerable number of problems with and holes in the theory of macro-evolution, to the extent that it has actually not even remotely been corroborated with any real, legitimate evidence. That is not dogma; that is simply a fact. There are a great number of books, videos, and lectures available from a wide variety of sources around the world that show just that, namely that all of the supposed evidence for evolution can be better explained in some other way, viz. in a way that has nothing to do with evolution. The bottom line is that macro-evolution makes no sense, because it is irrational to assume that something came from nothing, let alone that one species can evolve into another species and so on. But some people may think that the theory itself is coherent, even though it is not actually possible, but actually that is not even the case, for as we have seen the whole idea of natural selection is irrational, and natural selection is supposedly the driving force for macro-evolution. So, if it is not possible for anyone to accept as truth anything that they do not understand, other than to the extent that they understand it, and if macro-evolution is nonsensical as we just saw, and therefore impossible to *truly* understand on any level, then the media, the government, and the museums are trying to get us to do something that is impossible, namely to accept the truth proposition that "evolution is a proven fact," since it cannot be proven nor understood. What does this say about our public schools, about our government (especially the courts), about our media, about our museums? Basically it says that all of these organizations are teaching our children and us to be foolish, and they are damaging our ability to think critically and realistically by demanding such nonsense from us. It also shows us the incompetence and impudence of the organizations, as they either do not know that they are doing this or they know and yet they are doing it anyway, which in both cases is completely unacceptable. If we cannot trust these organizations, then how are we to feel safe and secure as a nation and as a society? As I said above, something must be done about this, and it must be done soon, very soon!

In 1982 there was a court case called *McLean vs. Arkansas Board of Education* in which it was debated whether or not opposing scientific theories should be taught in the public school systems, so as to give the students a balanced view of science and the available theories. Dr. Norman Geisler, the man who wrote the afterword for this book, gave a key testimony in support of the proposal that Creationism be taught alongside evolution for a balanced scientific view. However, not only did the court ignore Dr. Geisler's testimony, but they even refused to transcribe the testimony until after the court case was over and the verdict had been decided. This entire transcript of Dr. Geisler's testimony can be found in chapter 4 of his book *Creation & the Courts: Eighty Years of Conflict in the Classroom and the Courtroom*.[10] The courts essentially acted like his testimony did not even exist, even though to my knowledge it showed very clearly that Creationism should in fact be taught in the science classrooms, at least alongside evolution. This is the kind of thing that we need to fight against. We should not be censured simply because the courts disagree with us. That is not how this country is supposed to work, nor is it the way to uphold justice. Rather it is a sure way to choke out justice and to let presumption, arrogance, inanity, and foolhardiness win the day, which I certainly don't want, and I don't think that you want that either.

Conclusion

There have been many things discussed in this book, from evolution not being science to Intelligent

---

[10] Norman Geisler, *Creation & the Courts: Eighty Years of Conflict in the Classroom and the Courtroom* (Wheaton: Crossway, 2007), 147-181.

Design not being Creation sm to the impossibility of proving macro-evolution. Everyone who encounters this book would do well to remember this: false assertions made, after indeed having been proven false, speak volumes of one's character.

In closing, we should now be aware that evolution is a major problem in our nation, and that our government, as well as our courts, our public schools, and many of our museums and our media are propagating it as a proven fact, and that, quite simply, needs to be vigorously challenged until it changes. We have seen very clearly in this book many, many reasons why we cannot just sit back and watch our children, or even ourselves be lied to and taught nonsense by our nation's educational, media, and governmental institutions. We as Americans must stand up and fight to remind our government that it is against the law and our constitutional rights for them to dictate and mandate that a secular religious worldview, namely Darwinism, or any other particular religious worldview for that matter, be taught in our public schools, especially as fact. It is one thing for teachers to teach a scientific theory in our public schools. It is quite another for teachers to teach a government approved religion in our public schools and essentially demand that our children, and us, believe in it if we are to be deemed as credible in the eyes of the public. Such governmental bullying is no better or different than what Kim Jung III did to the North Korean citizens, or what Hitler did to the Jews and others in Germany, or what China does to their citizens. It is all just different manifestations of the same problem, namely a violation of our inherent human rights. If we as a nation do not stand up and let it be known that we will NOT stand for this kind of garbage, then it will not stop, but rather it will only continue to get worse and worse until it utterly destroys our nation. We MUST let our voices be heard, and we must make them heard NOW!!

Afterword

Trevor Slone's aim is to "shake things up" in America and get people thinking about reality and the facts. He wants people to stand up against the nonsense and the strong arming that is going on in the public schools, courts, news, and museums by the evolutionists that are trying to keep all opposing scientific views out of public sight and mind. That is the main point of this book. He believes that we should be teaching Intelligent Design (ID) in the public science classrooms, because it is science (as he argues in chapter 8). On all of this we completely agree, as I argued in my book *Creation in the Courts: Eighty Years of Conflict in the Classroom and the Courtroom* (Crossway, 2007).

Having been the lead witness in the famous "Scopes II Trial" in Arkansas (McLean, 1982), I can personally attest to the truth of much of what Trevor affirms in this book. One of the things that shocked me greatly was the bigotry of the evolutionists. Many times at the Scopes I trial (1925) creationists were called "bigots" by ACLU attorneys for not allowing evolution to be taught along side of creation in the Tennessee schools. So, I assumed (naively) that the ACLU would be in Arkansas defending the right to teach creation along with evolution. I was half right—they were there at the trial. To my surprise, however, they were now arguing the reverse of their contention at the Scopes I trial. Now they were insisting that creation should not be taught along side of evolution. I came to a simple conclusion: if it was bigotry in 1925 not to teach evolution along with creation in public schools when only creation was being taught, then it was still bigotry in 1981 when only evolution was being taught. I concluded that bigotry had not change, only the bigots had!

Legally and constitutionally, what happened in the Arkansas federal court (McClean, 1982) and in the later Supreme Court case (Edwards, 1987) was tragic. The courts ruled that teaching creation was an unconstitutional violation of the First Amendment. Since our country's Birth Certificate (1776) speaks of Creator, creation, and God-given moral absolutes (like the "unalienable right to live"), I found it profoundly strange to read the Court's decision declaring that creation cannot be taught in our public schools since creation implies a Creator and the concept of a Creator is inherently religious. That is like saying that *the Declaration of Independence* is unconstitutional! I find it difficult to believe that if Thomas Jefferson were to come back today, he who said "Taxation without representation is tyranny," that he would accept that he was being forced to pay taxes to a public school system that was teaching his children that the *Declaration of Independence* was unconstitutional! I have little doubt that Jefferson would help start another revolution.

Another irony stuck me every day during the nine day trial. The US Marshall would enter as we stood, and he said (prayed?): "God save the United States and this honorable court." I found it difficult to think of a court as honorable which had dishonorably dismissed the Creator of the universe whose name was inscribed on its national birth certificate. But the tragic truth is that with the Supreme Court's decision that creation could not be taught alongside of evolution in our country, which was founded on a Creator, creation, and God-given moral absolutes, we can no longer teach any of these things as true in the public schools, at least not until drastic change occurs within the system once again. The author of this book, Trevor Slone, is right: America does need to be shaken up. For unless we again recognize our Creator we are doomed, like many nations before us to be piled in the scrap-heap of history (Psa 9:17). As Thomas Jefferson declared: "God who gave us life gave us liberty. Can the liberties of a nation be secure when we have removed a conviction that these liberties are the gift of God?"

Dr. Norman L. Geisler

Professor of Apologetics

Veritas Evangelical Seminary

(www.VeritasSeminary.com)

Appendix

A Call To Christian Creationist Unity

"All Scripture is inspired by God and is profitable for teaching, for rebuking, for correcting, for training in righteousness, so that the man of God may be complete, equipped for every good work."

2 Timothy 3:16-17 (HCSB)

This passage from 2 Timothy is critical for a proper understanding of the authority of this appendix regarding Christian unity, for this appendix will revolve solely around Scripture, and it is, in the most formal sense, both a rebuke and an admonishment to Christians who are involved in the old earth/young earth debate. I was going to start this appendix off with an extremely disrespectful quote that I found by a particularly well known and respected Christian theologian. This individual is an avid old earth creationist who has gone out of his way to speak very vehemently toward young earth creationists regarding their scientific beliefs. To this I, a young earth creationist, take personal offense, and I would like that individual to know that I do not appreciate being demeaned because of something that I believe that is just as, if not more likely to be the truth than what he believes.

I do not think that R.C. Sproul, Norman Geisler, or any other giant in the modern Christian theological realm who finds Young Earth Creationism tenable would appreciate it either, especially if they saw the comment that I saw. However, I have also recently become aware that certain extremely prominent young earth creationists have also been incredibly disrespectful toward old earth creationists, and so for the sake of being fair to both sides of the argument I am not going to name names or quote from either side of the argument. Instead I decided to open this appendix with a few verses from the Scriptures that I hope and pray we will all, whether old or young earth proponents, accept with humility as the basis for what I am going to say in this appendix. I will try and be brief, as the message of this appendix is simple: We as Christians, especially well-educated Christians in the public eye, must seek unity in this matter of young vs. old earth Creationism, as it is a secondary matter and is not an essential of the faith. We are going to very briefly look at 6 passages from the New Testament and then end with a quote by the Prince of Preachers himself, Charles Haden Spurgeon, regarding the issue of science and the Bible. This is not intended to be an exposition of Scripture, but rather a basic overview and reiteration of some of the more conspicuous passages in the New Testament that discuss Christian unity.

Ephesians 4:1-16

Ephesians 4:1-16 says,

"Therefore I, the prisoner for the Lord, urge
you to walk worthy of the calling you have
received, with all humility and gentleness,
with patience, accepting one another in
love, diligently keeping the unity of the
Spirit with the peace that binds us. There is
one body and one Spirit —just as you were
called to one hope at your calling - one
Lord, one faith, one baptism, one God and
Father of all, who is above all and through
all and in all. Now grace was given to each
one of us according to the measure of the
Messiah's gift. For it says: When He
ascended on high, He took prisoners into
captivity; He gave gifts to people. But what
does 'He ascended' mean except that He
descended to the lower parts of the earth?
The One who descended is also the One
who ascended far above all the heavens,
that He might fill all things. And He
personally gave some to be apostles, some
prophets, some evangelists, some pastors
and teachers, for the training of the saints in
the work of ministry, to build up the body
of Christ, until we all reach unity in the faith
and in the knowledge of God's Son, growing
into a mature man with a stature measured

by Christ's fullness. Then we will no longer
be little children, tossed by the waves and
blown around by every wind of teaching, by
human cunning with cleverness in the
techniques of deceit. But speaking the truth
in love, let us grow in every way into Him
who is the head - Christ. From Him the
whole body, fitted and knit together by
every supporting ligament, promotes the
growth of the body for building up itself in
love by the proper working of each
individual part (HCSB)."

It is not hard to see in this passage that Paul, the
Apostle to the Gentiles, ordained by the Lord Jesus
Christ Himself, called the Church in this passage to
stand unified in the midst of a world that is openly
hostile to both our Christian mission and message.
This passage makes it clear that our goal as the
Church of Jesus Christ is "unity in the faith and in
the knowledge of God's son." In other words,
growing closer to one another as believers and
more knowledgeable about Christ as a community
is our main priority as the Church, the family of
God, along with preaching the gospel to and
making disciples in all the world (Matt. 28:18-20).
The bottom line here is that the last thing we need
to give this 21st century secular society is another
reason for them to hate us and therefore refuse to

accept the countlessly critical call to worship and love our great and holy God. It is a truly injudicious and utterly ridiculous thing to sacrifice both witness and wits for the glory of making a fellow believer look foolish over something that neither side can prove. The bottom line is that we as Christians, whether old earth or young earth creationists, have a transcendent obligation to unity in all non-essential matters over and above our scientific convictions, whatever they may be.

Romans 12:3-21

Romans 12:3-21 says,

"For by the grace given to me, I tell everyone among you not to think of himself more highly than he should think. Instead, think sensibly, as God has distributed a measure of faith to each one. Now as we have many parts in one body, and all the parts do not have the same function, in the same way we who are many are one body in Christ and individually members of one another. According to the grace given to us, we have different gifts: If prophecy, use it according to the standard of one's faith; if service, in service; if teaching, in teaching; if exhorting, in exhortation; giving, with generosity; leading, with diligence; showing mercy, with cheerfulness. Love must be without hypocrisy. Detest evil; cling to what is good. Show family affection to one another with brotherly love. Outdo one another in showing honor. Do not lack diligence; be fervent in spirit; serve the Lord. Rejoice in hope; be patient in affliction; be persistent in prayer. Share with the saints in their needs; pursue hospitality. Bless those who persecute you; bless and do not curse. Rejoice with those who rejoice; weep with those who weep. Be in agreement with one another. Do not be proud; instead, associate with the humble. Do not be wise in your own estimation. Do not repay anyone evil for evil. Try to do what is honorable in everyone's eyes. If possible, on your part, live at peace with everyone. Friends, do not avenge yourselves; instead, leave room for His wrath. For it is wr tten: Vengeance belongs to Me; I will repay, says the Lord. But if your enemy is hungry, feed him. If he is thirsty, give him something to drink. For in so doing you will be heaping fiery coals on his head. Do not be conquered by evil, but conquer evil with good (HCSB)."

This passage gives us a great number of *commands* as to how we are to act and treat each other, all of which clearly flow toward the goal of unity. This passage also tells us that no one is to think more highly of himself than he should, or in other words, arrogance is not a viable option for the Christian. No matter how credible one thinks himself (or his supposed evidence) to be; no matter how right he thinks his scientific convictions are; no matter how wrong or senseless he thinks everyone who disagrees with him is; the bottom line is that it doesn't matter. What matters is that we show respect and love to others, all others, and most especially our fellow Christian brothers and sisters. *No* amount or level of street or academic credibility, friendship, or anything else is worth damaging the bonds within the body of Christ. That is exactly what Satan wants us to do. We are to be gracious to one another, not insidious.

Romans 15:1-7

Romans 15:1-7 says,

"We who are strong ought to bear with the failings of the weak and not to please ourselves. Each of us should please our neighbors for their good, to build them up. For even Christ did not please himself but, as it is written: "The insults of those who insult you have fallen on me." For everything that was written in the past was written to teach us, so that through the endurance taught in the Scriptures and the encouragement they provide we might have hope. May the God who gives endurance and encouragement give you the same attitude of mind toward each other that Christ Jesus had, so that with one mind and one voice you may glorify the God and Father of our Lord Jesus Christ. Accept one another, then, just as Christ accepted you, in order to bring praise to God (HCSB)."

This passage shows us very clearly that those who insult Christians insult Christ Himself! That is most certainly not something that any of us as Christians should even remotely consider doing, for Christ is not only our Savior and Provider, but He is our Lord and King. **Christ** reigns supreme; not you, me, or anyone else, *just Christ, plain and simple*. As the above passage states, we are to accept one another, regardless of one's scientific beliefs, just as Christ has accepted us, and this acceptance includes a necessary disposition of love toward the ones being accepted. This is for the expressed purpose of bringing praise to our glorious and mighty King Jesus, and that is to now and forever be our single most important priority in life.

Colossians 3:12-17

Colossians 3:12-17 tells us,

"Therefore, God's chosen ones, holy and loved, put on heartfelt compassion, kindness, humility, gentleness, and patience, accepting one another and forgiving one another if anyone has a complaint against another. Just as the Lord has forgiven you, so you must also forgive. Above all, put on love - the perfect bond of unity. And let the peace of the Messiah, to which you were also called in one body, control your hearts. Be thankful. Let the message about the Messiah dwell richly among you, teaching and admonishing one another in all wisdom, and singing psalms, hymns, and spiritual songs, with gratitude in your hearts to God. And whatever you do, in word or in deed, do everything in the name of the Lord Jesus, giving thanks to God the Father through Him (HCSB)."

This passage admonishes us to exemplify compassion, kindness, humility, gentleness, patience, forgiveness, love, and to let the "peace of the Messiah" control our hearts. These are definitely not the types of things that this preposterous argument between old earth and young earth proponents is exhibiting! Rather, quite the contrary! We are called in this passage to do "everything in the name of the Lord Jesus." Now I know that not everyone is a genius like me (sarcasm intended), but it should not be hard for a true follower of Christ to realize that to ridicule and desecrate the name of a fellow believer "in the name of the Lord Jesus" is not exactly what this passage means, nor is it even theologically sound, let alone even remotely appropriate. Again, we are to befriend one another and set aside our scientific differences, regardless of how strongly we feel about our convictions, and we are commanded by God to maintain a strong level of cordiality regardless of how much we may or may not disagree with one another, *no matter what*. Glorifying Christ is our number one precedence, and we cannot do that by belittling fellow believers, no matter what the topic of discussion is.

Philippians 2:1-4

Philippians 2:1-4 states,

"If then there is any encouragement in Christ, if any consolation of love, if any fellowship with the Spirit, if any affection and mercy, fulfill my joy by thinking the same way, having the same love, sharing the same feelings, focusing on one goal. Do nothing out of rivalry or conceit, but in humility consider others as more important than yourselves. Everyone should look out not only for his own interests, but also for the interests of others (HCSB)."

This passage tells us exceptionally lucidly, "Do nothing out of rivalry or conceit, but in humility consider others as more important than yourselves." It is absolutely critical that this point be understood, for rivalry is at the heart of every argument, otherwise there would be no argument, and so rivalry is also fundamental to the feud between the old earth and the young earth creationists. This of course does not mean that all rivalry is sinful. After all we are at war with the world and Satan and his followers. Rather this passage is referring to sinful rivalry between believers, as unity is key to the proper functioning of the body, for just like all the systems and parts of the human body must work together In harmony for the body to properly function, so too must the various members of the body of Christ (Christians) work together peacefully so that the Church can act in accordance with the commands of Christ. It is one thing to disagree over something. It is quite another to harbor ill-intent toward a believer in such a disagreement. The latter is the type of rivalry being discussed in the above passage from Philippians. There is a divine command in the above passage to avoid such rivalry, and so if we are to remain true to our King and Lord, then we MUST stop this nonsense and come to the realization that whether old earth or young earth, the important issue is that the creation in the opening chapters of Genesis was a real event, and that it is our God who is that Creator.

1 Peter 3:8-12

Finally, 1 Peter 3:8-12 says,

"Now finally, all of you should be like-minded and sympathetic, should love believers, and be compassionate and humble, not paying back evil for evil or insult for insult but, on the contrary, giving a blessing, since you were called for this, so that you can inherit a blessing. For the one who wants to love life and to see good days must keep his tongue from evil and his lips from speaking deceit, and he must turn away from evil and do what is good. He must seek peace and pursue it, because the eyes of the Lord are on the righteous and His ears are open to their request. But the face of the Lord is against those who do what is evil (HCSB)."

In this final passage we see that Christians are to love believers and be compassionate and humble. This is similar to some of what we saw in the above passages. One cannot be loving, compassionate, and humble and at the same time be vicious, impertinent, and uncouth. We must choose the former over the latter always and forever, for this is a command from Scripture, and therefore it must not be overlooked or taken lightly! Also, we see in this passage that "the one who wants to love life and to see good days must keep his tongue from evil and his lips from speaking deceit, and he must turn away from evil and do what is good." The "one who wants to love life" is a euphemism for "the Christian." This is *not an option* for believers, but rather it is referring to all believers and what they *must* do as followers of Christ. We are all called to avoid saying mean, hurtful, and disrespectful things about fellow believers, and also about non-believers as well. It is one thing to call someone's beliefs foolish if there is overwhelming evidence in support of such a claim. It is quite another to claim that someone and/or their beliefs are foolish or impetuous when not only can such a claim not possibly be proven, but when there is, for all intents and purposes, virtually equal evidence on both sides of the argument, which happens to be the case in the old earth vs. young earth debate.

The Prince of Preachers

Charles Haden Spurgeon, also known as the Prince of Preachers, was a nineteenth century British preacher. While he was certainly not a scientist, he nevertheless was infatuated with the Scriptures and the reality that following the mandates in the Bible is not merely an option for believers, but rather they are absolutely and fundamentally *obligatory*. Spurgeon, in his sermon titled

"The Bible," had this to say as to what is the most important "science" of al ,

> "The science of Jesus Christ is the most excellent of sciences. Let no one turn away from the Bible because it is not a book of learning and wisdom. It is. Would ye know astronomy? It is here: it tells you of the Sun of Righteousness and the Star of Bethlehem. Would you know botany? It is here: it tells you of the plant of renown — the Lily of the Valley, and the Rose of Sharon. Would you know geology and mineralogy? You shall learn it here: for you may read of the Rock of Ages, and the White Stone with the name engraven thereon, which no man knoweth saving he that receiveth it. Would ye study history? Here is the most ancient of all the records of the history of the human race. Whate'er your science is, come and bend o'er this book; your science is here. Come and drink out of this fair fount of knowledge and wisdom, and ye shall find yourselves made wise unto salvation."[1]

---

[1] Charles H. Spurgeon, *Spurgeon's Sermons* (Peabody: Hendrickson Publisher's Marketing, LLC, 2011), 43.

We would all do well to remember these words by the Prince of Preachers and to realize that it is Christ and His Word that is superior to all science, for any truth that can be found in and by science must first and foremost find its genesis in the very nature and substance of God Almighty, our one true King Jesus. So let us all stop neglecting our God given responsibility of seeking unity in the Church and of loving our neighbor as our-self, and start showing the world that we are one in the body of Christ, that we support one another and bear each other's burdens, and that we are the epitome of Christ's compassion, holiness, and love for a world that has truly fallen so very far from Him. Let us set aside the age old debate (pun intended) over the age of the earth and universe and turn back to striving for unity in the midst of diversity in all things non-essential. It is one thing to debate an issue. It is quite another to divide over a non-essential one.

A Brief Note To You, the Reader

"For I have determined to know nothing among you except Jesus Christ and Him crucified."

- *1 Corinthians 2:2 (HCSB)*

1 Cor. 2:2. This is one of my tattoos that I have on my right arm, along with the New Testament Greek word for "boldness/confidence" and a large picture of the protein laminin, which is a protein that no multi-cellular living thing can live without, as it is the protein that holds cells together (this particular protein is shaped somewhat like a cross). You see, I have a very strong love for and fascination with Christian apologetics, and I have never been one to shy away from a necessary fight, let alone a fight involving my Lord and Savior Jesus Christ, my one and only truest and greatest Love (hence the boldness/confidence tattoo). I constantly read Christian and secular philosophy material; science information; information related to the historicity of the person of Jesus Christ and His life, death, crucifixion and bodily resurrection; information on world religions and cults; theology, psychology, anthropology, and many other similar subjects as well. But I also read a good deal about evangelism, church leadership (and general leadership), missions, and also information about the life and ministry of people like Charles Haden Spurgeon, Jonathan Edwards, and others, such as biographies and sermons by these individuals. Basically, I read a lot, both for school and on my own time. I also tend to write a lot about what I read and study, such as this book. However, a few years ago when I started studying Christian apologetics, I made a decision that no matter how much I learn, no matter how much I come to know, and no matter how many different things I may come to understand and engage in discussions about, my number one priority would always, *ALWAYS* be Christ and the mission of proclaiming the Gospel to the world. That is why I have "1 Cor. 2:2" tattooed on my right arm so that I will never forget what the most important thing in life is, which is Jesus Christ and Him crucified, for in 1 Corinthians 15:14-17 the Apostle Paul tells us that the resurrection of Christ is absolutely fundamental to the Christian faith and message, and there could be no resurrection without a crucifixion, since that is how Jesus died. So, even though this book is about the debate regarding Creationism, ID, and evolution/Darwinism, I wanted to take a few short moments and share with you, the reader, the greatest gift that you could ever possibly receive, and the one thing that you need above all else, and that, if you die without, you will be eternally lost and forever damned to spend eternity in Hell.

The beloved disciple of Jesus said this in John 3:16, "For God so loved the world that he gave his one and only Son, that whoever believes in him shall not perish but have eternal life (NIV)." You see, the Lord Jesus Christ came to earth, was born of a virgin by the Holy Spirit (Luke 1:30-35), lived a perfect life (Heb. 4:15), took upon Himself the sin of the world as He died on the cross, thereby atoning for the sins of the world so that we could find forgiveness and eternal life in Him (Rom. 4:25), and was buried and raised on the third day bodily (1 Cor. 15:3-8; Luke 24:42-43). All this was possible because Jesus is God Himself (John 10:30; Matt. 16:16-17; 26:63-64). As the passage from John above shows us, if one is willing to believe in Christ he can be eternally saved.

1 John 1:9-10 tell us this: "If we confess our sins, He is faithful and righteous to forgive us our sins and to cleanse us from all unrighteousness. If we say, 'We don't have any sin,' we make Him a liar, and His word is not in us (HCSB)." Also, Ephesians 2:8-9 tells us, "For you are saved by grace through faith, and this is not from yourselves; it is God's gift - not from works, so that no one can boast (HCSB)." You see, we are sinners, meaning that we have offended God; and since God is a holy, just, and perfect God, He must necessarily punish us for that sin, unless we turn to Him for forgiveness. We don't have to do anything to earn salvation, nor can we. The passage from Ephesians above makes it very clear that salvation is a gift of God, and that it has nothing to do with works. The passage from 1 John above, when coupled with John 3:16 and Ephesians 2:8-9, tells us that virtually anyone can be saved from Hell and given eternal life if they are willing to confess their sins to God and believe in the Son, Jesus. However, there

is one more thing that is required for eternal salvation besides confession of our sins and belief in Jesus, and that is repentance. In Luke 13:3-5, Jesus tells us, "I tell you; but unless you repent, you will all perish as well (HCSB)!" and in Acts 3:19 the Apostle Peter says, "Therefore repent and turn back, so that your sins may be wiped out (HCSB)." Jesus sums it up best (as if that should be surprising) when He says in Mark 1:15, "The time is fulfilled, and the kingdom of God has come near. Repent and believe in the good news (HCSB)!"

So, all you must do to become a Christian and gain eternal life is repent, confess your sins to God, and believe in the good news (when I say "all you must *do*" I am not claiming that anyone has this ability on their own, for these things are purely the result of the work of the Holy Spirit through the grace of God). Repent here means a change of position, more specifically a change of mind, of disposition toward sin and Christ. To truly repent of your sins you must decide to hate sin and instead love Jesus. You must decide that Jesus is worth more than anything else, period, to the extent that you are willing to give up everything in your life, including your very life itself, in exchange for Christ. As far as believing in the good news, the "good news" here is another way of saying "the gospel." The gospel consists of essentially everything that I have shared with you in the last few moments above.

Here is the bottom line: If you are willing to believe all of the things that I have shared with you in this brief message regarding Jesus and His life, death, and resurrection, and if you are willing to confess your sins to God and repent of them and change your mind from wanting to do what you want to do to instead wanting to do what God wants you to do, no matter what that may be, then you can be free from the eternal bondage of sin and the punishment and condemnation for that sin, namely eternal torment in Hell, for John 3:18 says, "Anyone who believes in Him is not condemned, but anyone who does not believe is already condemned, because he has not believed in the name of the One and Only Son of God (HCSB)," and Jesus is the Son of God. You can experience life like never before, for the first time ever, as Jesus says in John 6:47, "I assure you: Anyone who believes has eternal life (HCSB)," and in John 11:25, "I am the resurrection and the life. The one who believes in me will live, even though they die (NIV)." He is the one that we must believe in if we want to be saved from eternal Hell and damnation, for we are all sinners (Rom. 3:23) and we need Jesus to redeem us from our sins, but He will only do so if we are willing for Him to be not only our Savior, but more importantly our Lord, the One who is in charge of us and our lives wholeheartedly. If you will just do that, then you can experience love, freedom, and joy like never before.

Life as a Christian is not meant to be easy in this world that we do not belong to (John 18:36; Phil. 3:20), trust me, but the Lord Jesus promises to be with us always, no matter what (Heb. 13:5). God is the One who gave us life to begin with, as He is our Creator (Gen. 1), and so we owe Him that life in return. Make the choice before it's too late. Choose to follow and serve Christ! There will *NEVER* be a more important decision for you to make. Choose Christ, you won't be sorry. I guarantee it. *By the grace of God* I chose Christ over 24 years ago when I was 5 years old, and I guarantee you that I would not have made it (lived) past the age of 7 or 8 had I not done so due to my horrible past. The Lord has brought me through more than I could ever even begin to explain to you, and I am eternally stronger for all of it (Jam. 1:2-4). Won't you join me in the family of God? All you must do is submit your life to Christ by telling Him (and really mean it) that you believe all of the things discussed above, confess your sins and repent of them, and allow Him to be Lord and Master of your life, and by the grace of God you will be eternally saved (John 10:27-29; Rom. 8:38-39)! There is no special prayer that needs to be prayed, and there is no special way that you need to pray. Just talk to God like you would talk to anyone else who is standing right next to you, albeit with infinitely more respect and humility.

In Christ,

Trevor Ray Slone

1 Corinthians 2:2

Romans 1:16

James 1:2-4

1 Peter 3:15

Colossians 3:1-3

Galatians 6:14

2 Timothy 3:16

Bibliography

_____. A Scientific Descent From Darwinism.
http://www.dissentfromdarwin.org (accessed
August 4, 2012).

Ackerman, Paul D. *It's A Young World After All: Exciting
Evidences for Recent Creation.* Grand Rapids: Baker
Book House, 1986.

Agnes, Michael, ed. *Webster's New World Dictionary.* New
York: Pocket Books, 2003.

_____. *Answers to Evolution: 16 Reasons to Doubt
Darwinism.* Torrance: Rose Publishing, 2004.

Barrows, Edwards M. *Animal Behavior Desk Reference: A
Dictionary of Animal Behavior, Ecology, and
Evolution, Second Edition.* Boca Raton: CRC Press
LLC, 2001.

Beck, James R., and Bruce Demarest. *The Human Person in
Theology and Psychology.* Grand Rapids: Kregel,
2005.

Beckwith, Francis J. "Is Morality Relative?" in *Passionate Conviction: Contemporary Discourses on Christian Apologetics*. eds. Paul Copan and William Lane Craig. Nashville: B&H Academic, 2007, 211-226.

Behe, Michael J. *Darwin's Black Box: A Biochemical Challenge to Evolution*. New York: The Free Press, 1996.

Bickel, Bruce, and Stan Jantz. *World Religions and Cults 101*. Eugene: Harvest House Publishers, 2002.

Blood, D.C., V.P. Studdert, and C.C. Gay. *Saunders Comprehensive Veterinary Dictionary: Third Edition*. London: Elsevier Limited, 2007.

Carter, G.S. *Animal Evolution: A Study of Recent Views of Its Causes*. London: Sidgwick and Jackson Limited, 1951.

_____. *Dragons or Dinosaurs: Creation or Evolution*. Cloud Ten Pictures: 2010. DVD.

Corduan, Winfried. *In The Beginning God*. Nashville: Broadman-Holman, (forthcoming) 2013.

Corduan, Winfried. *No Doubt About It*. Nashville: Broadman-Holman, 1997.

Corduan, Winfried. "The Cosmological Argument." in *Reasons for Faith: Making a Case for the Christian Faith*. eds. Norman L. Geisler and Chad V. Meister. Wheaton: Crossway Books, 2007, 201-215.

Craig, William Lane. *On Guard: Defending Your Faith with Reason and Precision*. Wheaton: David C. Cook, 2010.

Danker, Frederick William. *The Concise Greek-English Lexicon of the New Testament*. Chicago: The University of Chicago Press, 2009.

Darwin, Charles. *Origin of Species: 6th edition*. New York: New York University Press, 1988. Quoted by Michael J. Behe. *Darwin's Black Box: A Biochemical Challenge to Evolution*. New York: The Free Press, 1996.

Darwin, Charles. *The Descent of Man: 2nd ed*. London: John Murray, 1887.

Darwin, Charles. To Asa Gray, cited by Adrian Desmond
and James Moore. *Darwin*. New York: W.W. Norton
and Co, 1991. Quoted by unknown author. *Answers
to Evolution: 16 Reasons to Doubt Darwinism*.
Torrance: Rose Publishing, 2004.

Darwin, Charles. In a letter to Asa Gray, June 5, 1861, in
Francis Darwin, ed. *The Life and Letters of Charles
Darwin*, 2 vols. New York: Basic Books, 1959.
Quoted by Geisler, Norman. *Creation & the Courts:
Eighty Years of Conflict in the Classroom and the
Courtroom*. Wheaton: Crossway Books, 2007.

Davis, John J. *Paradise to Prison: Studies in Genesis*. Salem:
Sheffield Publishing Company, 1998.

Dawkins, Richard. *The Greatest Show on Earth: The
Evidence For Evolution*. New York: Free Press, 2009.

Dembski, William. *The Design Revolution*. Downers Grove:
InterVarsity Press, 2004.

Dembski, William, and Sean McDowell. *Intelligent Design*.
Torrance: Rose Publishing, 2009.

Dewitt, David. *Unraveling The Origins Controversy.*
    Lynchburg: Creation Curriculum, L.L.C., 2007.

Evans, C. Stephen, and R. Zachary Manis. *Philosophy of*
    Religion: Thinking About Faith. Downers Grove:
    InterVarsity Press, 2009.

Forrest, Barbara, and Paul R. Gross. *Creationism's Trojan*
    Horse: The Wedge of Intelligent Design. New York:
    Oxford University Press, Inc., 2004.

_____. "Gallup Study: Engaged Employees Inspire
    Company Innovation." *Gallup Management*
    Journal. 12 October 2006.
    http://gmj.gallup.com/content/24880/Gallup-
    Study-Engaged-Employees-Inspire-Company-
    Innovation.aspx (accessed 2 July 2010). Quoted in
    John C. Maxwell. *The 5 Levels of Leadership: Proven*
    Steps to Maximize Your Potential. New York:
    Thomas Nelson Inc., 2011.

Geisler, Norman. *Christian Ethics: Contemporary Issues &*
    Options. Grand Rapids: Baker Academic, 2010.

Geisler, Norman. *Creation & the Courts: Eighty Years of Conflict in the Classroom and the Courtroom.* Wheaton: Crossway Books, 2007.

Geisler, Norman L. *Essential Doctrine Made Easy: Key Christian Beliefs.* Torrance: Rose Publishing, Inc., 2007.

Geisler, Norman L. "Old Testament Manuscripts." in *Baker Encyclopedia of Christian Apologetics.* Grand Rapids: Baker Academic, 1999. 548-553.

Geisler, Norman, and Abdul Saleeb. *Answering Islam: The Crescent in Light of the Cross, Updated and Revised Edition.* Grand Rapids: Baker Books, 2002.

Geisler, Norman L., and Ronald M. Brooks. *Come Let Us Reason: An Introduction to Logical Thinking.* Grand Rapids: Baker Books, 1990.

Geisler, Norman L., and William C. Roach. *Defending Inerrancy: Affirming the Accuracy of Scripture for a New Generation.* Grand Rapids: Baker Books, 2011.

Gerson, Carl W., and Randall J. Stephens. "The Evangelical Rejection of Reason." *New York Times*, October 17,

2011. Quoted by Casey Luskin. "The Campaign to Embarrass Christians into Accepting Darwinism." in *Christian Research Journal* 35. no.3 (2012): 50-53.

Gould, Stephen Jay. Cited in Jonathan Wells. *The Politically Incorrect Guide to Darwinism and Intelligent Design*. Washington, D.C.: Regenry, 2006. Quoted by Norman Geisler. *Creation & the Courts: Eighty Years of Conflict in the Classroom and the Courtroom*. Wheaton: Crossway Books, 2007.

Gove, Philip Babcock. *Webster's Third New International Dictionary of the English Language, Unabridged*. Springfield: Merriam-Webster, Incorporated, 2002.

Harris, Sam. *The Moral Landscape: How Science Can Determine Human Values*. New York: Free Press, 2010.

Hart-Davis, Adam, ed. *Science: The Definitive Visual Guide*. New York: Dorling Kindersley Limited, 2009.

Hasker, William. *Metaphysics: Constructing a World View*. Downers Grove: InterVarsity Press, 1983.

Hawking, Stephen. *The Grand Design*. New York: Random House, 2010.

Hexham, Irving. *Understanding World Religions: An Interdisciplinary Approach*. Grand Rapids: Zondervan, 2011.

Hitler, Adolf. *Mein Kampf*. New York: Reynal & Hitchcock, 1940. Quoted by Norman Geisler. *Creation & the Courts: Eighty Years of Conflict in the Classroom and the Courtroom*. Wheaton: Crossway Books, 2007.

Hobbes, Thomas. *Leviathan*, pt. 1, chap. 13. Quoted by Arthur F. Holmes *Ethics: Approaching Moral Decisions*. Downers Grove, InterVarsity Press, 2007.

Hodge, Charles. "What is Darwinism?" in *What Is Darwinism? And Other Writings on Science and Religion*. eds. Mark A. Noll and David N. Livingstone. Grand Rapids: Baker, 1994. Quoted by Norman Geisler. *Creation & the Courts: Eighty Years of Conflict in the Classroom and the Courtroom*. Wheaton: Crossway Books, 2007.

Holmes, Arthur F. *Ethics: Approaching Moral Decisions*. Downers Grove: InterVarsity Press, 2007.

Honderich, Ted, ed. *Philosophy: The Oxford Guide*. Oxford: Oxford University Press, 2005.

_____. "Intelligent Design Advocates." Wikipedia. http://en.wikipedia.org/wiki/Category:Intelligent_d esign_advocates (accessed May 31, 2012).

Isaacs, Derek. *Dragons or Dinosaurs?* Alachua: Bridge-Logos, 2010.

Johnson, George B., and Peter H. Raven. *Biology*. Austin: Holt, Rinehart, and Winston, 2004.

Kaiser Jr., Walter C. *Mission in the Old Testament: Second Edition*. Grand Rapids: Baker Academic, 2012.

Lewis, H.D. *The Elusive Self*. Philadelphia: Westminster, 1982. Quoted by James R. Beck and Bruce Demarest. *The Human Person in Theology and Psychology*. Grand Rapids: Kregel, 2005.

Lewontin, R. "Billions and Billions of Demons," review of *The Demon-Haunted World: Science as a Candle in the Dark,* by Carl Sagan, *New York Review of Books* (January 1997): 28-32.

Lott, Maxim. "Global warming skeptics as knowledgeable about science as climate change believers, study says." Fox News. http://www.foxnews.com/scitech/2012/05/28/global-warming-skeptics-know-more-about-science-new-study-claims/?cmpid=cmty_{linkBack}_Global_warming_s keptics_as_knowledgeable_about_science_as_clim ate_change_believers%2C_study_says. (accessed August 4, 2012).

Luskin, Casey. "Smelling Blood in the Water." in *God and Evolution: Protestants, Catholics, and Jews Explore Darwin's Challenge to Faith.* ed. Jay Richards. Seattle: Discovery Institute Press, 2010. Quoted by Casey Luskin. "The Campaign to Embarrass Christians into Accepting Darwinism." in *Christian Research Journal* 35. no. 3 (2012): 52.

Luskin, Casey. "The Campaign to Embarrass Christians into Accepting Darwinism." in *Christian Research Journal* 35. no.3 (2012): 52.

Lutzer, Erwin. *The Doctrines That Divide: A Fresh Look at the Historical Doctrines That Separate Christians.* Grand Rapids: Kregel, 1998.

Madigan, Michael T., and John M. Martinko. *Brock Biology of Microorganisms.* Upper Saddle River: Pearson Education, Inc., 2006.

Martin, Jobe. *Incredible Creatures That Defy Evolution 1.* Real Productions: 2000. DVD.

Mawdudi, Sayyid Abul A'la. *Let Us Be Muslims.* Leicester: Islamic Fountdation, 1991. Quoted by Irving Hexham. *Understanding World Religions: An Interdisciplinary Approach.* Grand Rapids: Zondervan, 2011.

Maxwell, John C. *The 5 Levels of Leadership: Proven Steps to Maximize Your Potential.* New York: Thomas Nelson Inc., 2011.

Mohler Jr., R. Albert. *The Disappearance of God: Dangerous Beliefs in the New Spiritual Openness.* Colorado Springs: Multnomah Books, 2009.

Mooney, Chris, and Sheril Kirshenbaum. *Unscientific America: How Scientific Illiteracy Threatens Our Future.* New York: Basic Books, 2009.

Moore, Malcom. "Husband of Chinese woman forced to have abortion 'disappears.'" The Telegraph. http://www.telegraph.co.uk/news/worldnews/asia/china/9356169/Husband-of-Chinese-woman-forced-to-have-abortion-disappears.html (accessed June 29, 2012).

Morris, John. *The Young Earth.* Green Forest: Master Books, 2007.

Morris, John D., and Frank J. Sherwin. *The Fossil Record: Unearthing Nature's History of Life.* Dallas: Institute of Creation Research, 2010.

Morris, John, and Steven A. Austin. *Footprints in the Ash: The Explosive Story of Mount St. Helens.* Green Forest: Master Books, 2003.

Muncaster, Ralph O. *Dismantling Evolution: Building the Case for Intelligent Design*. Eugene: Harvest House Publishers, 2003

Nink, Marco. "Employee Disengagement Plagues Germany." *Gallup Management Journal*, 9 April 2009. http://gmj.gallup.com/content/117376/Employee-Disengagement-Plagues-Germany.aspx (accessed 2 July 2010). Quoted by John C. Maxwell. *The 5 Levels of Leadership: Proven Steps to Maximize Your Potential*. New York: Thomas Nelson Inc., 2011.

_____. "Of faith and reason." in *Nature: Immunology* 11. no.5 (May 2010): 357.

Paley, William. *Natural Theology: Or Evidences of the Existence and Attributes of the Deity Collected from the Appearances of Nature*, reprinted. Boston: Gould and Lincoln, 1852 [1802]. Quoted by William Dembski and Sean McDowell. *Intelligent Design*. Torrance: Rose Publishing, 2009.

Pearson, Helen. "Raising the Dead." in *Nature* 483. (March 2012): 390-393.

Ruse, Michael. National Post. May 13, 2000.

Schirrmacher, Thomas P. "Human Rights and Christian Faith." Patrick Henry College. http://www.phc.edu/gj_schirrmacherv3n2.php (accessed July 24, 2012).

Sharp, Mary Jo. "Did Muhammad Believe in Women's Rights?" in *Christian Research Journal* 34. no.5 (2011): 21-27.

Simmons, Geoffrey. *Billions of Missing Links: A Rational Look At The Mysteries Evolution Can't Explain*. Eugene: Harvest House Publishers, 2007.

Smart, Ninian. "Towards a Definition of Religion." Unpublished paper, Lancaster University, 1970. Cf. Ninian Smart. *The World's Religions*. Englewood: Prentice-Hall, 1939. Quoted by Irving Hexham. *Understanding World Religions: An Interdisciplinary Approach*. Grand Rapids: Zondervan, 2011.

Spurgeon, Charles H. *Spurgeon's Sermons*. Peabody: Hendrickson Publisher's Marketing, LLC, 2011.

_____. Stanford Encyclopedia of Philosophy. "Scientific Realism." Stanford University. http://plato.stanford.edu/entries/scientific-realism/ (accessed May 23, 2012).

Stein, Ben. *Expelled: No Intelligence Allowed*. Vivendi Entertainment: 2008. DVD.

Tabbarah, Afif A. *The Spirit of Islam*. Beirut: Dar-El-Ilm Lilmalayin, 1978. Quoted by Irving Hexham. *Understanding World Religions: An Interdisciplinary Approach*. Grand Rapids: Zondervan, 2011.

Thomas, Robert L. *Evangelical Hermeneutics: The Old Versus the New*. Grand Rapids: Kregel Publications, 2002.

Thornhill, Randy, and Craig T. Palmer. *A Natural History of Rape: Biological Bases of Sexual Coercion*. Cumberland: MIT Press, 2000.

Todd, Scott C. "A view from Kansas on that evolution debate." in *Nature* 401. (September 1999): 423.

Turner, Derek. *Making Prehistory: Historical Science and the Scientific Realism Debate*. New York: Cambridge University Press, 2007.

_____. *Unlocking The Mystery Of Life*. Illustra Media: 2002. DVD.

Weil, Louis. "The Papacy: An Obstacle or a Sign for Christian Unity?" in *International Journal for the Study of the Christian Church* 4. no. 1 (2004) 6-20.

White, M.J.D. *Animal Cytology and Evolution*. New York: Cambridge University Press, 1954.

Williams, Peggy, Jessica Kuhn, and Rose Barlow, eds. *Biology: Concepts and Applications: Seventh Edition, Annotated Instructors Edition*. Belmont: Thomson Brooks/Cole, 2008.

Woodhouse, Mark B. *A Preface to Philosophy*. Belmont: Wadsworth, 2006

Zacharias, Ravi. *Jesus Among Other Gods: The Absolute Claims of the Christian Message*. Nashville: Thomas Nelson, 2000.

Zacharias, Ravi. *The Grand Weaver: How God Shapes Us Through the Events of Our Lives*. Grand Rapids: Zondervan, 2007.

Additional Information

Intelligent Design

Books

The Design and Complexity of the Cell, by Jeffrey P. Tomkins (2012)

Intelligent Design: The Bridge Between Science & Theology, by William A. Dembski and Michael Behe (2002)

Signature in the Cell: DNA and the Evidence for Intelligent Design, by Stephen C. Meyer (2010)

Intelligent Design Uncensored: An Easy-to-Understand Guide to the Controversy, by William A. Dembski and Jonathan Witt (2010)

Intelligent Design 101: Leading Experts Explain the Key Issues, edited by H. Wayne House (2008)

The Politically Incorrect Guide to Darwinism and Intelligent Design, by Jonathan Wells (2006)

The Cell's Design: How Chemistry Reveals the Creator's Artistry, by Fazale Rana (2008)

Science and Evidence for Design in the Universe (The Proceedings of the Wethersfield Institute Vol. 9), by

Michael J. Behe, William A. Dembski, and Stephen C. Meyer (2000)

The Design Revolution: Answering the Toughest Questions About Intelligent Design, by William A. Dembski and Charles W. Colson (2004)

Mere Creation: Science, Faith & Intelligent Design, by William Dembski (1998)

God and Stephen Hawking: Whose Design Is It Anyway?, by John C. Lennox (2011)

Pamphlets

Intelligent Design: Why Scientists are Abandoning Darwin, by William A. Dembski and Sean McDowell, published by Rose Publishing (2009)

Videos

Unlocking the Mysteries of Life, by Illustra media (2010)

DNA By Design, by Stephen C. Meyer (2010)

Metamorphosis: The Beauty and Design of Butterflies, by Illustra Media (2011)

Where Does The Evidence Lead, by Illustra Media (2004)

The Privileged Planet, by Illustra Media (2010)

Expelled: No Intelligence Allowed, with Ben Stein (2008)

Critiques of Darwinism

Books

Darwin's Black Box: The Biochemical Challenge to Evolution, by Michael J. Behe (2006)

The Edge of Evolution: The Search for the Limits of Darwinism, by Michael J. Behe (2007)

Darwin on Trial, by Phillip E. Johnson (2010)

Defeating Darwinism by Opening Minds, by Phillip E. Johnson (1997)

Fatal Flaws: What Evolutionists Don't Want You to Know, by Hank Hanegraaff and Phillip E. Johnson (2008)

Objections Sustained: Subversive Essays on Evolution, Law and Culture, by Phillip E. Johnson (2000)

Explore Evolution: The Arguments For and Against Neo-Darwinism, by Stephen C. Meyer, Scott Minnich, Jonathan Moneymaker, and Paul A. Nelson (2007)

What Darwin Didn't Know, by Hugh Ross, Fazale Rana, and Patti Townley-Covert (2009)

What Darwin Didn't Know: A Doctor Dissects the Theory of Evolution, by Geoffrey Simmons (2004)

Icons of Evolution: Science or Myth? Why Much of What We Teach About Evolution Is Wrong, by Jonathan Wells and Jody F. Sjogren (2002)

Darwin's Enigma, by Luther Sunderland (1998)

Billions of Missing Links: A Rational Look At The Mysteries Evolution Can't Explain, by Geoffrey Simmons (2007)

The Deniable Darwin and Other Essays, by David Berlinski (2010)

<u>Pamphlets</u>

Answers to Evolution: Response to Public Textbooks, 16 Reasons to Doubt Darwinism, published by Rose Publishing (2004)

Creation & Evolution: Major Challenges to Darwinian Evolution You Should Know, published by Rose Publishing (1999)

<u>Videos</u>

Darwin's Dilemma, by Illustra Media (2010)

Incredible Creatures That Defy Evolution, Vols. 1, 2, and 3, by Real Productions, with Dr. Jobe Martin (2006)

Young Earth Creationism

Books

What Is Creation Science, by Henry M. Morris and Gary E. Parker (1987)

One Human Family: The Bible, Science, Race, and Culture, by Carl Wieland (2011)

Footprints in the Ash: The Explosive Story of Mount St. Helens, by John Morris and Steven A. Austin (2009)

Exploring the Evidence for Creation, by Henry M. Morris III (2009)

The Fossil Record: Unearthing Nature's History of Life, by John D. Morris and Frank J. Sherwin (2010)

The Young Earth: The Real History of the Earth – Past, Present, and Future, by John Morris (2007)

A case for Young-Earth Creationism: A Zondervan Digital Short, by John Mark Reynolds and Paul Nelson (2012)

Thousands not Billions: Challenging the Icon of Evolution, Questioning the Age of the Earth, by Donald B. DeYoung (2005)

The Ultimate Proof of Creation: Resolving the Origins Debate, by Jason Lisle (2009)

The Biblical Basis for Modern Science: Revised and Updated, by Dr. Henry M. Morris (2010)

Biblical Creationism, by Henry M. Morris (2000)

Earth's Catastrophic Past, by Andrew Snelling (2009)

The Genesis Flood, by Henry Morris and John Whitcomb (2011)

In the Beginning: Compelling Evidence for Creation and the Flood (8th Edition), by Walter T. Brown (2008)

Coming to Grips with Genesis: Biblical Authority and the Age of the Earth, by Terry Mortenson and Thane H. Ury (2008)

Unraveling The Origins Controversy, by David A. Dewitt (2007)

<u>Videos</u>

Created Cosmos, by Answers in Genesis (2007)

Dragons or Dinosaurs: Creation or Evolution, by Cloud Ten Pictures (2010)

The New Answers DVD 1, 2, and 3, by Answers in Genesis (2010)

God of Wonders: Exploring the Wonders of Creation, Conscience, and the Glory of God, by Eternal Productions (2008)

Creation Not Confusion, by Creation Ministries International (2010)

Mysterious Islands: A Testimony to God's Handiwork in Creation, by Doug Phillips, Joshua Phillips, and John Erwin (2010) - This film is also a great critique of Darwinism, and it takes place in the Galapagos Islands, where Darwin first formed his theories of evolution.

Old Earth Creationism

Books

Origins of Life: Biblical and Evolutionary Models Face Off, by Fazale Rana and Hugh Ross (2004)

Who Was Adam?: A Creation Model Approach To The Origin Of Man, by Fazale Rana and Hugh Ross (2005)

Why The Universe Is The Way It Is, by Hugh Ross (2008)

A Biblical Case for an Old Earth, by David Snoke (2006)

A New Look At An Old Earth: Resolving the Conflict Between the Bible & Science, by Don Stoner (1997)

Seven Days That Divide the World: The Beginning According to Genesis and Science, by John C. Lennox (2011)

The Bible, Rocks, and Time: Geologic Evidence for the Age or the Earth, by Davis A. Young and Ralph Stearley (2008)

Relativism

Books

Relativism: feet Firmly Planted in Mid-Air, by Francis J. Beckwith and Gregory Koukle (1998)

How Do You Know You're Not Wrong?: Responding to Objections That Leave Christians Speechless, by Paul Copan (2005)

Is everything really relative?: Examining the assumptions of relativism and the culture of truth decay (RZIM critical questions series), by Paul Copan (2011)

A Refutation of Moral Relativism, by Peter Kreeft (2009)

A Refutation of Moral Relativism: Interviews with an Absolutist, by Peter Kreeft (1999)